# THE
# RELAXATION
## AND
# STRESS REDUCTION
# WORKBOOK

MARTHA DAVIS, Ph.D.,
ELIZABETH ROBBINS ESHELMAN, M.S.W.,
AND MATTHEW McKAY, Ph.D.

MJF BOOKS

NEW YORK

Significant contributions were made to the fourth edition by Kathy Dale, L.P.T.; Caryl B. Fairfull, R.D.; Cheryl Pierson-Carey; R.P.T.; and Nina Sonenberg.

Illustrations by Valerie Winemuller and Shelby Designs & Illustrates.
Text Design by Tracy Marie Powell-Zanca.

Published by MJF Books
Fine Communications
Two Lincoln Square
60 West 66th Street
New York, NY 10023

ISBN 1-56731-075-3

Printed by arrangement with New Harbinger Publications, Inc.

Manufactured in the United States of America

MJF Books and the MJF colophon are trademarks of Fine Creative Media, Inc.

10 9 8 7 6 5 4 3 2 1

# Contents

# Preface to the Fourth Edition

In preparing to revise this workbook for its fourth edition, we decided to find out how people are using it, what they find the most effective about it, and what they would like to see changed. We sent out surveys to 200 people who bought the book in 1993 and 64 people responded (a 32 percent response rate). We appreciate the feedback that we received and have incorporated many of the suggestions into this new edition.

In addition to using the workbook as a general reference book, respondents find it personally valuable in learning how to relax and manage stress. Over half of the respondents use the workbook to teach classes, seminars, workshops, psychoeducational groups, or individuals in a variety of settings, including colleges, schools, private practice, mental health clinics, hospitals, day care centers, cardiac rehabilitation programs, weight control programs, prisons, and chronic pain clinics. Clinicians use the workbook as an adjunct to therapy, recommending the book to their patients or copying certain sections for patient handouts.

Respondents indicate that they appreciate the organization, clarity, and simplicity of the workbook, which makes it easy to read and comprehend. Many respondents comment that the workbook is comprehensive, accurate, and professionally sound. Several respondents write that the techniques in the workbook are easy to teach because the material breaks down into simple-to-understand segments with clear explanations and applicable examples. These components also help students feel more competent.

The chapters that received the most suggestions for change in the survey were "How You React to Stress," "Breathing," "Self Hypnosis," "Time Management," "Biofeedback," "Nutrition," and "Exercise." There were requests for more information on how to cope with such problems as low self-esteem, anger, grief, test anxiety, somatic concerns, anxiety attacks, difficult people, and marital and family problems. Since this is a general book on stress management and relaxation and already fairly lengthy, we decided not to add chapters on new topics, but instead to add some examples and exercises that address these issues. For references on many subjects related to stress management, we suggest that you turn to the list of books and tapes at the end of each chapter and at the end of the book.

# How To Get the Most
# Out of This Workbook

This workbook is designed to teach you the most popular stress management and relaxation techniques and exercises used today. Consider it your guide to increasing your awareness of your personal reaction to stress and building your sense of control and mastery over the stressors in your life. We hope that this process will give you more pleasure and less frustration in your life.

Read chapters 1 and 2 first. They are the foundation upon which all of the other chapters are built. After you have read the first two chapters, you will know enough about stress and your personal reactions to stress to decide which chapters it will be most helpful for you to read next.

Chapters 3 through 12 teach techniques for relaxation. Chapters 13 through 15 help you with your stressful thoughts. Chapter 16 assists you managing your time more effectively so that you can free up time to relax and do more of what is most important to you. From chapter 17 you can learn to communicate more assertively and chapter 18 gives you many options to deal with environmental and interpersonal stress on the job. Chapters 19 and 20 teach the basics of nutrition and exercise and their relationship to stress management. Chapter 21 gives you some hints to increase motivation, deal with problems that come up along the way, and to stick to your plan.

A basic premise of this workbook is that the benefits of relaxation and stress reduction techniques can only be fully realized after they have been practiced regularly over a period of time. Intellectual understanding of most techniques is of little value, unless accompanied by first-hand experience. Whether you plan to use these techniques for yourself or in a professional setting to help others who are experiencing stress, your personal experience is key.

The purpose of regular practice is twofold. First, it will ensure that you will be able to consciously carry out the exercise instructions anytime you need to, without having to refer to written materials. Second, regular practice will help you develop the habits at an unconscious level.

The length of time required each day to practice the relaxation techniques in this workbook varies. To start, we suggest that you spend ten to fifteen minutes twice a day doing the exercises of your choice. Make a contract with yourself. Consider the time you spend practicing the exercises you find to be most helpful a reward or a break. You can decide to expand the time you give yourself to relax as you discover which exercises work best for you.

Choose a quiet place where you will not be interrupted to learn the techniques. Since this is new activity for you, it is wise to explain to the people around you what you are doing. Politely ask them to help you by leaving you alone without distractions. You'll find that family members, fellow office workers, and friends tend to be very supportive of these exercises once they understand what you are doing and why.

If you find it difficult to stick to a daily schedule or discover that barriers such as motivation or time get in your way, we have a couple of suggestions.

- Consider doing the exercises with another person. That way you can share your experiences and give and receive encouragement.

- If time is always the excuse, make an appointment with yourself just like you would make an appointment for a haircut or with a friend for lunch. If you have to cancel, immediately set up the next appointment or date.

If you still have trouble accomplishing what you set out to do, turn to chapter 21 for additional suggestions.

If you are over thirty or if your reaction to stress involves physical symptoms such as frequent headaches, stomach problems, or high blood pressure, make an appointment with your doctor for a physical examination before you begin these exercises. Tell your doctor or health-care provider that you intend to practice relaxation and stress management techniques and ask him or her to determine whether your physical symptoms are caused entirely by stress, or there are physiological causes as well. Your doctor can be a supportive partner in your efforts to live a more healthy life. Once you start your program, consult a physician if you experience any prolonged negative physical effects.

# 1

# How You React to Stress

Stress is an everyday fact of life. You can't avoid it. Stress is any change that you must adapt to, ranging from the negative extreme of actual physical danger to the exhilaration of falling in love or achieving some long-desired success. And in between, day-to-day living confronts even the most well-managed life with a continuous stream of potentially stressful experiences. All stress is not bad. In fact, stress is not only desirable, but also essential to life. Whether the stress you experience is the result of major life changes or the cumulative effect of minor everyday worries, it is how you respond to these experiences that determines the impact stress will have on your life.

You experience stress from four basic sources:

1. Your *environment* bombards you with demands to adjust. You must endure weather, noise, traffic, and pollution.

2. You also must cope with *social stressors* such as deadlines, financial problems, job interviews, presentations, disagreements, demands for your time and attention, and loss of loved ones.

3. A third source of stress is *physiological*. The rapid growth of adolescence, menopause in women, illness, aging, accidents, lack of exercise, poor nutrition, and sleep disturbances all tax the body. Your physiological reaction to environmental and social threats and changes can also result in stressful symptoms such as muscle tension, headaches, stomach upset, and anxiety.

4. The fourth source of stress is *your thoughts*. Your brain interprets and translates complex changes in your environment and body and determines when to turn on the "emergency response."

How you interpret and label your present experience and what you predict for the future can serve either to relax or to stress you. Interpreting a sour look from your boss to mean that you are doing an inadequate job is likely to be very anxiety provoking. Interpreting the same look as tiredness or preoccupation with personal problems will not be as frightening.

Stress researcher Richard Lazarus has argued that stress begins with your appraisal of a situation. You first ask how dangerous or difficult the situation is and what resources you have to help you cope with it. Anxious, stressed people often decide that (1) an event is dangerous, difficult, or painful and (2) they don't have the resources to cope.

## Fight or Flight Response

The groundwork for the modern meaning of "stress" was laid by Walter B. Cannon, a physiologist at Harvard around the turn of the century. He was the first to describe the "fight or flight response" as a series of biochemical changes that prepare you to deal with threats or danger. Primitive man needed quick bursts of energy to fight or flee such predators as a saber-toothed tiger. These days, when social custom prevents you from fighting or running away, this "emergency response" is rarely useful.

Hans Selye, the first major researcher on stress, was able to trace exactly what happens in your body during the fight or flight response. He found that any problem, imagined or real, can cause the cerebral cortex (the thinking part of the brain) to send an alarm to the hypothalamus (the main switch for the stress response, located in the midbrain). The hypothalamus then stimulates the sympathetic nervous system to make a series of changes in your body. Your heart rate, breathing rate, muscle tension, metabolism, and blood pressure all increase. Your hands and feet get cold as blood is directed away from your extremities and digestive system into the larger muscles that can help you fight or run. You experience butterflies in your stomach. Your diaphragm and your anus lock. Your pupils dilate to sharpen your vision and your hearing becomes more acute.

While all of this is going on, something else happens that can have long-term negative effects if left unchecked. Your adrenal glands start to secret corticoids (adrenaline, epinephrine, and norepinephrine) which inhibit digestion, reproduction, growth, and tissue repair and the responses of your immune and inflammatory systems. In other words, some very important functions that keep your body healthy begin to shut down.

The same mechanism that turned the stress response on can turn it off. This is called the *relaxation response*. As soon as you decide that a situation is no longer dangerous, your brain stops sending emergency signals to your brain stem, which in turn ceases to send panic messages to your nervous system. Three minutes after you shut off the danger signals, the fight or flight response burns out. Your metabolism, heart rate, breathing rate, muscle tension, and blood pressure all return to their normal levels. Herbert Benson (1975) suggests that you can use your mind to change your physiology for the better, improving your health and perhaps reducing your need for medication. He coined the term "the relaxation response" to refer to this natural restorative process.

## Chronic Stress and Disease

Of course there are times when the stress response is still adaptive today: you need it in the face of physical danger or when participating in sports that require fast, rigorous muscle activity. But neither of these situations demand a constant or prolonged stress response.

Chronic or persistent stress can occur when the stressors of life are unrelenting, as they are during a major reorganization or downsizing at work or while undergoing a messy divorce or coping with a chronic or life-threatening illness. Chronic stress also occurs when little stressors accumulate and you are unable to recuperate from any one of them. As long as the mind perceives a threat, the body remains aroused. If the stress response remains turned on, you can be increasing your chances of a stress-related disease.

Researchers have been looking at the relationship between stress and disease for the last fifty years. They have observed that people suffering from stress-related disorders tend to show hyperactivity in a particular "preferred system," such as skeletal-muscular, cardiovascular, or gastrointestinal system. For example, the evidence shows that chronic stress can result in muscle tension and fatigue for some people. For others, it can contribute to stress hypertension, migraine headaches, ulcers, or chronic diarrhea.

Almost every system in your body can be damaged by stress. Suppression of the reproduction system can cause amenorrhea (cessation of menstruation) and failure to ovulate in women, impotency in men, and loss of libido in both. Stress-triggered changes in the lungs increase the symptoms of asthma, bronchitis, and other respiratory conditions. Loss of insulin during the stress response may be a factor in the onset of adult diabetes. Stress suspends tissue repair and remodeling which in turn causes decalcification of the bones, osteoporosis, and susceptibility to fractures. Inhibition of immune and inflammatory systems makes you more susceptible to colds and flu and can exacerbate some diseases such as cancer and AIDS (Acquired Immunodeficiency Syndrome). In addition, a prolonged stress response can worsen conditions such as arthritis, chronic pain, and diabetes. There is also some evidence that the continued release and depletion of norepinephrine during a state of chronic stress can contribute to depression.

The relationship between chronic stress, disease, and aging is another area of research. Aging experts are looking at the changing patterns of disease and the emergence of degenerative disorders. Over just a few generations, the threat of infectious diseases such as typhoid, pneumonia, and polio have been replaced with such "modern plagues" as cardiovascular disease, cancer, arthritis, respiratory disorders such as asthma and emphysema, and a pervasive incidence of depression. As you age normally, you expect a natural slowing down of your body's functioning. But many of these mid- to late-life disorders are stress-sensitive diseases. Researchers and clinicians are each now asking how stress accelerates the aging process and what can be done to counteract this process.

## Tactics for Coping With Stress

As a member of modern society, you have available to you a variety of methods to cope with the negative effects of stress. Doctors treat your stress-related symptoms and diseases. Over-the-counter remedies reduce your pain, help you sleep, keep you awake, enable you to relax, and counter your acid indigestion and nervous bowels. You can consume food, alcohol, and recreational drugs to help block feelings of disease. You have diversions such as TV, movies, hobbies, and sports. You can withdraw from the world into your home to avoid all but the most necessary contact with the stressful world around you.

Our society rewards people who deal with stress by working harder and faster to produce more in a shorter time. Cardiologists Friedmand and Rosenman refer to such people as "Type A" personalities. The Type A has a strong sense of time urgency, is highly competitive, and is easily angered when he doesn't get his way. Although Type A personalities may be very successful, they have a significantly higher rate of cardiovascular disease than "Type B" personalities. Unlike their hard-driving, aggressive counterparts, Type B's don't suffer from chronic time urgency. They can play and relax without guilt and are not hostile or excessively competitive. Type B's can be just as ambitious as Type A's and often are more successful. Presidents of companies are apt to be clever Type B's who employ Type A's to do their work for them.

In contrast to anxious, chronically stressed people, certain individuals are less vulnerable to stress, according to University of Chicago research psychologist Suzanne Kobasa. These "stress-hardy" individuals have a lower frequency of illness and work absenteeism. They view stressors as challenges and chances for new opportunities and personal growth rather than as threats. They feel in control of their life circumstances, and they perceive that they have the resources to make choices and influence events around them. They also have a sense of commitment to their homes, families, and work that makes it easier for them to be involved with other people and in other activities. According to Herbert Benson and Eileen Steward, authors of *The Wellness Book*, the incidence of illness is even lower in individuals who have these "stress-hardy" characteristics and who also have a good social support system, exercise regularly and maintain a healthy diet.

## Knowing Your Goal

The goal of stress management is not merely stress reduction. Life would be boring without stress. While you usually think of stressful events or stressors as being negative, such as the injury or death of a loved one, they can also be positive. For instance, getting a new home or a promotion at work brings with it the stress of change of status and new responsibilities. The physical exertion of a good workout, the excitement of coming up with a solution to a difficult problem, or the pleasure of watching a beautiful sunset are all examples of "eustress" or positive stress. Distress or negative stress occurs when you perceive that the challenge facing you is dangerous, difficult, painful, or "unfair" and you are concerned that you may lack the resources to cope with it. You can actually increase your ability to deal with distress by integrating into your everyday life positive activities such as stopping to view a colorful garden or landscape, regular exercise and re- laxation, enjoyable social contacts, sensible dietary practices, optimistic and rational thinking, and humor and play.

Research shows that performance and efficiency actually improve with increased stress, until performance peaks as the stress level becomes too great. Stress management involves finding the right types and amounts of stress, given your individual personality, priorities, and life situation, so that you can maximize your performance and satisfaction. By using the tools presented in this workbook, you can learn how to cope more effectively with distress as well as add more eustress or stimulating challenges, pleasure, and excitement to your life.

## Schedule of Recent Experience

The first step in reducing stress is to acknowledge the impact of large and small changes in your life. These changes may be positive or negative, forced on you from without or initiated by you. What they share in common is that you must adapt to them and reestablish an equilibrium in your life. Thomas Holmes, M.D., and his research associates at the University of Washington have found that people are more likely to develop illnesses or clinical symptoms after experiencing a period when they have had to adapt to many life events.

Dr. Holmes and his associates have developed the *Schedule of Recent Experience,* which allows you to quantify how many changes you have experienced in the past year and consider how these stressful events may increase your vulnerability to illness. The purpose of this scale is to increase your awareness of stressful events and their potential impact on your health so that you can take steps to reduce the stress level in your life.

## Schedule of Recent Experience

**Instructions.** Think back on each possible life event listed below and decide how many times, if at all, it has happened to you within the last year. Write that number in the "Number of Times" column. (If an event happened more than than four times, give it a score of four.)

| Event | Number of Times | x | Mean Value | = | Your Score |
|---|---|---|---|---|---|
| 1. A lot more or a lot less trouble with the boss. | | x | 23 | = | |
| 2. A major change in sleeping habits (sleeping a lot more or a lot less or a change in time of day when you sleep). | | x | 16 | = | |
| 3. A major change in eating habits (eating a lot more or a lot less or very different meal hours or surroundings). | | x | 15 | = | |
| 4. A revision of personal habits (dress, manners, associations, and so on). | | x | 24 | = | |
| 5. A major change in your usual type or amount of recreation. | | x | 19 | = | |
| 6. A major change in your social activities (e. g., clubs, dancing, movies, visiting, and so on). | | x | 18 | = | |

| Event | Number of Times | x | Mean Value | = | Your Score |
|---|---|---|---|---|---|
| 7.  A major change in church activities (attending a lot more or a lot less than usual). | | x | 19 | = | |
| 8.  A major change in the number of family get-togethers (a lot more or a lot less than usual). | | x | 15 | = | |
| 9.  A major change in your financial state (a lot worse off or a lot better off). | | x | 38 | = | |
| 10. Trouble with in-laws. | | x | 29 | = | |
| 11. A major change in the number of arguments with spouse (a lot more or a lot less than usual regarding child rearing, personal habits, and so on). | | x | 35 | = | |
| 12. Sexual difficulties. | | x | 39 | = | |
| 13. Major personal injury or illness. | | x | 53 | = | |
| 14. Death of a close family member (other than spouse). | | x | 63 | = | |
| 15. Death of spouse. | | x | 100 | = | |
| 16. Death of a close friend. | | x | 37 | = | |
| 17. Gaining a new family member (through birth, adoption, oldster moving in, and so on). | | x | 39 | = | |
| 18. Major change in the health or behavior of a family. | | x | 44 | = | |
| 19. Change in residence. | | x | 20 | = | |
| 20. Detention in jail or other institution. | | x | 63 | = | |

| Event | Number of Times | x | Mean Value | = | Your Score |
|---|---|---|---|---|---|
| 21. Minor violations of the law (traffic tickets, jaywalking, disturbing the peace, and so on). | | x | 11 | = | |
| 22. Major business readjustment (merger, reorganization, bankruptcy, and so on). | | x | 39 | = | |
| 23. Marriage. | | x | 501 | = | |
| 24. Divorce. | | x | 73 | = | |
| 25. Marital separation from spouse. | | x | 65 | = | |
| 26. Outstanding personal achievement. | | x | 28 | = | |
| 27. Son or daughter leaving home (marriage, attending college, and so on). | | x | 29 | = | |
| 28. Retirement from work. | | x | 45 | = | |
| 29. Major change in working hours or conditions. | | x | 20 | = | |
| 30. Major change in responsibilities at work (promotion, demotion, lateral transfer). | | x | 29 | = | |
| 31. Being fired from work. | | x | 47 | = | |
| 32. Major change in living conditions (building a new home or remodeling, deterioration of home or neighborhood). | | x | 25 | = | |
| 33. Spouse beginning or ceasing to work outside the home. | | x | 26 | = | |

| Event | Number of Times | x | Mean Value | = | Your Score |
|---|---|---|---|---|---|
| 34. Taking out a mortgage or loan for a major purchase (purchasing a home or business and so on). | | x | 31 | = | |
| 35. Taking out a loan for a lesser purchase (a car, TV, freezer, and so on). | | x | 17 | = | |
| 36. Foreclosure on a mortgage or loan. | | x | 30 | = | |
| 37. Vacation. | | x | 13 | = | |
| 38. Changing to a new school. | | x | 20 | = | |
| 39. Changing to a different line of work. | | x | 36 | = | |
| 40. Beginning or ceasing formal schooling. | | x | 26 | = | |
| 41. Marital reconciliation with mate. | | x | 45 | = | |
| 42. Pregnancy. | | | 40 | = | |
| Your total score | | | | | |

**Scoring.**    Multiply the mean score by the number of times an event happened, and enter the result in the "Your Score" column. (Remember, if an event happened more than four times within the past year, give it a score of four.) Add up your scores to get your total score and enter it at the bottom of the schedule.

According to Dr. Holmes and his associates, the higher your total score, the greater your risk of developing stress related symptoms or illnesses. Of those people with a score of over 300 for the past year, almost 80 percent get sick in the near future; with a score of 200 to 299, about 50 percent get sick in the near future; and with a score of 150-199, only about 30 percent get sick in the near future. A score of less than 150 indicates that you have a low chance of becoming ill. So the higher your score, the harder you should work to stay well.

Since individuals vary in their perception of a given life event as well as in their ability to adapt to change, we recommend that you use this standardized test only as a rough predictor of your increased risk.

Stress can be cumulative. Events from two years ago may still be affecting you now. If you think that past events may be a factor for you, repeat this test for the events of the preceding year and compare your scores.

## Prevention

Here are some ways that you can use the Schedule of Recent Experience to maintain your health and prevent illness:

1. Remind yourself of the amount of change that has happened to you by posting the Schedule of Recent Experience where you and your family can easily see it.

2. Think about the meaning of each change for you and try to identify some of the feelings you experience.

3. Think about ways that you can best adjust to each change.

4. Take your time in making decisions.

5. Try to anticipate life changes and plan for them well.

6. Pace yourself. Don't rush. It will get done.

7. View accomplishments as part of daily life rather than as a "stopping point" or a "time to let down."

In addition, we recommend:

8. Be compassionate and patient with yourself. It is not uncommon for people to become overwhelmed by all the stresses in their lives. It takes a while to put into effect coping strategies to deal with stress.

9. Acknowledge what you can control and what you cannot control, and when possible choose which changes you take on.

10. Try out the stress management and relaxation techniques presented in this book and incorporate the ones that work best for you into your own personalized stress management program.

## Symptoms Checklist

The major objective of this workbook is to help you achieve symptom relief using relaxation and stress reduction techniques. So that you can determine exactly which symptoms you want to work on, complete the following checklist.

After you have used this workbook to master stress reduction techniques that work best for you, return to this checklist and use it to measure your symptom relief.

**Instructions.** Rate your stress-related symptoms below for the degree of discomfort that they cause you, using this ten-point scale:

| Slight discomfort | | | | Moderate discomfort | | | | Extreme discomfort | | |
|---|---|---|---|---|---|---|---|---|---|---|
| 1 | 2 | 3 | 4 | 5 | 6 | 7 | 8 | 9 | 10 |

| *Symptom*<br><br>*(Disregard those that you don't experience)* | *Degree of discomfort (1-10) now* | *Degree of discomfort (1-10) after mastering relaxation and stress reduction techniques* |
|---|---|---|
| Anxiety in specific situations<br>  Tests<br>  Deadlines<br>  Interviews<br>  Other | _____<br>_____<br>_____<br>_____ | _____<br>_____<br>_____ |
| Anxiety in personal relationships<br>  Spouse<br>  Parents<br>  Children<br>  Other | _____<br>_____<br>_____<br>_____ | |
| General anxiety (regardless of the situation or the people involved) | | |
| Depression | | |
| Powerlessness | | |
| Poor self-esteem | | |
| Hostility | | |
| Anger | | |
| Irritability | | |
| Resentment | | |
| Phobias | | |
| Fears | | |
| Obsessions, unwanted thoughts | | |

| Symptom  (Disregard those that you don't experience) | Degree of discomfort (1-10) now | Degree of discomfort (1-10) after mastering relaxation and stress reduction techniques |
|---|---|---|
| Muscular tension | | |
| High blood pressure | | |
| Headaches | | |
| Neckaches | | |
| Backaches | | |
| Indigestion | | |
| Irritable bowel | | |
| Ulcers | | |
| Chronic constipation | | |
| Chronic diarrhea | | |
| Muscle spasms | | |
| Tics | | |
| Tremors | | |
| Fatigue | | |
| Insomnia | | |
| Sleeping difficulties | | |
| Obesity | | |
| Physical weakness | | |
| Job stress | | |
| Other | | |
| | | |
| | | |

**Important.** Physical symptoms may have purely physiological causes. You should have a medical doctor eliminate the possibility of such physical problems before you proceed on the assumption that your symptoms are completely stress related.

## Symptom Effectiveness

Now that you have identified your stress-related symptoms, it is time to choose the one or two that bother you the most and to select the techniques that you will use to relieve them. Since everyone reacts differently to stress, it is hard to say which techniques will work best for you. However, the chart on the following pages will give you a general idea of what to try first and where to go from there.

Chapter headings for each stress reduction method are across the top, and typical stress-related symptoms are listed down the side. (Note that you may have only one or several of these symptoms.)

As you can see, more than one stress reduction technique is indicated as effective in treating most symptoms. The most effective techniques for a particular symptom are marked with a boldface **X**, while other helpful techniques for that same symptom are indicated by a smaller and lighter x.

Also note that the techniques fall into roughly two categories: relaxation techniques that focus on relaxing the body and stress reduction techniques that condition the mind to handle stress effectively. Your mind, body, and emotions are interrelated. In seeking relief from stress, you will probably obtain the best results by using at least one technique from each of these two broad categories. For example, if your most painful stress symptom is general anxiety, you might practice progressive relaxation and breathing exercises to calm your body and do exercises from the chapter on refuting irrational ideas to reduce your mental and emotional stress.

Before you move to the chapter on the technique in which you are most interested, read chapter 2. Body awareness is the key to everything else in this workbook, and without it you cannot use any of these techniques effectively.

**Further Reading**

Amundson, M. E., C. A. Hart, and T. A. Holmes. 1986. *Manual for the Schedule of Recent Experience (SRE)*. Seattle, WA: University of Washington Press.

Benson, H. 1975. *The Relaxation Response*. New York: Morrow.

———. 1984. *Beyond the Relaxation Response*. New York: Time Books.

Benson, H., and E. Stuart. 1992. *The Wellness Book*. New York: Birch Lane Press.

Kobasa, S., S. Maddi, M. Puccetti, and M. Zola. 1985. "Effectiveness of Hardiness, Exercise and Social Support as Resources Against Illness." *Journal of Psychosomatic Research* 29:505-33.

Lazarus, R. S. 1984. *Stress Appraisal and Coping*. New York: Springer Publishing.

Lorig, K., H. Holman, D. Sobel, et al. 1994. *Living a Healthy Life With Chronic Disease*. Palo Alto: Bull Publishing.

Miller, L. H., A. Smith, and L. Rothstein. 1993. *The Stress Solution: An Action Plan To Manage the Stress in Your Life*. New York: Pocket Books.

Ornstein, R., and D. Sobel. 1989. *Healthy Pleasures*. Menlo Park: Addison-Wesley.

———. 1987. *The Healing Brain*. New York: Simon & Schuster.

Sapolsky, R. M. 1994. *Why Zebras Don't Get Ulcers: A Guide to Stress, Stress Related Diseases, and Coping*. New York: W.H. Freeman.

Selye, Hans. 1956. *The Stress of Life*. New York: McGraw Hill.

———. 1974. *Stress Without Distress*. New York: Dutton.

# Symptom Effectiveness Chart

Chapter headings for each stress reduction method are across the top, and typical stress-related symptom are listed down the side. The most effective techniques for a particular symptoms are

**Techniques**

| Symptoms | Breathing | Progressive Relaxation | Meditation | Visualization | Appplied Relaxation | Self-Hypnosis | Auto-genics |
|---|---|---|---|---|---|---|---|
| Anxiety in specific situations (tests, deadlines, interviews, etc.) | X | X | x | x |  | x |  |
| Anxiety in your personal relationships (spouse, parents, children, etc.) | X | X |  |  |  | x |  |
| Anxiety, general (regardless of the situation or the people involved) | X | X | X | x | X |  | x |
| Depression, hopelessness, powerlessness, poor self-esteem | x | x | X |  |  |  |  |
| Hostility, anger, irritability, resentment | X |  | x |  |  |  | x |
| Phobias, fears |  | X |  |  | X |  |  |
| Obsessions, unwanted thoughts | x |  | X |  |  |  |  |
| Muscular tension | X | X |  | x |  | x | X |
| High blood pressure | x | X | x |  |  |  | X |
| Headaches, neckaches, backaches | x | X |  | X | X | X | x |
| Indigestion, irritable bowel, ulcers, chronic constipation | x | X |  |  |  | X | X |
| Muscle spasms, tics, tremors |  | X |  | x | X | x |  |
| Fatigue, tired all the time | X | x |  |  |  | X | x |
| Insomnia, sleeping difficulties | x | X |  |  | X | X | x |
| Obesity | x |  |  |  |  | x |  |
| Physical weakness | x |  |  |  |  |  |  |
| Job stress | x |  |  |  |  |  |  |
| Chronic pain | X | x | X | X | x | X | x |
| Chronic illness | X |  | X | X |  | x | x |

marked with a boldface **X**, while other helpful techniques for that same symptom are indicated by a lighter x.

**Important:** Physical symptoms may have purely physiological causes. You should have a medical doctor eliminate the possibility of such physical problems before you proceed on the assumption that your symptoms are completely stress-related.

| Brief Combination Techniques | Bio-feedback | Thought Stopping | Refuting Irrational Ideas | Coping Skills Training | Goal Setting and Time Management | Assertive-ness Training | Job Stress Manage-ment | Nutrition | Exercise |
|---|---|---|---|---|---|---|---|---|---|
| x |  | **X** | x | **X** | x | x |  |  |  |
| x |  |  | x | x |  | **X** |  |  |  |
| x | **X** | x | **X** | x |  |  |  |  | x |
|  |  | **X** | **X** |  |  | **X** |  | x | x |
|  | x |  | **X** |  | **X** | **X** |  | x | x |
|  | x | **X** | **X** | **X** | x | x |  |  |  |
|  |  | **X** | **X** | x | x |  |  |  |  |
| x | **X** |  |  |  | x |  |  |  | **X** |
| x | **X** |  |  |  | x | x |  | **X** | x |
|  | **X** |  |  |  | x |  |  | x | **X** |
| x | x |  |  |  | x | x |  | **X** | x |
|  | **X** |  |  |  | x |  |  |  | x |
|  |  |  |  |  | x |  |  | x | x |
|  | x | **X** |  |  |  |  |  | x | x |
|  |  |  | x |  |  |  |  | **X** | **X** |
|  |  |  | x |  |  |  |  |  | **X** |
| **X** |  |  | **X** | x | x | x | **X** |  |  |
| x | **X** | **X** |  | x |  | x |  | **X** | **X** |
| x | **X** | **X** |  |  |  | x |  | **X** | **X** |

# 2

# Body Awareness

The ability to recognize how your body reacts to the stressors in your life can be a powerful skill, although most people are more aware of the weather, the time of day, or their bank balance than they are of the tension in their own bodies or their personal stress response. Your body registers stress long before the conscious mind does. Muscle tension is your body's way of letting you know that you are under stress, and body awareness is the first step toward acknowledging and reducing stress.

The importance of body states, their effect on consciousness, and their relationship to stress have been emphasized for many centuries by eastern philosophies such as Zen, Yoga, and Sufi. During this century, the work of Wilhelm Reich, originally a student of Freud, kindled western psychiatry's interest in the body's interaction with emotional conditions. Two modern therapies that concentrate on the body and its relationship to emotional stress are the Gestalt Therapy of Fritz Perls and the Bioenergetic Therapy of Alexander Lowen. Both of these therapie. work closely with the mind-body relationship.

Lowen noted that you inevitably tense your body when you experience stress. When the stress is removed, the tension will also go away. He found that chronic muscular tension occurs in people with particular beliefs or attitudes and tends to tighten specific muscle groups. For example, a woman who believes that it is bad to express anger is likely to have chronic neck tension and pain, while a man experiencing a lot of anxiety about the future may develop chronic stomach problems. This chronic muscular tension restricts digestion, limits self-expression, and decreases energy. Every contracted muscle blocks movement.

Perls believed in the importance of differentiating between your external awareness and internal awareness in order to separate the world from your physical reaction to it. External awareness includes all stimulation to the five senses from the outside world. Internal awareness refers to any physical sensation, feeling, emotional discomfort, or comfort inside your body. Much of the tension in your body isn't felt because most of your awareness is directed to the outside world. In the body inventory, you will experience Gestalt exercises designed to locate and explore your body tension.

# Body Inventory

The following exercises promote body awareness, and will help you identify areas of tension.

## Internal Versus External Awareness

1.  First focus your attention on the outside world. Start sentences with "I am aware of." (For example, "I am aware of the cars going by outside the window, papers moving, the coffee perking, the breeze blowing and the blue carpet.")

2.  After you have become aware of everything that is going on around you, shift to focusing your attention on your body and your physical sensations, your internal world. (For example, "I am aware of feeling warm, my stomach gurgling, tension in my neck, nose tickling, and a cramp in my foot.")

3.  Shuttle back and forth between internal and external awareness. (For example, "I am aware of the chair pushing into my buttocks, the circle of yellow light from the lamp, my shoulders hunching up, the smell of bacon.")

4.  Used at free moments through the day, this exercise allows you to separate and appreciate the real difference between your inner and outer worlds.

## Body Scanning

Close your eyes. Starting with your toes and moving up your body, ask yourself, "Where am I tense?" Whenever you discover a tense area, exaggerate it slightly so you can become aware of it. Be aware of the muscles in your body that are tense. Then, for example, say to yourself, "I am tensing my neck muscles . . . I am hurting myself . . . I am creating tension in my body." Note that all muscular tension is self-produced. At this point, be aware of any life situation that may be causing the tension in your body and what you could do to change it.

## Letting Go of Your Body

Lie down on a rug or a firm bed and get comfortable. Pull your feet up until your feet rest flat on the floor and close your eyes. Check yourself for comfort. (This may require shifting your body around.) Become aware of your breathing . . . Feel the air move into your nose, mouth, and down your throat into your lungs. Focus on your body and let all of the parts come into your awareness spontaneously. What parts of your body come into awareness first? What parts are you less aware of? Become aware of which parts of your body you can easily feel and which parts of your body have little sensation. Do you notice any difference between the right and left side of your body? Now become aware of any physical discomfort you are feeling. Become aware of this discomfort until you can describe it in detail. Focus and be aware of what happens to this discomfort. It may change . . . Let your body do whatever it wants to do. Continue letting go for five to ten minutes, allowing your body to take over.

## Stress Awareness Diary

Some parts of the day are more stressful than others, and some stressful events are more likely to produce physical and emotional symptoms than others. Certain types of stressful events often produce characteristic symptoms. It is useful to keep a record of stressful events as well as symptoms that may have been a stress reaction.

Keep a stress awareness diary for two weeks. Make a note of the time that a stressful event occurs and the time you notice a physical or emotional symptom that could be related to the stress.

The following stress awareness diary is from the Monday of a department store clerk:

| Time | Stressful event | Symptom |
|------|-----------------|---------|
| 8:00 | Alarm doesn't go off, late, rushing | |
| 9:30 | | Slight headache |
| 11:00 | Customer is rude and insulting | |
| 11:15 | | Anger, tightness in stomach |
| 3:00 | Return of three big-ticket items, much paper work | |
| 3:15 | | Depression, slight headache |
| 5:30 | Heavy commute traffic | |
| 6:30 | Irritable with son | Anger, pounding headache |
| 6:35 | Wife defends son | Tightness in stomach |

As you can see, the diary identifies how particular stresses result in predictable symptoms. Interpersonal confrontations may characteristically be followed by stomach tension. Rushing may be causing vasoconstriction (tightening of the blood vessels) for this individual, and therefore resulting in irritability and headaches. You can use your stress awareness diary to discover and chart your stressful events and characteristic reactions.

After using these body awareness exercises, you will begin to recognize where your body stores muscular tension. When you allow yourself increased awareness, you can find ways to let go of the tension you discover. Along with the release of tension, you will experience increased energy and a sense of well-being.

After your stress awareness diary has helped you identify your reactions to stress, you should continue to record your progress with the other relaxation techniques in this workbook.

# Stress Awareness Diary

Date _____ Day of the week _____

| Time | Stressful event | Symptom |
| --- | --- | --- |
| _____ | _____ | _____ |
| _____ | _____ | _____ |
| _____ | _____ | _____ |
| _____ | _____ | _____ |
| _____ | _____ | _____ |
| _____ | _____ | _____ |
| _____ | _____ | _____ |
| _____ | _____ | _____ |
| _____ | _____ | _____ |
| _____ | _____ | _____ |
| _____ | _____ | _____ |
| _____ | _____ | _____ |
| _____ | _____ | _____ |
| _____ | _____ | _____ |
| _____ | _____ | _____ |
| _____ | _____ | _____ |
| _____ | _____ | _____ |
| _____ | _____ | _____ |
| _____ | _____ | _____ |
| _____ | _____ | _____ |
| _____ | _____ | _____ |

To keep a convenient record of how you feel before and after your relaxation exercises, use the following record of general tension.

## Record of General Tension

Rate yourself on this 10-point scale before and after you do your relaxation exercise.

| 1 | 2 | 3 | 4 | 5 |
|---|---|---|---|---|
| totally relaxed no tension | very relaxed | moderately relaxed | fairly relaxed | slightly relaxed |

| 6 | 7 | 8 | 9 | 10 |
|---|---|---|---|---|
| slightly tense | fairly tense | moderately tense | very tense | extremely tense (the most uncomfortable you could be) |

| Week of | Before session | After session | Comments |
|---|---|---|---|
| Monday | | | |
| Tuesday | | | |
| Wednesday | | | |
| Thursday | | | |
| Friday | | | |
| Saturday | | | |
| Sunday | | | |

Your personal mind-body connection and the interactions between your thoughts, body, and social environment are an integral part of beginning to manage the stress in your life, as opposed to letting it manage you. This chapter will help you begin that process.

### Further Reading

Benson, H., and E. Stuart. 1992. *The Wellness Book.* New York: Birch Lane Press.

Borysenko, J. 1987. *Minding the Body, Mending the Mind.* Reading, MA: Addison-Wesley.

Coleman, D., and J. Gurin. 1993. *Mind Body Medicine: How To Use Your Mind for Better Health.* Yonkers, NY: Consumer Reports Books.

Lorig, K., et al. 1994. *Living a Healthy Life With Chronic Conditions.* Palo Alto, CA: Bull Publishing.

Lowen, Alexander. 1976. *Bioenergetics.* New York: Viking-Penguin.

Scheller, Mary Dale. 1992. *Growing Older, Feeling Better.* Palo Alto, CA: Bull Publishing.

# 3

# Breathing

Breathing is a necessity of life that most people take for granted. With each breath of air, you obtain oxygen and release the waste product carbon dioxide. Poor breathing habits diminish the flow of these gases to and from your body, making it harder for you to cope with stressful situations. Improper breathing contributes to anxiety, panic attacks, depression, muscle tension, headaches, and fatigue. As you learn to be aware of your breathing and practice slowing and normalizing your breaths, your mind will quiet and your body will relax. Breathing awareness and good breathing habits will enhance your psychological and physical well-being, whether you practice them alone or in combination with other relaxation techniques.

Let's examine a breath. When you inhale, air is drawn in through your nose, where it is warmed to body temperature, humidified, and partially cleansed. Your diaphragm, a sheet-like muscle separating the lungs and the abdomen, facilitates your breathing by expanding and contracting as you breathe in and out.

Your lungs are like a tree with many branches (bronchial tubes) that carry air to elastic air sacs (alveoli). The alveoli have the balloon-like ability to expand when air is taken into the lungs and contract when air is let out. Small blood vessels (capillaries) surrounding the alveoli receive oxygen and transport it to your heart.

The blood that your heart pumps carries oxygen to all parts of your body. An exchange occurs in which blood cells receive oxygen and release carbon dioxide, a waste product that is carried back to your heart and lungs and exhaled. This efficient method of transporting and exchanging oxygen is vital to sustain life.

When you breathe, you typically use one of two patterns: (1) chest or thoracic breathing and (2) abdominal or diaphragmatic breathing.

Chest or thoracic breathing is often associated with anxiety or other emotional distress. It is also common in people who wear restricted clothing or lead sedentary or stressful lives. Chest breathing is shallow and often irregular and rapid. When air is inhaled, the chest expands and the shoulders rise to take in the air. Anxious people may experience breathholding, hyper-ventilation or constricted breathing, shortness of breath, or fear of passing out. If an insufficient

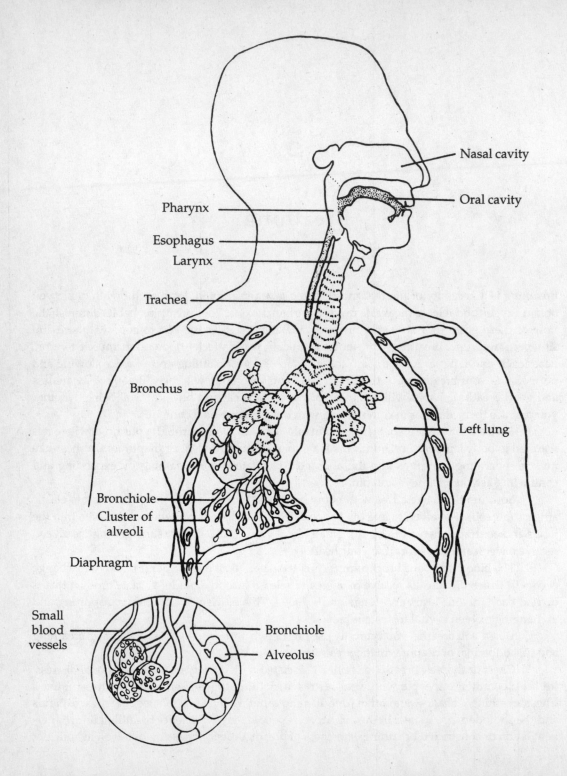

Adapted from *The Anatomy Coloring Book* by Wynn Kapit and Lawrence M. Elson, Harper & Row, New York, 1977.

amount of air reaches your lungs, your blood is not properly oxygenated, your heart rate and muscle tension increase, and your stress response is turned on.

Abdominal or diaphragmatic breathing is the natural breathing of newborn babies and sleeping adults. Inhaled air is drawn deep into the lungs and exhaled as the diaphragm contracts and expands. Breathing is even and nonconstricting. The respiratory system is able to do its job of producing energy from oxygen and removing waste products.

By increasing your awareness of your own breathing patterns and shifting to more abdominal breathing, you can reduce the muscle tension and anxiety present with stress-related symptoms or thoughts. Diaphragmatic breathing is the easiest way of eliciting the relaxation response.

## Symptom Relief

Breathing exercises have been found to be effective in reducing generalized anxiety disorders, panic attacks and agoraphobia, depression, irritability, muscle tension, headaches, and fatigue. They are used in the treatment and prevention of breathholding, hyperventilation, shallow breathing, and cold hands and feet.

## Time for Mastery

While a breathing exercise can be learned in a matter of minutes and some benefits experienced immediately, the profound effects of the exercise may not be fully appreciated until after months of persistent practice. After you have tried the exercises presented in this chapter, develop a breathing program incorporating those exercises you find most beneficial and follow your program with patience and persistence.

## Instructions

This chapter is divided up into four sections: (1) breathing for awareness and relaxation, (2) breathing to release tension, (3) breathing to stimulate alertness, and (4) breathing for symptom control.

## 1. Breathing for Awareness and Relaxation

Your first step is to increase your awareness of your breathing habits and to learn how to use breathing as a relaxation skill.

### Breathing Awareness

1. Close your eyes. Put your right hand on your abdomen, right at the waistline, and put your left hand on your chest, right in the center.

2. Without trying to change your breathing, simply notice how you are breathing. Which hand rises the most as you inhale—the hand on your chest or the hand on your belly?

If your abdomen expands, then you are breathing from your abdomen or diaphragm. If your belly doesn't move or moves less than your chest, then you are breathing from your chest.

The trick to shifting from chest to abdominal breathing is to make one or two full exhalations that push out the air from the bottom of your lungs. This will create a vacuum that will pull in a deep, diaphragmatic breath on your next inhalation.

## Diaphragmatic or Abdominal Breathing

1. Lie down on a rug or blanket on the floor in a "dead body" pose—your legs straight and slightly apart, your toes pointed comfortably outward, your arms at your sides and not touching your body, your palms up, and your eyes closed.

2. Bring your attention to your breathing and place your hand on the spot that seems to rise and fall the most as you inhale and exhale.

3. Gently place both of your hands or a book on your abdomen and follow your breathing. Notice how your abdomen rises with each inhalation and falls with each exhalation.

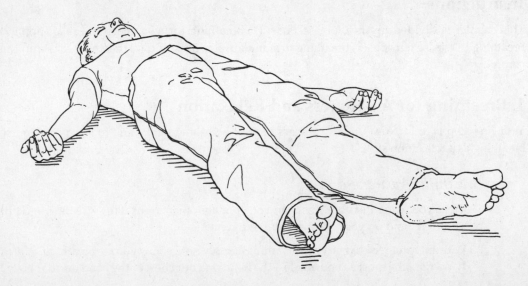

4. Breathe through your nose. (If possible, always clear your nasal passages before doing breathing exercises.)

5. If you experience difficulty breathing into your abdomen, press your hand down on your abdomen as you exhale and let your abdomen push your hand back up as you inhale deeply.

6. Is your chest moving in harmony with your abdomen or is it rigid? Spend a minute or two letting your chest follow the movement of your abdomen.

7. If you continue to experience difficulty breathing into your abdomen, an alternative is to lie on your stomach, with your head rested on your folded hands. Take deep abdominal breaths so you can feel your abdomen pushing against the floor.

## Deep Breathing

1. Although this exercise can be practiced in a variety of poses, the following is recommended: lie down on a blanket or rug on the floor. Bend your knees and move your feet about eight inches apart, with your toes turned slightly outward. Make sure that your spine is straight.

2. Scan your body for tension.

3. Place one hand on your abdomen and one hand on your chest.

4. Inhale slowly and deeply through your nose into your abdomen to push up your hand as much as feels comfortable. Your chest should move only a little and only with your abdomen.

5. When you feel at ease with step 4, smile slightly and inhale through your nose and exhale through your mouth, making a quiet, relaxing, whooshing sound like the wind as you blow gently out. Your mouth, tongue and jaw will be relaxed. Take long, slow, deep breaths that raise and lower your abdomen. Focus on the sound and feeling of breathing as you become more and more relaxed.

6. Continue deep breathing for about five or ten minutes at a time, once or twice a day, for a couple of weeks. Then, if you like, extend this period to twenty minutes.

7. At the end of each deep breathing session, take a little time to once more scan your body for tension. Compare the tension you feel at the conclusion of the exercise with that which you experienced when you began.

8. When you become at ease with breathing into your abdomen, practice it any time during the day when you feel like it and you are sitting down or standing still. Concentrate on your abdomen moving up and down, the air moving in and out of your lungs, and the feeling of relaxation that deep breathing gives you.

9. When you have learned to relax yourself using deep breathing, practice it whenever you feel yourself getting tense.

### Complete Natural Breathing

1. Begin by sitting or standing up straight in a good posture.

2. Breathe through your nose.

3. As you inhale, *first* fill the lower section of your lungs. (Your diaphragm will push your abdomen outward to make room for the air.) *Second,* fill the middle part of your lungs as your lower ribs and chest move forward slightly to accommodate the air. *Third,* fill the upper part of your lungs as your raise your chest slightly and draw in your abdomen a little to support your lungs. (You might imagine you're blowing up a balloon.) These three steps can be performed in one smooth, continuous inhalation, which with practice can be completed in a couple of seconds.

4. Now hold your breath for a few seconds to experience your full lungs.

5. As you slowly exhale, pull your abdomen in slightly and slowly lift it up as your lungs empty. When you have completely exhaled, relax your abdomen and chest.

6. Now and then at the end of the inhalation phase, raise your shoulders and collarbone slightly so that the very top of your shoulders are sure to be replenished with fresh air.

## 2. Breathing To Release Tension

Use the following exercises to enhance relaxation and release tension.

### Breath Counting

1. Sit or lie in a comfortable position with your arms and legs uncrossed and your spine straight.

2. Breathe in deeply into your abdomen. Let yourself pause before you exhale.

3. As you exhale, count "One" to yourself. As you continue to inhale and exhale, count each exhalation by saying "Two . . . three . . . four."

4. Continue counting your exhalations in sets of four for five to ten minutes.

5. Notice your breathing gradually slowing, your body relaxing, and your mind calming as you practice this breathing meditation.

### The Relaxing Sigh

During the day, you probably catch yourself sighing or yawning. This is generally a sign that you are not getting enough oxygen. Sighing and yawning are your body's way of remedying the situation. A sigh is often accompanied by a sense that things are not quite as they should be and a feeling of tension. Since a sigh actually does release a bit of this tension, you can practice sighing at will as a means of relaxing.

1. Sit or stand up straight.

2. Sigh deeply, letting out a sound of deep relief as the air rushes out of your lungs.

3. Don't think about inhaling—just let the air come in naturally.

4. Take eight to twelve of these relaxing sighs and let yourself experience the feeling of relaxation. Repeat whenever you feel the need for it.

### Letting Go of Tension

1. Sit comfortably in a chair with your feet on the floor.

2. Breathe in deeply into your abdomen and say to yourself, "Breathe in relaxation." Let yourself pause before you exhale.

3. Breathe out from your abdomen and say to yourself, "Breathe out tension." Pause before you inhale.

4. Use each inhalation as a moment to become aware of any tension in your body.

5. Use each exhalation as an opportunity to let go of tension.

6. You may find it helpful to use your imagination to picture or feel the relaxation entering and the tension leaving your body.

## 3. Breathing To Stimulate Alertness

These exercises can be used to stimulate and tone your entire breathing apparatus and refresh your whole body.

### Purifying Breath

This exercise can be practiced by itself or combined with other breathing exercises.

1. Begin by sitting or standing up straight in a good posture.

2. Inhale a complete natural breath.

3. Hold this breath for a few seconds.

4. Pretend that you are blowing through a straw and exhale a little of the air with considerable force through the small opening between your lips. Stop exhaling for a moment and then blow out a bit more air. Continue this procedure until all the air is exhaled in small, forceful puffs.

### The Windmill

When you have been bent over your work for several hours and are feeling tense, this exercise will relax you and make you more alert.

1. Stand up straight with your arms out in front of you.

2. Inhale and hold a complete natural breath.

3. Swing your arms backward in a circle several times and then reverse directions. For variety, try rotating them alternately like a windmill.

4. Exhale forcefully through your mouth.

5. Practice a couple of purifying breaths.

6. Repeat this exercise as often as you like.

### Bending

This exercise is a useful one to use when you feel stiff and tense. It has the added benefit of stretching your torso, making it more flexible for breathing.

1. Stand up straight with your hands on your hips.

2. Inhale and hold a complete natural breath.

3. Let the lower part of your body remain stiff. Bow forward as far as you can, slowly exhaling completely through your mouth.

4. Stand up straight again. Inhale and hold another complete natural breath.

5. Bend backwards as you slowly exhale.

6. Stand up straight again and inhale and hold another complete natural breath.

7. Continue this exercise, first bending backwards and then to the left and right sides.

8. After each round of four bends, practice one purifying breath.

9. Do four full rounds.

## 4. Breathing for Symptom Control or Release

### Abdominal Breathing and Imagination

This exercise combines the relaxing benefits of complete natural breathing with the curative value of positive autosuggestions.

1. Lie down on a rug or blanket on the floor in a "dead body" pose.

2. Place your hands gently on your solar plexus (the point where your ribs start to separate above your abdomen) and practice complete natural breathing for a few minutes.

3. Imagine that energy is rushing into your lungs with each incoming breath of air and being immediately stored in your solar plexus. Imagine that this energy is flowing out to all parts of your body with each exhalation. Form a mental picture of this energizing process.

4. Continue on a daily basis for at least five to ten minutes a day.

**Alternatives to step 3:**

3a. Keep one hand on your solar plexus and move the other hand to a point on your body that hurts. As you inhale, imagine energy coming in and being stored. As you exhale, imagine the energy flowing to the spot that hurts and stimulating it. As you continue to inhale more energy, imagine this energy driving out the pain with each exhalation. Keep a clear picture of this process in your mind as you alternately stimulate the spot that hurts and then drive out the pain.

3b. Keep one hand on your solar plexus and move the other hand to a point on your body that has been injured or is infected. Imagine the energy coming in and being stored as you inhale. As you exhale, imagine that you are directing energy to the affected point and stimulating it, driving out the infection or healing it. Picture this process in your mind's eye.

## Alternative Breathing

While this relaxation exercise is generally useful, people suffering from tension or sinus headaches often find it particularly beneficial.

1. Sit in a comfortable position with good posture.

2. Rest the index and second finger of your right hand on your forehead.

3. Close your right nostril with your thumb.

4. Inhale slowly and soundlessly through your left nostril.

5. Close your left nostril with your ring finger and simultaneously open your right nostril by removing your thumb.

6. Exhale slowly and soundlessly and as thoroughly as possible through your right nostril.

7. Inhale through your right nostril.

8. Close your right nostril with your thumb and open your left nostril.

9. Exhale through your left nostril.

10. Inhale through your left nostril.

11. Begin by doing 5 cycles. Then slowly raise the number to from 10 to 25 cycles.

## Breath Training

This exercise, which has been adapted from Nick Masi's 1993 audiocassette, *Breath of Life*, has also been called "breathing retraining" and "controlled breathing." Individuals with panic disorder or agoraphobia have found it particularly helpful. When most people feel panic, they have a tendency to gasp, take in a breath, and hold onto it. The resulting sensation of fullness and inability to get enough air in turn produces quick, shallow breathing or hyperventilation.

The hyperventilation triggers the panic attack. Breath training provides a crucial counting or pacing procedure that helps to counteract this process. Here are the steps to follow.

1. *Exhale first.* At the first sign of nervousness or panic, at the first "what if" thought that you might pass out, have a heart attack, or be unable to breathe, *always exhale.* It is important to exhale first so that your lungs open up and it feels like there's plenty of room to take a good deep breath.

2. Inhale and exhale through your nose. Exhaling through your nose will slow down your breathing and prevent hyperventilation. As an alternative to breathing through your nose, inhale through your mouth and make a purifying exhalation through your mouth by pretending that you are blowing out through a straw.

3. Lie on your back with your hand over your abdomen, and the other hand on your chest. *Exhale first,* and then breathe in through your nose, counting "One . . . two . . . three." Pause a second, and then breathe out through your mouth, counting "One . . . two . . . three . . . four." Make sure that your exhalation is always longer than your inhalation. This will protect you from taking short, gasping panic breaths.

Alternative breathing

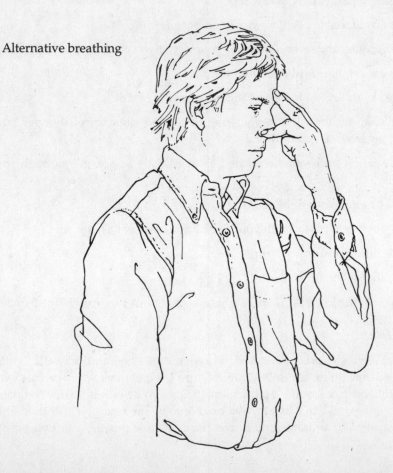

4. After you feel comfortable with step 3, you can slow your breathing even further. Breathe in and count "One . . . two . . . three . . . four"; pause and breathe out, counting "One . . . two . . . three . . . four . . . five." Keep practicing these slow deep breaths, pushing the hand on your abdomen up, but allowing very little movement for the hand on your chest. When your minds drifts, refocus on your breathing.

**Alternative positions:**

1a. Lie on your stomach with your hands folded under your head. Continue to count "One . . . two . . . three" as you breathe in and "One . . . two . . . three . . . four" as you breathe out. As in step 4 above, breathe even more slowly by counting to four as you inhale and to five as you exhale.

2a. Step 4 can also be done while you are standing, walking, and sitting. Pace your steps to match the same slow rate of your breathing.

When paced breathing feels comfortable and natural, you can replace counting with the words "in" as you inhale and "calm" as you exhale. Maintain the same pace, making each exhalation last slightly longer than each inhalation. Breathe in through your nose and breathe out through your mouth. *Always exhale first.*

## Controlled Breathing

If you find that it is difficult to use the counting techniques described above, you can make a pacing tape that will teach you controlled breathing. First you need to decide how to set the breathing rate that is best for you. Depending on how slowly you breathe when you are at rest, your rate can be set at either eight or twelve breaths a minute. To determine which interval will be better for you, relax and count how many breaths you take over a period of three minutes. If you counted more than thirty breaths, follow the instructions for a twelve breaths per minute tape. If you counted thirty or fewer, follow the instructions for an eight breaths per minute tape.

**To make a twelve breaths per minute pacing tape:**

1. Say the word "in" for two seconds.

2. Say the word "out" for two seconds.

3. Pause for one second.

4. Continue to repeat "in" for two seconds and "out" for two seconds, followed by a one-second pause.

5. Keep the tape going for about five minutes.

**To make an eight breaths per minute pacing tape:**

1. Say the word "in" for three seconds.

2. Say the word "out" for three seconds.

3. Pause for one second.

4. Continue to repeat that sequence for about five minutes.

After you have made your pacing tape, practice breathing with the tape four times per day. When you feel comfortable, practice controlled breathing with the tape off for thirty seconds and then turn the tape back on for one minute to see if your pace is still matched to the tape. If your breath rate remains the same, try turning the tape off for two minutes at a time, and then for five minutes. Each time you finish breathing on your own, turn the tape back on again to see if your pace is still matched to the tape.

## Further Reading

Benson, H., and E. Stuart. 1992. *The Wellness Book: The Comprehensive Guide to Maintaining Health and Treating Stress-Related Illness*. Secaucus, NJ: Birch Lane Press.

Borysensko, J. 1987. *Minding the Body, Mending the Mind*. Reading, MA: Addison-Wesley.

Loehr, J., and J. Migdow. 1986. *Take a Deep Breath*. New York: Villard Books.

Saraswati, Swami Janakananda. 1976. *Yoga, Tantra and Meditation*. New York: Ballantine.

Spreads, Carol. 1978. *Breathing—The ABC's*. New York: Harper and Row.

## Audiotapes

Masi, Nick. 1993. *Breath of Life*. Plantation, FL: Resource Warehouse.

*Progressive Relaxation and Breathing*. 1987. Oakland, CA: New Harbinger Publications.

*Ten Minutes to Relax*. 1990. Manhasset, NY: Vital Body Marketing Company.

# 4

# Progressive Relaxation

You cannot have the feeling of warm well-being in your body and at the same time experience psychological stress. Progressive relaxation of your muscles reduces pulse rate and blood pressure as well as decreasing perspiration and respiration rates. Deep muscle relaxation, when successfully mastered, can be used as an anti-anxiety pill.

Edmund Jacobson, a Chicago physician, published the book *Progressive Relaxation* in 1929. In this book he described his deep muscle relaxation technique, which he asserted required no imagination, willpower or suggestion. His technique is based on the premise that the body responds to anxiety-provoking thoughts and events with muscle tension. This physiological tension, in turn, increases the subjective experience of anxiety. Deep muscle relaxation reduces physiological tension and is incompatible with anxiety: The habit of responding with one blocks the habit of responding with the other.

## Symptom Relief

Excellent results have been found in the treatment of muscular tension, anxiety, insomnia, depression, fatigue, irritable bowel, muscle spasms, neck and back pain, high blood pressure, mild phobias, and stuttering.

## Time for Mastery

One to two weeks. Two fifteen minute sessions per day.

## Instructions

Most people do not realize which of their muscles are chronically tense. Progressive relaxation provides a way of identifying particular muscles and muscle groups and distinguishing between sensations of tension and deep relaxation. Four major muscle groups will be covered:

1. Hands, forearms, and biceps

2. Head, face, throat, and shoulders, including concentration on forehead, cheeks, nose, eyes, jaws, lips, tongue, and neck. Considerable attention is devoted to your head, because from the emotional point of view, the most important muscles in your body are situated in and around this region.

3. Chest, stomach, and lower back.

4. Thighs, buttocks, calves, and feet.

Progressive relaxation can be practiced lying down or in a chair with your head supported. Each muscle or muscle grouping is tensed from five to seven seconds and then relaxed for twenty to thirty seconds. This procedure is repeated at least once. If an area remains tense, you can practice up to five times. You may also find it useful to use the following relaxing expressions when untensing:

*Let go of the tension.*

*Throw away the tension—I am feeling calm and rested.*

*Relax and smooth out the muscles.*

*Let the tension dissolve away.*

Once the procedure is familiar enough to be remembered, keep your eyes closed and focus attention on just one muscle group at a time. The instructions for progressive relaxation are divided into two sections. The first part, which you may wish to tape and replay when practicing, will familiarize you with the muscles in your body which are most commonly tense. The second section shortens the procedure by simultaneously tensing and relaxing many muscles at one time so that deep muscle relaxation can be achieved in a very brief period.

## Basic Procedure

Get in a comfortable position and relax. Now clench your right fist, tighter and tighter, studying the tension as you do so. Keep it clenched and notice the tension in your fist, hand, and forearm. Now relax. Feel the looseness in your right hand, and notice the contrast with the tension. Repeat this procedure with your right fist again, always noticing as you relax that this is the opposite of tension—relax and feel the difference. Repeat the entire procedure with your left fist, then both fists at once.

Now bend your elbows and tense your biceps. Tense them as hard as you can and observe the feeling of tautness. Relax, straighten out your arms. Let the relaxation develop and feel that difference. Repeat this, and all succeeding procedures at least once.

Turning attention to your head, wrinkle your forehead as tight as you can. Now relax and smooth it out. Let yourself imagine your entire forehead and scalp becoming smooth and at rest. Now frown and notice the strain spreading throughout your forehead. Let go. Allow your brow to become smooth again. Close your eyes now, squint them tighter. Look for the tension. Relax your eyes. Let them remain closed gently and comfortably. Now clench your jaw, bite hard, notice the tension throughout your jaw. Relax your jaw. When the jaw is relaxed, your lips will be slightly parted. Let yourself really appreciate the contrast between tension and relaxation. Now press your tongue against the roof of your mouth. Feel the ache in the back of your mouth. Relax. Press your lips now, purse them into an "O." Relax your lips. Notice that your forehead, scalp, eyes, jaw, tongue and lips are all relaxed.

Press your head back as far as it can comfortably go and observe the tension in your neck. Roll it to the right and feel the changing locus of stress, roll it to the left. Straighten your head and bring it forward, press your chin against your chest. Feel the tension in your throat, the back of your neck. Relax, allowing your head to return to a comfortable position. Let the relaxation deepen. Now shrug your shoulders. Keep the tension as you hunch your head down between your shoulders. Relax your shoulders. Drop them back and feel the relaxation spreading through your neck, throat and shoulders, pure relaxation, deeper and deeper.

Give your entire body a chance to relax. Feel the comfort and the heaviness. Now breathe in and fill your lungs completely. Hold your breath. Notice the tension. Now exhale, let your chest become loose, let the air hiss out. Continue relaxing, letting your breath come freely and gently. Repeat this several times, noticing the tension draining from your body as you exhale. Next, tighten your stomach and hold. Note the tension, then relax. Now place your hand on your stomach. Breathe deeply into your stomach, pushing your hand up. Hold, and relax. Feel the contrast of relaxation as the air rushes out. Now arch your back, without straining. Keep the rest of your body as relaxed as possible. Focus on the tension in your lower back. Now relax, deeper and deeper.

Tighten your buttocks and thighs. Flex your thighs by pressing down your heels as hard as you can. Relax and feel the difference. Now curl your toes downward, making your calves tense. Study the tension. Relax. Now bend your toes toward your face, creating tension in your shins. Relax again.

Feel the heaviness throughout your lower body as the relaxation deepens. Relax your feet, ankles, calves, shins, knees, thighs, and buttocks. Now let the relaxation spread to your stomach, lower back, and chest. Let go more and more. Experience the relaxation deepening in your shoulders, arms, and hands. Deeper and deeper. Notice the feeling of looseness and relaxation in your neck, jaws, and all your facial muscles.

## Shorthand Procedure

The following is a procedure for achieving deep muscle relaxation quickly. Whole muscle groups are simultaneously tensed and then relaxed. As before, repeat each procedure at least once, tensing each muscle group from five to seven seconds and then relaxing from 15 to 30 seconds. Remember to notice the contrast between the sensations of tension and relaxation.

1. Curl both fists, tightening biceps and forearms (Charles Atlas pose). Relax.

2. Wrinkle up forehead. At the same time, press your head as far back as possible, roll it clockwise in a complete circle, reverse. Now wrinkle up the muscles of your face like a walnut: frowning, eyes squinted, lips pursed, tongue pressing the roof of the mouth, and shoulders hunched. Relax.

3. Arch back as you take a deep breath into the chest. Hold. Relax. Take a deep breath, pressing out the stomach. Hold. Relax.

4. Pull feet and toes back toward face, tightening shins. Hold. Relax. Curl toes, simultaneously tightening calves, thighs and buttocks. Relax.

## Special Considerations

1. If you make a tape of the basic procedure to facilitate your relaxation program, remember to space each procedure so that time is allowed to experience the tension and relaxation before going on to the next muscle or muscle group.

2. Most people have somewhat limited success when they begin deep muscle relaxation, but it is only a matter of practice. Whereas twenty minutes of work might initially bring only partial relaxation, it will eventually be possible to relax your whole body in a few moments.

3. Sometimes in the beginning, it may seem to you as though relaxation is complete. But although the muscle or muscle group may well be partially relaxed, a certain number of muscle fibers will still be contracted. It is the act of relaxing these additional fibers that will bring about the emotional effects you want. It is helpful to say to yourself during the relaxation phase, "Let go more and more."

4. Caution should be taken in tensing the neck and back. Excessive tightening can result in muscle or spinal damage. It is also commonly observed that overtightening the toes or feet results in muscle cramping.

5. People new to this technique sometimes make the error of relaxing tension gradually. This slow-motion release of tension may look relaxed, but it actually requires sustained tension. When you release the tension in a particular muscle, let it go instantly, as though you had just turned off an electrical current. Let your muscles become suddenly limp.

### Further Reading

Jacobson, Edmund. 1974. *Progressive Relaxation.* Chicago: The University of Chicago Press, Midway Reprint.

Wolpe, Joseph. 1982. *The Practice of Behavior Therapy.* 3rd ed. New York: Pergamon Press.

# 5

# Meditation

Meditation is the practice of uncritically attempting to focus your attention on one thing at a time. Exactly what that thing is is relatively unimportant and varies from one tradition to the next. Often the meditator repeats, either aloud or silently, a syllable, word, or group of words. This is known as mantra mediation. Gazing at a fixed object such as a flame or flower can also anchor the attention. Many meditators find that a convenient and relaxing point of focus is the rising and falling of their own breath. But you can use anything as an object of meditation . . . Aunt Mary's maiden name, the calendar on your desk, or even the tip of your nose.

It is important to understand that the heart of meditation lies not simply in focusing on one object to the exclusion of all other thought, but rather in the *attempt* to achieve this type of focus. The nature of the mind is such that it does not want to stay concentrated. Myriads of thoughts will appear and seemingly interfere with the meditation. A typical meditation might go something like this (the meditator in this case has chosen the task of counting to three repeatedly):

> One . . . two . . . This isn't so hard . . . one . . . two . . . three . . . one . . . I'm not having many thoughts at all . . . Oh, oh, I just had a thought . . . That was another one . . . two . . . My nose itches . . . one . . . I wonder if it's okay to scratch it . . . Darn, there was another thought. I've got to try harder . . . one . . . two . . . three . . . one . . . two . . . I was judging myself pretty harshly. I'm not supposed to do that . . . one . . . two . . . three . . . one . . . I'm hungry . . . Wonder what I'll cook tonight . . . one . . . two . . . three . . . I'm having way too many thoughts . . . I'll never get this right . . . one . . . two . . . Now don't judge . . . one . . . two . . . three . . . one . . .

Each time this meditator realizes that his mind has drifted to other thoughts, he chooses instead to dwell on the original object of his attention. By repeating this one moment of awareness, a moment which consists of noticing the thought and then refocusing the attention, over time a number of surprising realizations will become apparent:

- It is impossible to worry, fear, or hate when your mind is thinking about something other than the object of these emotions.

- It isn't necessary to think about everything that pops into your head. You have the ability to choose which thoughts you will think about.

- The seemingly diverse contents of your mind can really fit into a few simple categories, such as: grudging thoughts, fearful thoughts, angry thoughts, wanting thoughts, planning thoughts, memories, and so on.

- You act in certain ways because you have certain thoughts which, over your lifetime, have become habitual. Habitual patterns of thought and perception will begin to lose their influence over your life once you become aware of them.

- Emotion, aside from the thoughts and pictures in your mind, consists entirely of physical sensations in your body.

- Even the strongest emotion will become manageable if you concentrate on the sensations in your body, and not the content of the thought that produced the emotion.

- Thought and emotion are not permanent. They pass into and out of your body and mind. They need not leave a trace.

- When you are awake to what is happening *right now,* the extreme highs and extreme lows of your emotional response to life will disappear. You will live life with equanimity.

Members of many Eastern religions have long realized the benefits of meditation, but most Westerners have approached the practice with a skeptical eye. Weren't the only people who practice meditation members of non-Christian religions? That in itself was reason enough for many to view it with suspicion. And anyone who touted meditation as a sure way to achieve mental and physical well being was seen as a fanatic trying to make a quick buck from a totally untested method.

In 1968, Dr. Herbert Benson and his colleagues at Harvard Medical School decided to put meditation to the test. Volunteer practitioners of Transcendental Meditation were tested to see if meditation really could counter the physiological effects of stress. Benson scientifically proved that: (1) Heart beat and breathing rates slow down. (2) Oxygen consumption falls by 20 percent. (3) Blood lactate levels drop. (This level rises with stress and fatigue.) (4) Skin resistance to electrical current, a sign of relaxation, increases fourfold. (5) EEG ratings of brain wave patterns indicate increased alpha activity, another sign of relaxation.

Benson went on to prove that any meditational practice could duplicate these physiological changes as long as four factors were present: (1) a relatively quiet environment, (2) a mental device that provides a constant stimulus, (3) a comfortable position, and (4) a passive attitude (this aspect will be discussed in depth later).

## Symptom Effectiveness

Meditation has been used successfully in the treatment and prevention of high blood pressure, heart disease, migraine headaches, and autoimmune diseases such as diabetes and arthritis. It has proved helpful in curtailing obsessive thinking, anxiety, depression, and hostility.

## Time for Mastery

You can learn to meditate within a few minutes. Immediately your body will use less oxygen (a sign of deep relaxation) while you are meditating. However, as with most things, the benefits of meditation increase with practice. Levels of relaxation deepen. Attention becomes more steady. You become more adept at living in the present moment. Therefore, it is important to meditate regularly.

## Instructions

### Establishing Your Posture

**A.** From the following, select a position that is comfortable for you:

- In a chair with your knees comfortably apart and your hands resting in your lap.

- Tailor-fashion (cross-legged) on the floor. This position is most comfortable and stable when a cushion is placed under your buttocks so that both knees touch the floor.

- Japanese fashion on your knees with your big toes touching and your heels pointed outward so that your buttocks rest on the soles of your feet. Again, if you place a cushion between your feet on which your buttocks can rest, you will be able to hold the position for a much longer period of time.

- The yoga full lotus position. This position requires so much physical conditioning that it is not recommended for beginners.

**B.** Sit with your back straight (but not ramrod rigid) and let the weight of your head fall directly down upon your spinal column. This can be accomplished by pulling your chin in slightly. Allow the small of your back to arch.

**C.** Rock briefly from side to side, then from front to back and establish the point at which your upper torso feels balanced on your hips.

**D.** Close your mouth and breathe through your nose. Place your tongue on the roof of your mouth.

### Centering Yourself
#### A. Grounding

Close your eyes and focus on the place where your body touches the cushion or chair. What are the sensations there? Next notice the places where your body

# Establishing Your Posture

Yoga lotus position

Japanese-fashion

Tailor-fashion

touches itself. Are your hands crossed? Your legs? Pay attention to the sensation at these places of contact. Finally focus on the way your body takes up space. Does it take up a lot of space? A small amount? Can you feel the boundary between your body and space? Notice the feelings there.

**B. Breathing**

With your eyes closed, take several deep breaths and notice the quality of your breathing. Is it fast or slow? Deep or shallow? Notice where your breath rests in your body. Is it up high in your chest? In the midsection around your stomach? Down low in your belly? Try moving your breath from one area to the other. Breathe into your upper chest, then into your stomach, then drop your breath into your lower belly. Feel your abdomen expand and contract as the air goes in and out. Notice how the upper chest and stomach areas seem almost still. This "dropped breath" is the most relaxing stance from which to meditate. However, if you have difficulty taking deep belly breaths, pay this no mind. Your breath will drop of its own accord as you become more practiced in meditation.

## Attitude

Maintaining a passive attitude during meditation is perhaps the most important element in eliciting relaxation. It is important to realize that, especially as a beginner, you will have many thoughts and relatively few moments of clear concentration. This is natural and to be expected. Realize that your thoughts are not really interruptions, but are an integral part of meditation. Without thoughts, you would not be able to develop the ability to let them go.

A passive attitude includes a lack of concern about whether you are doing things correctly, whether you are accomplishing any goals, or whether this meditation is right for you. Sit with the intention of "I'm going to put in my time here, just sitting, and whatever happens is exactly what should happen."

## A Word About Time

In general, any amount of time spent in meditation is more relaxing than not meditating at all. When you first begin to practice, maintain the meditation for only as long as is comfortable, even if this is only for five minutes a day. If you feel that you are forcing yourself to sit, you may develop an aversion to practicing meditation at all. As you progress in your practice and meditation becomes easier, you will find yourself wanting to extend your time. In terms of relaxation, twenty to thirty minutes once or twice a day is sufficient.

# Exercises

The following exercises are divided into five groups.

**Group 1** explains the mechanics of three basic meditations. Try each one a few times, then settle on the one you like best. Practice it regularly, at least once a day.

**Group 2** consists of meditational exercises which will help you to develop the skill of relaxing muscle groups at will.

**Group 3** introduces minor irritants into the basic sitting practice you selected from Group 1. In real life you may often find yourself in the presence of minor pain, annoyances, or disappointments which cause you to tense up. By practicing feeling relaxed around small irritations while you meditate, you will become more adept at handling life's larger irritations when they occur.

**Group 4** contains exercises that can be practiced inconspicuously. You may often be in situations where you feel tense but don't have the opportunity to sit in a quiet place and relax. These exercises will help you to relax while blending in with your everyday world.

**Group 5** teaches you how to let go of obsessive thoughts and feelings that make it difficult to relax because your mind wants to hold on to an idea or emotion that you experienced at an earlier time.

# Group 1. Three Basic Meditations

### 1. *Mantra Meditation*

This is the most common form of meditation throughout the world. Before you begin, select a word or syllable that you like. It may be a word which has meaning for you. Or it may be two nonsense syllables, the sound of which you find pleasant. Benson recommended using the word "one." Many meditators prefer the universal mantra, "OM."

**A.** Find your posture and center yourself. Take several deep breaths.

**B.** Chant your mantra silently to yourself. Say the word or syllables over and over within your mind. When your thought strays, note that, then bring your attention back to your mantra. If you notice any sensations in your body, note the feeling, then return to the repetition of your own special word. You needn't force it. Let your mantra find its own rhythm as you repeat it over and over again.

**C.** If you have the opportunity, you may want to try chanting your mantra aloud. Let the sound of your own voice fill you as you relax. Notice whether the sensations in your body are different from those you felt when you chanted silently. Which is more relaxing?

**D.** Remember, meditation is to be practiced with awareness. You may find that the repetition of a mantra, especially when repeated silently, can easily become mechanical. When this happens, you may have the sense that an inner voice is repeating your mantra while you are actually lost in thought or rapidly approaching sleep. Try to stay aware of each repetition of each syllable.

### 2. *Breath Counting Meditation*

This is perhaps the most relaxing form of meditation. Following the gentle ins and outs of the breath creates a sense of peace and restfulness.

**A.** Find your posture and center yourself. Take several deep breaths. Either close your eyes or fix them on a spot on the floor about four feet in front of you. Your eyes may or may not be focused.

**B.** Take deep but not forced belly breaths. As you do, focus your attention on each part of the breath: the inhale, the turn (the point at which you stop inhaling and start exhaling), the exhale, the pause (between the exhale and inhale), the turn (the point at which you start to inhale), the inhale, and so on. Pay careful attention to the pause. What are the sensations in your body as you pause between breaths?

**C.** As you exhale, say "one." Continue counting each exhale by saying "two . . . three . . . four." Then begin again with "one." If you lose count, simply start over with "one."

**D.** When you discover that your mind has slipped into thought, note this, then gently return to the counting of your breath.

**E.** If a particular sensation in your body catches your attention, focus on the sensation until it recedes. Then return your attention to the inhale and the exhale and the counting of your breath.

**F.** If you wish, try the following variation. Begin by counting your breath for several minutes. Then stop the actual counting and put your attention on the sensations of breathing. Focus on your abdomen as it expands and contracts. Can you sense how the size of the empty space in your abdomen grows and shrinks as your breath goes in and out of your belly? At first, you may have more thoughts when you practice this way than you had when you were counting breaths. The counting kept your mind returning in a small circle of numbers which left less room for rising thoughts. Do not be disturbed by this. Simply note each thought and then return your awareness to the sensations of your breath. Every now and then, you may come across a thought that you find enticing and want to contemplate. Tell yourself you will consider this thought when the meditation period is over and let it go. Sensations other than breathing may call your attention from time to time : a strain in your shoulder, or the pins and needles of your legs falling asleep. When this happens, let your attention focus on these new sensations until they fade into the background. Then go back to your breath. The sounds of the outside world will cross and recross the boundaries of your awareness. Note their passing and return to your breath.

## 3. *Gazing*

This form of meditation involves fixing your gaze on an object without thinking about it in words. Select a small object that you like. A stone, a candle, a piece of wood, or anything else that you feel is appropriate.

**A.** Find your posture, center yourself and take several deep breaths.

**B.** Set your object on a surface which is at eye level and about a foot or so away from you. Look at it carefully. Gaze rather than stare. Keep your eyes soft and relaxed, without frowning. Notice the object's color, texture, size, and shape. Trace its edges with your eyes. Cover every inch that is visible to you, and see if you can have the feeling of experiencing its qualities. Allow yourself to become totally involved in the exploration, as though you had never seen this object before.

C.  As thoughts or words you associate with the object pop up, simply note them and let them go. Return your attention to your object.

D.  If sensations in your body attract your attention, allow yourself to stay with the sensations until they fade while continuing to gaze at your object.

**Special Considerations**

1.  It is not necessary to feel as though you are relaxing while you meditate in order for you to actually become relaxed. You may feel as though you are thinking thousands of thoughts and are very restless. However, when you open your eyes at the end of your meditation, you will realize you feel much more relaxed than you did before meditating.

2.  As your mind quiets with meditation, old or hidden pain can arise from your subconscious. If you find that when you meditate you suddenly feel angry, depressed, or frightened, try to gently allow yourself to experience the feeling while resisting the temptation to make sense out of your feelings. If you feel the need, talk to a friend, counselor, or meditation teacher.

3.  You may hear or read about ideal conditions for meditation: that you should meditate only in a quiet place. Or meditate only two hours after you've eaten. Or meditate only in a position that you can hold comfortably for twenty minutes, and so on. Yes, these are ideal conditions, but life is seldom ideal. If the place isn't absolutely quiet or the only time you have to meditate is right after lunch, don't let these small obstacles keep you from meditating. If you find yourself being particularly bothered by noises or the rumblings of a full stomach, simply incorporate the annoying sensation in with the object of your meditation.

4.  If you adopt a daily sitting practice, you may find that there are stretches of time during which you will not want to meditate. Do not expect that your desire to meditate will grow constantly with your practice. If you feel discouraged, be gentle with yourself and try to work creatively on ways to make your practice more comfortable. Know that these periods of discouragement will go away by themselves in time. For helping to maintain a schedule, the value of finding a group with which you can meditate at least once a week cannot be overstated.

# Group 2. Releasing Muscular Tension

## 1. *The Moving Band Meditation*

A.  Find your posture, center yourself and take several deep breaths.

B.  Imagine that a three-inch-wide band encircles the top of your head. Focus your attention on that part of your head which is surrounded by the imaginary band. Notice the sensations. Is there any tension in your forehead? If so, try to relax it. Are there any other sensations in this area? Focus on them for a moment.

**C.** Lower the imaginary band three inches—the width of the band. Again focus your attention on the area encompassed by the band. Really try to feel around in there. What does the back of your eyeball feel like? Or the right wall of your nose? How are the muscles of your upper lip set? Any tension? Try to completely relax this area of your head. Breathe deeply and whisper to yourself, "Let it go, let it all go."

**D.** Continue to move the band down your body. Focus intently on any sensations. Wherever you notice tension, try to release it. As you do, take several deep belly breaths and relax. See if you can be aware of how the muscles feel as they relax.

**E.** When the band gets down to your torso, imagine that the band goes around one arm, then across your upper body, around the other arm, then across your back. Scan a section of each arm and your torso at the same time as though they were one part. Notice the sensations where the arms are separate from the body. What do these boundaries feel like? Can you make the sensation of the boundaries less distinct so that your arms feel like they are merging with your torso? Is there any tension? In the shoulders? The back? If so, relax these areas.

**F.** Move the band down your torso and arms to your legs, noting tension and releasing it. Focus on the sensation where your legs touch each other (if they do), and where they touch the floor. Again, feel the sensations at the points of contact, then try to experience the sensation of your legs merging together.

**G.** This exercise can be practiced in two different ways:

1. Move the band slowly down your body, carefully experiencing each sensation, noting all the points of tension and letting them go.

2. Quickly lower the band down your body. Move it as soon as your attention has given the encompassed area a brief scan. If practiced this way, repeat the entire exercise several times in a row.

Try both ways and see which is more relaxing.

## 2. *The Inner Exploration*

**A.** Find your posture and center yourself. Take two or three deep breaths.

**B.** Pick a part of your body on which to focus your attention. Explore it thoroughly with your awareness. For example, if you were concentrating on your jaw bone, you would want to have an idea about what it looks like. How is it attached to your head? Where are the muscles that move it? Can you tense and relax these muscles? What are the sensations when the jaw moves? When is it still? How are the teeth attached to it? What do your teeth feel like? The left front tooth? The last molar on the right? In what position is your jaw most relaxed?

**C.** It is helpful to explore any part of your body with the focal point of your mind, but especially those that fit into the following categories:

1. Parts of your body that are prone to hold tension. Some of these are the brow, jaw, neck, shoulders, and lower back.

2. Internal areas that tend to hold tension. Pay special attention to your stomach, chest, lower abdomen, and heart.

3. Areas of your body that you almost never think about in your daily life, such as your middle toe, your elbow, or the back of your knee.

# Group 3. Softening

People usually respond to pain, irritation, or any discomfort by trying to build a solid wall of tightness around it, attempting to block off the feeling. However, the more you resist pain, the more it hurts. And the more it hurts, the more you will try to resist it. This vicious circle produces one big knot of pain and resistance that is extremely difficult to untie.

An alternative way to deal with pain is to learn to soften around it. This means you first acknowledge pain's presence, and then simply allow yourself to experience, physically and mentally, whatever it is that hurts. Be your own good nurse, hold your own hand, tell yourself it's all right, and then sit with yourself compassionately as you experience sensations of discomfort.

When you soften around an irritation, you consciously relax your tense, clenched muscles around the spot that hurts. You focus on the hurting itself, without all the tightness you tend to add to it.

Softening also means that you notice but disregard your thoughts about how awful the discomfort is, how you have to move, how you have to scratch, how you can't stand it, and so on.

A metaphor may help you understand softening. It's like working the hard lumps out of a mound of clay so that you can feel a tiny pearl in the center. It's like removing screens placed around a candle flame so that you can see it clearly. It's like thawing out the frozen core of a large piece of meat so that you can remove the bone. It's like cleaning layers of grime off of the outside of a window so that you can see what's inside more clearly.

The following exercises introduce minor irritations into your basic meditation. By practicing with small irritations in a safe setting, you can begin to understand the process of softening.

## 1. *Don't Move*

A. Find your posture and center yourself. Take several deep breaths.

B. Make an agreement with yourself that for a preset period of time you will not move. Then begin your basic meditation.

C. As time passes, you may find yourself moving your head or shifting in your seat without realizing it. This is fine. Note the movement and return to your meditation. After a while you will be able to notice your intention to move a part of your body before you actually move it.

**D.** Once you are able to identify your intention to move, try to focus on what exactly your desire is. Do you want to squirm around in your chair? Stretch your back muscles? Maybe you have an itch, or an ant is crawling across your foot. Try to precisely identify the uncomfortable sensation. Remember now, don't move.

**E.** As you focus on the discomfort, try to soften around it. If muscle groups are tightening, try to relax them. Check these muscle groups often. They will not want to stay relaxed. Where is your breath? Is it high in your chest? If so, try to drop it into your belly. Focus on the sensation of discomfort. What is the feeling here? Stay with it for a while.

**F.** When time is up, move your body slowly to the position in which you've been wanting to sit. Focus on the sensations. Is the relief immediate? Is the relief gradual? In what way does your body feel better? Is there any tension? If so, release it.

## 2. *The Lifted Arm*

**A.** Find your posture and center yourself. Take several deep breaths.

**B.** Place your left hand on your lap. Bend your right arm at your elbow and lift the arm so that the tips of your fingers are about even with the top of your head. In other words, raise your hand as though you want to answer a question.

**C.** Begin your basic meditation. As the right arm begins to tire, focus on the sensation of tiredness. Which muscles are actually holding the arm up? Can you find a way to relax them somewhat without letting the arm fall? Scan your body and see if other groups are tightening. Are your legs tensing because your arm hurts? If so, can you relax them? Focus on your heart, stomach and lungs. Are you beginning to feel a little anxious? If so, can you find a way to calm yourself? Take several deep breaths and say to yourself gently, "Relax," or "Let it go."

**D.** When you've finished meditating, lower your right arm very slowly until it rests in your lap. As you lower it, focus on the sensations. Which muscles are strained and which are not? Can you find the point at which the muscles that held up the arm relax? How does the discomfort change? Does it go away as soon as the arm moves? Does it go away gradually? Is there any discomfort as your hand rests in your lap? Can you still feel the muscles you were so aware of when your arm was raised? Scan your body for tension, take several deep breaths, and relax.

## 3. *Warming Up and Cooling Down*

This exercise involves working with temperatures that are slightly warmer or slightly cooler than those with which you are comfortable. Find an area where you can meditate that's a little warmer or cooler than you would normally like it. This could be in your living room before you turn on the heat in the morning. Or perhaps in front of (but not too close to) a fireplace or heater. Or this could be a matter of putting on or taking off an extra sweater. The point is to be *slightly* warmer or cooler than usual.

A. Find your posture and center yourself. Take several deep breaths. Practice your basic meditation.

B. As the warmth or coolness around you becomes irritating, focus on your body's reaction to it. Are your muscles tensing? Which ones? Is perspiration about to form? If so, what does this feel like? Or is your body beginning to shiver? If so, how does it do this? What tightens? Does it stay tight? Does your whole body shiver or only certain parts? Can you find a way to soften your body's reaction to the temperature? Can you concentrate on your object of meditation and not notice your reactions to the temperature?

C. When you have finished meditating, find an area that's comfortably heated and spend a few minutes quietly noticing how your body adjusts from discomfort to comfort.

Any irritating sound or sensation can be used as a focal point for meditation. Focusing on your body's minor aches, or the sound of a lawn mower, or a dog barking, can teach you how your body responds to life's irritations. Once you realize this, you can begin to learn how to soften around them.

## Group 4. Being Present in the Present

Most stress comes from thinking about the past or worrying about the future. When you live in the present moment, when all of your attention is focused on what you are doing *right now*, there is no room for anything else to enter—including fears, desires, or anything that could be stressful.

In the meditative state all of your attention is focused on the present moment: the inhale, the exhale, the mantra, the object of meditation. When thoughts of past or future, desires or aversions, or anything else arise, you note this and then turn your awareness gently back to the present. It is this concentration on the *now* which allows your body and mind to enter a state of relaxation.

But you needn't go off by yourself and sit in silence in order to concentrate. In fact, the odds are that you have moments every day which demand and get your complete attention. What about those times you try to make a left-hand turn across the path of heavy oncoming traffic? Or when your four-year-old runs home with tears in his eyes and a cut on his elbow? Where is your attention when you are watching the best movie you ever saw in your life?

The following exercises will show you how to focus your attention on the present even in the midst of a busy world. They can be practiced anywhere and can be very helpful in calming your body as it responds to stress throughout the day.

### 1. *Eating Meditation*

You eat every day, but how often do you really pay attention to what you are eating while you are eating it? Do you usually eat with other people? In front of TV? While reading a book? Can you usually finish a three-course meal in ten minutes or less?

This is a conscious eating meditation. Try it some place where it is unlikely anyone will want to come over and eat with you. For the sake of this exercise, the food in question is a cheese sandwich.

**A.** Sit down in front of your food and take several deep breaths. Note the color, shape, and texture. Does it seem appealing to you? Can you barely restrain yourself from gobbling it up? Whatever your feeling is, notice it.

**B.** Be aware of your intention to begin eating. Move your hand slowly toward the sandwich. As you do this, make a quiet mental note of the action. You may say to yourself, "Reaching . . . reaching . . . reaching." By labeling your actions you are more likely to keep in mind your purpose—to stay aware. As you pick up the sandwich, notice that you are "lifting . . . lifting . . . lifting."

**C.** Watch your hand move the sandwich closer to your mouth. When it nears your mouth, take a moment to smell the food. What smells do you recognize? Can you smell the mayonnaise? How is your body reacting to the smell? Is your mouth watering? Notice the sensation of your body desiring food.

**D.** As you take your first bite, feel your teeth penetrate the bread. When the bite is complete, how is the food positioned in your mouth? How does your tongue position the food so that it's in between your teeth? Begin chewing slowly. What are the sensations in your teeth? Your tongue? How does your tongue move when you chew? What tastes are you experiencing? The tomato? The cheese? What part of your tongue experiences the taste? And where is your arm? Did you put it back on the table? If so, did you notice the motion?

**E.** When you swallow, try to be aware of how the muscles in your esophagus contract and relax as they push the food to your stomach. Where is the food when you have finished swallowing? Can you feel the sensations in your stomach? Where is your stomach? What size is it? Is it empty, full, or somewhere in between?

**F.** As you continue to eat your sandwich, try to stay aware of as many sensations as you can. Silently label each movement if this helps. If you eat with the hand you don't normally use, the awkwardness may serve as a reminder to pay attention. As with your basic meditation, when thoughts arise, notice them. Then return your attention to your food.

## 2. *Walking Meditation*

Most people cover miles in the course of their daily routines. This makes walking a good activity on which to practice one-pointed concentration. The following exercise incorporates walking, breathing, and counting as a focal point.

**A.** Stand up and relax your abdominal muscles. Take several deep belly breaths. Feel your abdomen expand and contract with each breath. As you practice this exercise, try to continue breathing from this dropped stance. Mentally repeat the word "in" with each inhalation and "out" with each exhalation.

**B.** Without controlling your breathing too much, try to arrange it so that one of your feet touches the ground at the beginning of each *in* breath and each *out* breath. Now, see how many steps it seems natural to take during each inhalation and each exhalation.

**C.** Count your steps in time with your breathing as you walk. If you are taking three steps during each inhalation and exhalation, mentally say to yourself, "In . . . two . . . three. Out . . . two . . . three. In . . . two . . . three . . . " and so on. Your *in* breaths may be longer or shorter than your *out* breaths and therefore may accommodate either more or fewer steps. Or your step count may vary from breath to breath. Just pay attention and readjust your walking to the ins and outs of your breathing as is needed.

**D.** As with all meditations, when thoughts or images interrupt your counting, make a mental note of this and then return to your walking and counting and breathing.

**E.** A different way of practicing this meditation is, instead of counting steps, to pay attention to the sensations of walking. Concentrate on your feet and lower legs. Notice which muscles contract and which relax as you lift your legs up and down. Which part of your foot touches the ground first? Pay attention to how your weight shifts from one foot to the other. What are the feelings in your knees as they bend and straighten? And, while you're at it, pay attention to the ground. What is its texture? Is it hard or soft? Notice any cracks or stones. How does the sensation of walking on grass differ from that of walking on a sidewalk? Catch the thoughts, let them go, and notice everything.

## 3. *Gazing*

Basic instructions were given earlier for using a small object such as a stone or candle as a focal point for meditation. This same exercise can be practiced anywhere using a variety of objects, both large and small. You can gaze during a meeting, on a bus, or in a waiting room. It is a wonderfully inconspicuous practice.

**A.** Find an object within your line of vision on which you want to fix your eyes. Take several belly breaths as you glue your eyes to the object. Let it capture your interest, as though it were the only object around you. (For more detailed instructions, see Meditation 3 in the Basic Meditation section.)

**B.** Try not to judge what you are seeing or have any thoughts about it at all. See if you can have the experience of "just seeing." When thoughts arise, note them, then return your focus to the object.

**C.** Try practicing this exercise with different types of objects. Here are a few suggestions:

- Concrete objects—objects with a definite size and shape that are usually stationary.

- Natural objects—such as clouds, sand, a pile of dry leaves, the ocean, and so on.

- Vastness—any large, uniform surface such as a wall or a finely patterned rug.

- Moving objects—a crowd of people, cars on a busy street, and so on. With objects of this nature, don't follow individual shapes with your eyes. Instead, fix your eyes on a point in space and let the movement pass in front of you.

Any simple activity can become a meditation when you try to continuously focus your attention on it. A good mindfulness exercise is to choose an activity you do every day, preferably a short one. Concentrate on every action and every sensation involved in the activity. Use the type of mental notation discussed in the Eating Meditation if that helps. You could practice concentrating when you shave, brush your teeth, wash dishes, fold clothes, or pull up weeds. As thoughts occur, note them, and then go back to the task with renewed concentration. It is often helpful to switch to your unaccustomed hand (you might not want to do this while shaving). The resulting awkwardness will serve as a constant reminder that you want to concentrate on what you are doing.

## Group 5. Letting Go of Thoughts

This highly structured exercise is found in many cultures in one form or another. In it, you passively observe the flow of your thoughts, feelings, and perceptions, one after another, without being concerned with their meaning or their relationship to one another. This will allow you to literally see what's on your mind and then let it go.

**A.** Find your posture and center yourself. Take several deep breaths.

**B.** Close your eyes and imagine yourself sitting at the bottom of a deep pool of water. When you have a thought, feeling, or perception, see it as a bubble and let it rise away from you and disappear. When it's gone, wait for the next one to appear and repeat the process. Don't think about the contents of the bubble. Just observe it. Sometimes the same bubble may come up many times, or several bubbles will seem related to each other, or the bubbles may be empty. That's okay. Don't allow yourself to be concerned with these thoughts. Just watch them pass in front of your mind's eye.

**C.** If you feel uncomfortable imagining being under water, imagine that you are sitting on the bank of a river, watching a leaf drift slowly downstream. Observe one thought, feeling, or perception as the leaf, and then let it drift out of sight. Return to gazing at the river, waiting for the next leaf to float by with a new thought. Or, if you prefer, you can imagine your thoughts rising in puffs of smoke from a campfire.

### Further Reading

Friedman, Lenore. 1987. *Meetings With Remarkable Women.* Boston: Shambala Publications.

Goldstein, Joseph. 1987. *The Experience of Insight.* Boston: Shambala Publications.

Goldstein, Joseph, and Jack Kornfield. 1987. *Seeking the Heart of Wisdom.* Boston: Shambala Publications.

Harp, David. 1990. *The Three Minute Meditator.* San Francisco: Mind's i press. (This book is particularly recommended as an excellent introduction to meditation practice.)

Hewitt, James. 1989. *The Complete Yoga Book.* New York: Shocken Books.

Kabit-Zinn, J. 1990. *Full Catastrophe Living: Using the Wisdom of Your Body and Mind To Face Stress, Pain, and Illness*. New York: Delacorte.

———. 1994. *Wherever You Go There You Are: Mindfulness Meditation in Everyday Life*. New York: Hyperion.

LeShan, Lawrence. 1974. *How To Meditate*. New York: Bantam Books.

Locke, Steve and Douglas Colligan. 1986. *The Healer Within*. New York: E. P. Dutton.

Saraswati, Swami Janakananda. 1975. *Yoga, Tantra, and Meditation*. New York: Ballantine.

Smith, Jonathan. 1986. *Meditation: A Sensible Guide to a Timeless Discipline*. Champaign, IL: Research Press.

# 6

# Visualization

You can significantly reduce stress with something enormously powerful: your imagination. The practice of positive thinking in the treatment of physical symptoms was popularized by Emil Coué, a French pharmacist, around the turn of this century. He believed that the power of the imagination far exceeds that of the will. It is hard to will yourself into a relaxed state, but you can imagine relaxation spreading through your body, and you can visualize yourself in a safe and beautiful retreat.

Coué asserted that all of your thoughts become reality—you are what you think you are. For example, if you think sad thoughts, you feel unhappy. If you think anxious thoughts, you become tense. In order to overcome the feeling of unhappiness or tension, you can refocus your mind on positive, healing images. When you predict that you are going to be lonely and miserable, it is likely your prediction will come true, because your negative thoughts will be reflected in asocial behavior. A woman who predicts that she will get a stomach ache when she is yelled at by her boss is likely to have her thoughts take a somatic form. Coué found that organic diseases such as fibrous tumors, tuberculosis, hemorrhages, and constipation are often worsened when you focus on them. He recommended to his patients that they repeat twenty times to themselves on waking, mechanically moving their lips, the now-famous phrase, "Every day in every way I am getting better and better."

Coué also encouraged his patients to get into a comfortable, relaxed position upon retiring, close their eyes, and practice general relaxation of all their muscles. As they started to doze off in the "stage of semi-consciousness," he suggested that they introduce into their minds any desired idea, for example, "I am going to be relaxed tomorrow." This is a way of bridging your conscious and unconscious minds and allowing your unconscious to make a wish come true.

Carl Jung, in his work in the early part of this century, used a technique for healing which he referred to as "active imagination." He instructed his patients to meditate without having any goal or program in mind. Images would come to consciousness which the patient was to observe and experience without interference. Later, if he or she wanted, the patient could actually communicate with the images by asking them questions or talking to them. Jung used active imagination to help the individual appreciate his or her own rich inner life and learn to draw on its healing power in times of stress. Jungian and Gestalt therapists have since devised several stress-reduction techniques using the intuitive, imaginative part of the mind.

Visualization is practiced and studied in cancer and pain centers throughout the country. Stephanie Matthews and O. Carl Simonton, who pioneered the use of visualization with cancer patients, wrote *Getting Well Again* in 1980. Two other visualization scientists, therapists, and writers are Jeanne Achterberg, who wrote *Imagery in Healing* in 1985, and Connecticut surgeon and Yale professor Bernie S. Siegel, who wrote *Love, Medicine, and Miracles* in 1986.

Shakti Gawain, author of *Creative Visualization and Living in the Light*, states that visualization is a form of energy creating life and life's happenings. Everything is energy and our mind creates our world, much as a movie projector projects a world upon a blank screen.

## Symptom Relief

Visualization is effective in treating many stress-related and physical illnesses, including headaches, muscle spasms, chronic pain, and general or situation-specific anxiety.

## Time for Mastery

Symptom relief can be immediate or take several weeks of practice.

## Instructions

### Kinds of Visualization

Everybody visualizes. Daydreams, memories, and inner talk are all types of visualization. You can harness your visualizations and consciously employ them for bettering yourself and your life. Visualizations or mental sense impressions that you create consciously can train your body to relax and ignore stress.

There are three types of visualization for change:

1. **Receptive visualization.** Here you relax, empty your mind, sketch a vague scene, ask a question, and wait for a response. You might imagine you are on the beach, the breeze is caressing your skin. You can hear and smell the sea. You can ask, "Why can't I relax?" The response might surface into your consciousness, "Because you can't say no to people," or "Because you can't detach yourself from your husband's depression."

2. **Programmed visualization.** Create an image, replete with sight, taste, sound, and smell. Imagine a goal that you want to attain or a healing that you want to accelerate. Harriet used programmed visualization when she started to run. For her first race, she not only practiced, but after one run on the course, she daily would visualize her race on that course. She would feel the pressure to run up a hill, the exhaustion after several miles, the sprint to the finish line. When she ran that race she set a state record for 40- to 49-year-old women.

3. **Guided visualization.** Again visualize your scene in detail, but omit crucial elements. Then wait for your subconscious, or your inner guide, to supply the missing pieces in your puzzle. Jane imagines visiting a special place where she likes to relax. She constructs the smells, tastes, sounds, touch, sights associated with this place, a forest clearing that she used to visit with the Girl Scouts. She sees herself roasting marshmallows over a campfire at twilight. (There are no mosquitoes.) She imagines her Girl Scout leader, someone whom Jane loves, and asks her teacher how she can relax. Sometimes her leader reminds her of some songs Jane loves and tells Jane to sing them whenever she feels tense. Sometimes her leader reminds Jane of some old jokes and old times that made Jane laugh, and tells Jane that she needs to laugh more. Often the leader gives Jane a hug, to remind her that she is loved and that she needs to search for affirmations of that love.

## Rules for Effective Visualization

1. Loosen your clothing, lie down in a quiet place, and close your eyes softly.

2. Scan your body, seeking tension in specific muscles. Relax those muscles as much as you can.

3. Form mental sense impressions. Involve all your senses: sight, hearing, smell, touch, and taste. For instance, imagine the sights of a green forest with the trees, blue sky, white clouds, and pine needles underfoot. Then add the sounds: wind in the trees, water running, birdcalls, and so on. Include the feel of the ground under your shoes, the smell of pine, and the taste of chewing a grass stem or mountain spring water.

4. Use affirmations. Repeat short, positive statements that affirm your ability to relax now. Use the present tense and avoid negatives such as "I am *not* tense" in favor of positive versions such as "I am letting go of tension." Here are some other examples of affirmations:

   *Tension flows from my body.*

   *I can relax at will.*

   *I am in harmony with life.*

   *Peace is within me.*

5. Visualize three times a day. Visualization practice is easiest in the morning and night while lying in bed. After some practice, you will be able to visualize while waiting in the doctor's office, at the service station, before going into a parent-teacher conference, or during an IRS audit.

# Basic Tension and Relaxation Exercises

## 1. *Eye Relaxation (Palming)*

Put your palms directly over your closed eyes. Block out all light without putting too much pressure on your eyelids. Try to see the color black. You may see other colors or images, but focus on the color black. Use a mental image to remember the color black (black fur, black object in the room).

Continue this way for two to three minutes, thinking and focusing on black. Lower your hands and slowly open your eyes, gradually getting accustomed to the light. Experience the sense of relaxation in the muscles that control the opening and closing of your eyes.

Color imagery and eye relaxation can be done when you need a technique and don't have very much time. They are designed to be fun and provide you with some alternatives to keep "relaxing" interesting. Try to slip one of these into your regular activities every now and then.

## 2. *Metaphorical Images*

Lie down, close your eyes, and relax. Visualize an image for tension and then supplant it with an image for relaxation. The best images are those you make up yourself. But to get you started, images for tension might include:

- The color red
- The screech of chalk on a blackboard
- The tension of a cable
- The scream of a siren in the night
- The glare of a searchlight
- The smell of ammonia
- The confinement of a dark tunnel
- The pounding of a jackhammer

These tension images during visualization can soften, expand, fade, creating relaxation and harmony.

- The color red can fade to pale blue.
- The chalk can crumble into powder.
- The cable can slacken.
- The siren might soften to a whisper of a flute.
- The searchlight might fade into a soft rosy glow.
- The dark tunnel might open into a light, airy beach.
- The jackhammer can become the hands of a masseuse kneading your muscles.

As you scan your body, apply a tension image to a tense muscle. Allow it to develop into your relaxation image. For example, if your neck is tense, you may visualize a tightened vise. Imagine the vise opening as you say an affirmation such as "Relax," or "I can relax at will."

End by reciting your affirmation. Speak to the specific tenseness as you apply your relaxation image. Watch the tension disappear.

## 3. *Creating Your Special Place*

In creating your own special place you will be making a retreat for relaxation and guidance. This place may be indoors or out. In structuring your place, follow a few guidelines:

- Allow a private entry into your place.

- Make it peaceful, comfortable and safe.

- Fill your place with sensuous detail. Create a midground, a foreground, and a background.

- Allow room for an inner guide or other person to comfortably be with you.

A special place might be at the end of a path that leads to a pond. Grass is under your feet, the pond is about 30 yards away and mountains are in the distance. You can feel the coolness of the air in this shady spot. The mockingbird is singing everyone's song. The sun is bright on the pond. The honeysuckle's pungent odor attracts the bee buzzing over the flower with its sweet nectar.

Or your special place might be a sparkling clean kitchen, with cinnamon buns baking in the oven. Through the kitchen window you can see fields of yellow wheat. A window chime flutters in the breeze. At the table is a cup of tea for your guest.

Try taping this exercise and playing it, or have a friend read it to you slowly.

To go to your safe place, lie down, be totally comfortable. Close your eyes . . . Walk slowly to a quiet place in your mind . . . Your place can be inside or outside . . . It needs to be peaceful and safe . . . Picture yourself unloading your anxieties, your worries . . . Notice the view in the distance . . . What do you smell? . . . What do you hear? . . . Notice what is before you . . . Reach out and touch it . . . How does it feel? . . . Smell it . . . Hear it . . . Make the temperature comfortable . . . Be safe here . . . Look around for a special spot, a private spot . . . Find the path to this place . . . Feel the ground with your feet . . . Look above you . . . What do you see? . . . Hear? . . . Smell? . . . Walk down this path until you can enter your own quiet, comfortable, safe place.

You have arrived at your special place . . . What is under your feet? . . . How does it feel? . . . Take several steps . . . What do you see above you? . . . What do you hear? . . . Do you hear something else? . . . Reach and touch something . . . What is its texture? . . . Are there pens, paper, paints nearby, or is there sand to draw in, clay to work? . . . Go to them, handle them, smell them. These are your special tools, or tools for your inner guide to reveal ideas or feelings to you . . . Look as far as you can see . . . What do you see? . . . What do you hear? . . . What aromas do you notice?

Now you need to find a place for your inner guide and a path from which your guide can enter.

Sit or lie in your special place . . . Notice its smells, sounds, sights . . . . . . This is your place and nothing can harm you here . . . If danger is here, expel it   . . . Spend three to five minutes realizing you are relaxed, safe and comfortable.

Memorize this place's smells, tastes, sights, sounds . . . You can come back and relax here whenever you want . . . Leave by the same path or entrance . . . Notice the ground, touch things near you . . . Look far away and appreciate the view . . . Remind yourself this special place you created can be entered whenever you wish. Say an affirmation such as, "I can relax here," or "This is my special place. I can come here whenever I wish."

Now open your eyes and spend a few seconds appreciating your relaxation.

## 4. *Finding Your Inner Guide*

Your Inner Guide is an imaginary person or animal that clarifies and instructs. This being is your link to your inner wisdom and subconscious. Your Inner Guide can tell you how to relax and can clarify what is causing your stress. With practice, you can meet your Inner Guide in your special place whenever you want.

Perhaps you already have an Inner Guide, a deceased parent or other spiritual presence. If so, invite this person into your special place and ask him or her to show you how to relax.

Try this exercise using your tape recorder or a friend.

Relax and follow the path to your special place, as you have been doing. Invite an Inner Guide to your place. Wait. Watch your guide's path. Notice a speck in the distance. Wait. Watch your guide's approach. Listen to its footfalls. Can you smell its fragrance? As your guide gains shape and clarity, if you feel unsafe, send it away. Wait for other guides until you find one you like, even though its appearance may surprise you or seem odd.

When your guide is comfortable, ask it questions. Wait for its answers. An answer may be a laugh, a saying, a feeling, a dream, a frown, a purr. Ask your guide, "How can I relax? What is causing my tension?" When your Guide answers, you will probably be surprised at the simplicity, yet clarity of its answers.

Before your guide leaves you, or immediately after, say your affirmation to yourself. Affirm your ability to relax with a simple, "I can relax here," or "I can relax at will."

Do this exercise several times a day for at least seven days. By the seventh day, you will probably have found a guide and some answers.

A student who has lost his mother and his house and has a father unable to care for him, uses his mother as his Inner Guide. He goes to her to relax, to seek guidance when pressure from life and his peers is overwhelming. She doesn't say much, but her presence and her look of approval or disapproval is often enough.

One person's guide creates relaxation because of the emptying of the mind that occurs in her presence. Rarely are words spoken, but her actions in small stories guide her.

Each person's inner guide is different and instructs them in a unique manner.

## 5. *Listening to Music*

Listening to music is one of the most common forms of relaxation. Each person gives his own meaning to music. It is important, therefore, that you select music that you find peaceful and soothing when you want to listen to music for the purpose of relaxation. If possible, make a half-hour tape of uninterrupted relaxing music that you can play daily or whenever you decide to use music to relax. Repetition of the same music that helped you to relax in the past carries with it a positive association that is likely to be beneficial in the future.

To get the most out of your music session, find a half-hour of uninterrupted time alone. Put on the music you have chosen, settle back in a comfortable position, and close your eyes. Mentally scan your body, noting areas of tension, pain, and relaxation. Be aware of your mood as you focus your attention on the music. Each time an unrelated thought enters your head, note it and then discard it, remembering your goal of focusing on the music and relaxing. Say an affirmation such as "Relax," or "Music relaxes me." When the music ends, allow your mind to again scan your body and become aware of how it feels. Does your body feel different from how it felt before you started? Is there any difference in your mood?

## Special Considerations

**A.** If you have trouble getting impressions from all senses, work on your strongest sense first. The rest will improve in time.

**B.** Practice often—three times a day. And be patient, it takes time.

**C.** If recording your own tapes doesn't work, you might want to buy a prerecorded tape. See the list of tapes offered by New Harbinger at the end of the book.

**D. Laughter.** Laughter reduces emotional and physical tension by producing an internal message. Laughing stimulates your circulatory, respiratory, vascular, and nervous systems. When the internal spasms subside, the release of pressure reduces muscle tension and creates a feeling of well-being.

In his book, *Anatomy of an Illness*, Norman Cousins describes how he used laughter to overcome a rare and painful illness. His laughter therapy included watching old Marx Brothers movies and Candid Camera shows. He says that laughter has astounding rejuvenating effects on mind and body and "serves as a bulletproof vest that protects you against the ravages of negative thinking."

It is difficult to remain anxious, angry or depressed when you are laughing. Laughter gets your attention off yourself and your situation. It gives you the distance necessary to gain a perspective on a situation you are probably taking too seriously. Besides serving these useful functions, laughter is just plain fun to do. Give yourself more opportunities to laugh as a break from your stressful life.

Here's a humor exercise.

Close your eyes . . . experience yourself becoming more and more relaxed as the tension gradually leaves your body . . . once you are relaxed, begin imagining yourself using humor in a difficult situation . . . it might be telling your boss you made a mistake . . . or presenting a paper you have written. Choose something that is happening in your life right now and create a humorous alternative to your usual stress response.

**E. Creativity.**  Accessing or learning to "turn on" the imaginative, creative aspect of the brain can be a powerful stress management tool and a relief from anxiety, worrying, and negative thinking. Scientific research done since the 1950's supports the value and validity of creative thought and has demonstrated that there are two distinct hemispheres in the human brain that mediate and process different kinds of tasks and problems.

The left brain or hemisphere, named the major or dominant brain by scientists, controls verbal and numerical information processed sequentially in a linear fashion. The left brain is the active, verbal, logical, rational, and analytic part of our brain. In contrast, the right brain or hemisphere manages the intuitive, experimental, nonverbal part of our brain and deals in images and holistic patterns and structures. It deals in dreams, metaphors, analogies, and new combinations of ideas. The key concept is that there are two ways of perceiving the world, and the right brain mode is more conducive to the relaxation response.

In her book, *Drawing on the Right Side of the Brain*, Betty Edwards, an art teacher and researcher on the relationship of drawing and brain-hemisphere process, states that anyone can draw. Ms. Edwards writes, "It is not a matter of 'talent,' but a process of developing and turning on the perceptual skills available in the right hemisphere." In her work with beginning art students, Ms. Edwards uses upside down or inverted drawing to force a cognitive shift from the dominant left brain to the subdominant right brain. This shift takes the student out of the labeling, rational, abstract mode, and puts them in the nonverbal, visual, concrete, intuitive mode which allows them to learn the artist's way of perceiving and attending to visual information that the left brain cannot or will not process. After experiencing this shift, the students reported less time urgency, less attachment to meaning, and a heightened sense of alertness, while feeling relaxed, calm, confident, and exhilarated. This pleasurable experience is derived from resting the left hemisphere, stopping its chatter, and keeping it quiet for a change. Visualization and guided imagery are methods of accessing the right brain and using its relaxing power.

Here is an exercise taken in part from *Drawing on the Right Side of the Brain* by Betty Edwards.

Find a quiet place to draw where no one will disturb you . . . play music if you like . . . From an art book choose a drawing that interests you . . . Turn the drawing you are going to copy upside down . . . Do not turn the drawing rightside up until you have finished . . . Finish the drawing in one sitting . . . Allow 30 to 40 minutes to complete the drawing . . . You might want to set a timer so you can forget about keeping time.

Look at the upside-down drawing for a minute . . . Regard the angles and shapes and lines . . . You can see the lines all fit together . . . Where one line ends another starts . . . When you begin to draw start at the top and copy each line . . . moving from line to adjacent line, putting it all together just like a jigsaw puzzle . . . Stay away from naming parts.

Begin to draw . . . work your way through the drawing by moving from line to line, part to adjacent part . . . Take your time . . . Don't make the exercise too complicated . . . Allow your movements to be slow and easy.

After you have finished, notice your state of mind . . . Do you feel calm and relaxed? . . . Did you lose track of time and meaning? . . . Did you turn off the chatter? . . . Were you able to get away from labeling and focus on the whole rather than the parts of the drawing? . . . Turn your drawing rightside up . . . You will probably be quite surprised by how well your drawing came out . . . Give yourself a pat on the back.

## Further Reading

Achtneberg, J. 1985. *Imagery in Healing: Shamanism and Modern Medicine.* Boston: New Science Library.

Cousins, N. 1990. *Head First: The Biology of Hope and the Healing Power of the Human Spirit.* New York: Penguin Books.

Epstein, Gerald. 1989. *Healing Visualization: Creating Health Through Imagery.* New York: Bantam.

Fanning, Patrick. 1988. *Visualization for Change.* Oakland, CA: New Harbinger Publications.

Gawain, Shakti. 1978. *Creative Visualization.* Mill Valley, CA: Whatever Publishing.

Klein, Allen. 1988. *The Healing Power of Humor.* Los Angeles: J. P. Tarcher.

Ornstein, Robert. 1986. *The Psychology of Consciousness.* San Francisco: W. H. Freeman.

Russman, Martin. 1987. *Healing Yourself.* New York: Pocket Books. (Books and tapes.)

Samuels, Mike, and Nancy Samuels. 1975. *Seeing With the Mind's Eye.* New York: Random House.

Siegel, Bernie. 1988. *Love, Medicine, and Miracles.* New York: Harper & Row.

Simonton, O. C., S. Matthews-Simonton, and J. L. Creighton. 1980. *Getting Well Again.* New York: Bantam Books.

Wells, V. 1990. *The Joy of Visualization: 75 Creative Ways To Enhance Your Life.* Vancouver: Raincoast Books.

## Tape Publishers

Health Journeys, Image Paths, Inc.
    P. O. Box 5714
    Cleveland, OH 44101
    1-800-800-8661

Sources
    P. O. Box W
    Stanford, CA 94305
    1-800-521-TAPES

*Available tapes include guided imagery and relaxation tapes by Emmett E. Miller, M. D.*

# 7

# Applied Relaxation Training

Applied relaxation training brings together a number of proven relaxation techniques, including many covered in this book. The combined effect is both rapid and powerful, helping you to reverse the effects of high stress in under a minute. You will need to invest some time in learning the steps that make up applied relaxation before you can enjoy its full benefits. Since the program is progressive, you will be adding new features to the exercise over the course of several weeks, while taking away other features once they have come habitual. Eventually you will be able to achieve deep relaxation in twenty to thirty seconds, calming both your body and your mind in any stressful situation you encounter.

Applied relaxation was developed by the Swedish physician L. G. Öst in the late 1980s. Öst worked with phobic patients, who needed rapid and reliable methods to cut through the anxiety that struck when they encountered phobic situations. Finding that the technique could achieve high rates of success even with severely phobic patients, Öst realized that applied relaxation could be helpful in a variety of life situations, from daily fights and frustrations to difficulty falling asleep at night.

As with other stress reduction techniques, applied relaxation works best when you can recognize stress at its earliest stages. (Chapter 2 on "Body Awareness" can help you tune in to your body's own stress warning signals.) The later stages of applied relaxation training ask you to focus on the physiological changes that accompany stress, such as increased heart rate, rapid breathing, and sweating. Once you notice these, you'll apply patterns that you've learned to slow your breathing and calm your body. When your body returns to a state of relaxation, your thoughts and outlook will automatically become more peaceful too. The negative cycle of building anxiety is replaced by a cycle of deepening relaxation and control.

Applied relaxation training progresses through six stages:

1. Progressive relaxation

2. Release-only relaxation

3. Cue-controlled relaxation

4.  Differential relaxation

5.  Rapid relaxation

6.  Applied relaxation

In general, the program first teaches you to relax by using a physical relaxation process. You then progress to a conditioned relaxation response and finally learn to relax on command. You will also progress from practicing in a relaxed exercise setting to using the technique in real-life situations.

## Symptom Relief

Although applied relaxation was developed to treat patients with phobias, it has a wide range of applications in other areas, including panic disorder, generalized anxiety disorder, headache (tension, migraine, and mixed), back and joint pain, epilepsy both in children and adults, and tinnitus. In clinical practice, applied relaxation training has also proved useful for sleep-onset insomnia and "cardiac neurosis" and for cancer patients with chemotherapy-induced nausea (Öst 1987). Öst found that almost everyone can learn applied relaxation and that 90 to 95 percent of the patients in his studies experienced benefits from the training.

## Time for Mastery

You will experience the benefits of deep relaxation after just a few sessions of applied relaxation training, and even sooner if you have already mastered progressive muscle relaxation. Remember that this is a progressive program. Each new stage will help you to relax more quickly and more deeply, until you can relax at will in less than a minute. Don't rush yourself. You'll want to master each step of the program before you move on to the next step. Allow yourself one to two weeks, with two practice sessions a day, to feel comfortable with each step. If this sounds like a lot of time, keep in mind that your practice sessions can become the most refreshing part of your day.

Clinical applications of applied relaxation have ranged from an unusually quick two-week course for in-patients suffering from tinnitus (Scott et al. 1985) to a fourteen-week program for in-patients with panic disorders (Öst 1987). A middle range is more usual: you can expect to spend from six to eight weeks progressing through the program. Bear in mind that the early stages may require more time and practice than the later ones.

## Instructions

Applied relaxation training involves learning six separate stages. Each stage builds on the one before it, so be sure to follow all six stages in their listed order.

You may find it useful to record a cassette tape to guide yourself through the exercises that follow. A tape will help you focus on relaxing your body and free you to close your eyes. To make a tape, use the instructions for each step as your script; parenthetical notes have been included to let you know when to skip something or how much time to leave yourself on your tape. Speak in a slow, even voice and be sure not to rush through the process. (Chapter 11 offers some additional tips on recording relaxation exercises.) If you'd prefer to order a prerecorded tape, see the end of this chapter for information on an audiotape dovetailing with the exercises presented here.

## 1. *Progressive Muscle Relaxation*

Progressive muscle relaxation will help you to recognize the difference between tension and relaxation in each of the major muscle groups. Surprising as it may sound, these distinctions are easy to overlook. Once you can really feel the difference between a tense muscle and a deeply relaxed one, you will be able to identify your chronic trouble spots and consciously rid them of their locked-in tension. You will also be able to bring your muscles to a deeper state of relaxation after you relax them than you could have if you hadn't tensed them first.

Progressive muscle relaxation is described in chapter 4 of this book. Follow the "Basic Procedure" section, focusing on these muscle groups:

*Session one:* Hands, arms, face, neck, and shoulders

*Session two:* Chest, stomach, back, buttocks, legs, and feet

If you like, you can begin progressive muscle relaxation by doing the first group of muscles in the morning and the second group in the evening. Or you can take a bit longer for each session and work through your entire body. Strive to work through both groups in each session as you become more comfortable with progressive muscle relaxation.

Give yourself one to two weeks to master the technique, with two fifteen-minute practice sessions per day. Your goal should be to relax your entire body in one fifteen-to- twenty-minute session.

## 2. *Release-Only Relaxation*

Now that you've felt the difference between tensing and relaxing each muscle group, you're ready to move on to the next stage of applied relaxation training. As you might guess from its name, release-only relaxation cuts out the first step in progressive muscle relaxation: the tensing step. This means that you can cut the time down by half or more that you need to achieve deep relaxation in each muscle group.

With practice, you'll find that mental focus alone is enough to drain your muscles of their tension, with no need for you to tense them first. Developing this skill depends on your ability to recognize the difference between clenched muscles and deeply relaxed ones. Be sure that you're comfortable with progressive muscle relaxation before you begin the release-only instructions.

**A.** Sit in a comfortable chair with your arms at your side and move around a bit until you're comfortable.

**B.** Begin to focus on your breathing. Breathe in deeply and feel the pure air fill your stomach, your lower chest, and your upper chest. Hold your breath for a moment as you sit up straighter . . . and then breathe out slowly through your mouth, feeling all tension and worry blow out in a stream. After you've exhaled completely, relax your stomach and your chest. Continue to take full, calm, even breaths, noticing that you become more relaxed with each breath.

C. Now relax your forehead, smoothing out all the lines. Keep breathing deeply . . . and now relax your eyebrows. Just let all the tension melt away, all the way down to your jaw. Let it all go. Now let your lips separate and relax your tongue. Breathe in and breathe out and relax your throat. Notice how peaceful and loose your entire face feels now.

D. Roll your head gently and feel your neck relax. Release your shoulders. Just let them drop all the way down. Your neck is loose, and your shoulders are heavy and low. Now let the relaxation travel down through your arms to your fingertips. Your arms are heavy and loose. Your lips are still separated because your jaw is relaxed too.

E. Breathe in deeply and feel your stomach expand and then your chest. Hold your breath for a moment and then breathe out slowly in a smooth stream through your mouth.

F. Let the feeling of relaxation spread to your stomach. Feel all the muscles in your abdomen release their tension as it assumes its natural shape. Relax your waist and relax your back. Continue to breathe deeply. Notice how loose and heavy the upper half of your body feels.

G. And now relax the lower half of your body. Feel your buttocks sink into the chair. Relax your thighs. Relax your knees. Feel the relaxation travel through your calves to your ankles, to the bottoms of your feet, all the way down to the tips of your toes. Your feet feel warm and heavy on the floor in front of you. With each breath, feel the relaxation deepen.

H. Now scan your body for tension as you continue to breathe. Your legs are relaxed. Your back is relaxed. Your shoulders and arms are relaxed. Your face is relaxed. There's only a feeling of peace and warmth and relaxation.

I. If any muscle felt hard to relax, turn your attention to it now. Is it your back? Your shoulders? Your thighs? Your jaw? Tune in to the muscle and now tense it. Hold it tighter and release. Feel it join the rest of your body in a deep, deep relaxation.

The directions for release-only relaxation may seem simpler than those for progressive muscle relaxation, but the tasks involved are actually a bit more complex. Be certain that you are draining all of the tension out of each muscle you focus on. Don't let the tension creep back in as you turn your attention to different muscles. When you stand up after a session of release-only, you should feel as relaxed if not more than you did after a session of progressive muscle relaxation.

Of course, you don't want to stress yourself out by pushing yourself through a set of strict directions. Try to *allow* your body to relax, rather than forcing it. If you have trouble with a particular step, take a deep breath and try it again—or skip it. Let negative, critical thoughts blow away with each breath and hold on to the feeling of success and deepening peace.

Allow yourself one to two weeks with two practice sessions a day to master release-only relaxation. When you can relax your entire body in one five-to-seven-minute session, you're ready to move on to step three.

## 3. *Cue-Controlled Relaxation*

Cue-controlled relaxation reduces the time you need to relax even further: down to two or three minutes in most cases. In this stage, you will focus on your breathing and condition yourself to relax exactly when you tell yourself to. The instructions will help you build an association between a cue—for example, the command "Relax"—and true muscle relaxation. Be sure that you are comfortable with release-only relaxation before you begin.

**A.** Make yourself comfortable in your chair, with your arms at your sides and your feet flat on the ground. Take a deep breath and hold it for a moment. Concentrate on blowing the worries of the day far, far away as you release the air in a smooth stream from your mouth. Empty your lungs entirely and then feel your stomach and your chest relax.

**B.** Now begin to relax yourself, from your forehead all the way down to your toes, using the release-only technique you practiced in step two. See if you can relax yourself completely in thirty seconds. If you need more time, that's fine too. *(If you're making a tape, pause here for half a minute to allow time to relax.)*

**C.** You feel peaceful and at ease now. Your stomach and chest are moving in and out with slow, even breaths. With each breath, the feeling of relaxation deepens.

**D.** Continue to breathe deeply and regularly, saying "breathe in" to yourself as you inhale and "relax" as you exhale. *(If you're making a tape, record these words on the tape, allowing about eight seconds for each repetition.)*

Breathe in . . . relax . . .

Breathe in . . . relax . . .

Breathe in . . . relax . . .

Breathe in . . . relax . . .

Breathe in . . . relax . . .

Feel each breath bring peace and calm in and float worry and tension out.

**E.** Continue to breathe this way for several minutes now, saying the words "breathe in" and "relax" as you breathe. *(Do not record the words again on your tape; this section is most effective when you say the words to yourself in silence.)* Focus all your attention on the words in your head and on the process of breathing. Feel your muscles relax more and more deeply with each breath. Let the word "relax" crowd every other thought from your mind. Close your eyes, if you can, to deepen your focus. *(If you're making a tape, allow one to two minutes of silence before continuing to record the instructions.)*

**F.** Now listen to the words again as you continue to breathe in . . . and relax.

Breathe in . . . relax . . .

Breathe in . . . relax . . .

Breathe in . . . relax . . .

Breathe in . . . relax . . .

Breathe in . . . relax . . .

**G.** Continue to breathe, saying these words in your head, for a few minutes now. Feel each breath bring peace and calm in and float worry and tension out. *(Stop recording the tape here.)*

**H.** If you have time, repeat the entire process of cue-controlled relaxation after a recovery period of from ten to fifteen minutes.

Practice cue-controlled relaxation twice a day, as you did with the earlier stages. After each session, you may want to make a note of the time that it took you to relax and how deeply relaxed you became. Most people find that the actual time that it takes them to relax at this stage is shorter than they imagine. Aim to relax completely using cue-controlled relaxation within two to three minutes before moving on to step four.

## 4. *Differential Relaxation*

At this point in applied relaxation training you are able to sit down in a comfortable chair at any point during the day and achieve deep relaxation in a matter of minutes. While this is a valuable skill, it's undeniable that many stressful life situations happen when you're far from your favorite chair and perhaps unable to sit down at all.

The aim of this stage of applied relaxation training is to help you relax while you're still involved in your daily activities. Most activities, such as writing or walking, require you to tense some of your muscles, but not all of them. Differential relaxation will help you to isolate those muscles that you need for whatever activity you're doing and relax the rest of your body. It will also let you do this in a variety of settings.

Differential relaxation builds on the skills you've been practicing in the first three stages. Be sure that you feel comfortable with the third stage, cue-controlled relaxation, before you begin.

The exercises below consist of a series of movements that you repeat, in a relaxed state, in a number of locations. First you'll progress from the comfortable chair that you've been using to a stiff-backed chair, and then from a chair at a desk to standing and walking postures.

**Part One**

**A.** Sit in a comfortable chair, with your arms at your sides and your feet flat on the floor. Take some time to relax yourself thoroughly, using the cue-controlled technique you practiced in step three. *(If you're listening to a tape, stop the tape now and press "play" again when you're in a calm and relaxed state.)*

**B.** You feel peaceful and easy. You are breathing slowly and deeply. Now open your eyes. Without moving your head, begin to look around the room. Move your eyes all the way up to the ceiling and all the way down to the floor. Look to the left and look to the right. The muscles in your neck are still relaxed. Continue to move your eyes around the room, as though you were tracing big, loopy circles from ceiling to floor and from side to side. Your jaw is relaxed too. Let your lips fall apart.

**C.** Now it's time to move your head too. Look all the way up and let your head tilt slowly back to follow your eyes. Now move your eyes down and bring your chin in slowly to your chest. Center your head and then turn all the way to the right. Bring your head back to center and turn all the way to the left with one smooth motion of your neck. Your shoulders are still loose. Now move your head loosely around and feel how the strain moves around your neck. The rest of your body is still and loose and relaxed.

**D.** Notice how comfortable you are in your chair. When you stop moving, the muscles that were straining join the rest of your body in deep, heavy relaxation. You breathe in and relax. Each regular breath helps the relaxation spread.

**E.** Slowly begin to lift your left arm. Imagine that a string is pulling up on your left wrist until your hand is even with your shoulders. Straighten your arm out in front of you and now flex your left hand, stretching your fingers all the way out. Your other arm is still and loose and heavy, resting at your side. Notice how the only tension in your body is in your left arm and hand. Now relax your hand and bring your arm slowly in and down. Keep breathing the calming, cleansing air in regular breaths.

**F.** Slowly lift your right arm. Feel the string on your wrist pull it up. Now stretch out your arm and your hand and flex all of your fingers. Scan your other arm for tension and relax your neck. Relax your jaw. Now relax your hand. Let your arm come slowly down to rest at your side. Clear away all the tension from it and notice how heavy and still both of your arms are now. Your whole body is at rest.

**G.** Move your attention down to your legs. Lift your left leg slowly, keeping your knee bent. Imagine a string pulling up from your left knee. Feel the muscles in your thigh working and feel your calf muscles as you flex your left foot up. Check your shoulders and your back for tension. Hold for a moment and now relax your foot and slowly put your leg down. Your ankle may tingle, and your thigh may tingle, but your whole leg feels peaceful and heavy.

**H.** Now begin to lift your right leg up. Imagine a string from the ceiling pulling on your right knee. Notice the muscles in your thigh straining. Flex your right foot up. Make sure that your jaw and your shoulders are still loose. And now relax your foot and let your leg come slowly back to rest. Your right leg is once again heavy and loose.

These are the movements that you will continue to practice in differential relaxation. Work through a few sessions in a comfortable chair until you achieve a feeling of deep relaxation in both your mind and your muscles. Aim for a time frame of from sixty to ninety seconds for deep, full relaxation. Then choose an upright chair with a stiff back to sit in. Go through the same exercises, checking to make sure that your back stays at ease when it is not needed. After several sessions, when you are able to remain relaxed in an upright chair, move the chair to a desk where you have a pen and some writing paper handy. Complete the same movements again and then continue with part two of the instructions. (As usual, you'll find a tape helpful here.)

**Part Two**

**A.** You are seated at a desk, comfortable in your chair. Your lower back is tensing a little bit to keep you sitting straight, but your shoulders are loose. Your arms are loose and at your sides. Now lift the hand that you write with to the desk. Your other hand may remain in your lap or it may come up to the top of the desk too. Breathe in and relax. Remain loose and easy as you reach out to pick up a pen. Grasp the pen and feel your hand come to life. Relax your wrist and your shoulders. Now begin to write. Only your hand is working and the arm muscles that you need for writing. Your other arm is still loose and heavy. Notice the difference between your working hand and your relaxed arm.

**B.** Put the pen down. Feel how heavy your wrist is. Let both of your shoulders relax.

In your next session, go back to the beginning of the differential relaxation exercises and do them while standing up. It's a good idea to stand near a wall, with your back to it. As you move through each separate motion, notice which muscles have to remain tense and which ones you can relax.

You can think about differential relaxation while you are walking too. Feel your muscles tense in the leg that you begin to lift and then relax as your foot comes smoothly and solidly down. Feel the strain move from one leg to the other. Notice how relaxed your shoulders and your arms can remain. Let your breathing come as calmly and evenly as your steps.

Allow yourself one to two weeks to master differential relaxation, progressing from the comfortable chair to the stiff-backed chair to the desk and then to the standing and walking positions. When you can keep most of your muscles relaxed in every position and relax yourself in sixty to ninety seconds, you are ready to move on to the next-to-last stage of applied relaxation training.

## 5. *Rapid Relaxation*

Rapid relaxation can bring the time you need to relax down to thirty seconds. Being able to relax that quickly can mean real relief during stressful life situations. It's a good idea to practice rapid relaxation many times a day as you move through different activities and states of mind.

Rapid relaxation asks you to pick a special relaxation cue. Choose something that you see regularly throughout the day, such as your watch or a certain clock or the picture you pass as you walk down the hall to the bathroom. If you can, mark that special cue with a piece of colored tape while you're practicing this technique.

When you're ready to begin, look at your special cue. Breathe in and relax. Breathe in and relax. Continue to look at your cue and think "relax." Breathe in and relax. You are breathing deeply and evenly, and you continue to think "relax" each time you exhale. Let the relaxation spread throughout your body. Scan your body for tension and relax as much as possible in every muscle that is not needed for any present activity.

Every time you look at your cue throughout the day, go through these simple steps:

1. Take two or three deep, even breaths, exhaling slowly through your mouth.

2. Think "relax" each time you exhale, as you continue to breathe deeply.

3. Scan your body for any tension. Focus on muscles that need to relax and empty them of tension.

Try to use your relaxation cue fifteen to twenty times a day to relax quickly in natural, nonstressful situations. This will instill the habit of checking yourself for anxiety and moving back to a state of deep relaxation throughout the day. After your first few days of practice, you may want to change the color of the tape on your relaxation cue—or even change the cue altogether. This will keep the idea of relaxation fresh in your mind. Finally, see if you can use rapid relaxation to calm yourself during one or two particularly stressful moments of the day. (The next stage will help you to refine this ability, but it's a good idea to open yourself up early to the idea of relaxation during crisis.)

When you feel comfortable with rapid relaxation and are able to achieve a state of deep relaxation in twenty to thirty seconds many times during the day, you are ready to move on to the final stage of applied relaxation training.

## 6. *Applied Relaxation*

The final stage of applied relaxation training involves relaxing quickly in the face of anxiety-provoking situations. You will use the same techniques that you practiced in rapid relaxation, beginning your deep breathing the moment you notice an anxiety reaction setting in.

If you're unsure of your body's particular stress warning signs—such as rapid breathing, sweating, or an increased heart rate—turn to the exercises for body awareness in chapter 2. The earlier you can identify the physiological signs that accompany stress, the more effectively you can cut in on an anxiety reaction before it builds.

As soon as you note a sign of anxiety—if you catch your breath, feel your heart leap, or feel a flush of heat—begin your three steps:

1. Take two to three deep, even breaths.

2. Think these calming words to yourself as you continue to breathe deeply:

    Breathe in . . . relax . . .

    Breathe in . . . relax . . .

    Breathe in . . . relax . . .

    If you prefer, you need only hear yourself think "relax" each time you exhale.

3. Scan your body for tension and concentrate on relaxing the muscles that you don't need to continue your activity.

To begin coming close to the feeling of anxiety, start by practicing these instructions after you have run up a flight of stairs. As you feel more confident, you may want to try visualizing a stressful situation: a fight with your spouse, an encounter with your boss, or a moment looking down from a high place or caught in an enclosed space. (Chapter 6 offers ideas and exercises to help you build your visualization skills.) Finally, you'll want to turn to the three steps above when you encounter a stressful situation in real life. Take a brief moment to collect yourself and remember the three steps and then put them into effect immediately. No one but you needs to know what you're doing, and you and those around you will all benefit from the calmness with which you approach the crisis at hand.

Be patient with yourself. It takes time to learn each of these stages, and this is especially true for one that involves relaxing during moments of high stress. Applied relaxation is a skill, and as with other skills you will refine your ability with practice. Chances are that you won't feel complete relief the first time you try to cut through a deeply stressful situation with applied relaxation. Notice the improvements that you do make. Most people are able to stop anxiety from increasing with relatively little practice. From that point, it's just a few short steps to actually decreasing the anxiety and replacing panic with a feeling of calm and control.

## Special Considerations

If you have progressed methodically from one step of applied relaxation to the next, you have the control you need to bring your body to a state of deep and full relaxation. You can control your breathing and your thoughts and separate appropriate tension from tension you don't need.

As with any other skill, you'll want to practice applied relaxation regularly to keep yourself in top form. Make it a habit to scan your body for tension at least once a day. Focus on ridding your body of that tension, using the rapid relaxation technique. Whatever activity you may be doing, bring yourself to a calm and deep relaxation.

If there are times when your anxiety doesn't seem to respond or you worry that you've forgotten the skill you once had, remember that setbacks happen. No treatment can guarantee permanent freedom from anxiety attacks or moments of deep stress. But if you can learn to see setbacks as an opportunity to practice applied relaxation, you'll have taken a great stride toward converting stress into useful and productive energy. At other times, remember the feeling of deep, deep relaxation that you have achieved. Remember that you can bring yourself there whenever you need to.

### Audio Tape

Fanning, P., M. McKay, and N. Sonenberg. 1991. *Applied Relaxation Training.* 1991. Oakland, CA: New Harbinger Publications.

### Further Reading

Öst, Lars-Göran. 1987. "Applied Relaxation: Description of a Coping Technique and Review of Controlled Studies." *Behaviour Research Therapy* 25:397-409.

———. 1988. "Applied Relaxation vs. Progressive Relaxation in the Treatment of Panic Disorder." *Behaviour Research Therapy* 26:13-22.

# 8

# Self-Hypnosis

Self-hypnosis is a powerful technique that you can quickly and easily learn to counteract stress and stress-related illness. In addition to helping you relax, you can use it to introduce and reinforce positive changes in your life.

*Hypnosis* is a term derived from the Greek word for sleep. In some ways, hypnosis is similar to sleep: there is a narrowing of consciousness, accompanied by inertia and passivity. Hypnosis is very relaxing. But unlike sleep, you never completely loose awareness during hypnosis. When hypnotized, you are able to respond if necessary to things going on around you. While hypnosis is usually done with eyes closed to facilitate concentration and imagination, it can be done with eyes opened.

Hypnosis allows you to experience your thoughts and images as real. During hypnosis you willingly suspend disbelief for the moment, just as you do when you become absorbed in a compelling fantasy or play. For instance, when you are watching a violent chase scene in a movie, your mind and body respond in many ways as though you are actually participating in the chase: your muscles tense, your stomach knots, your heart rate increases, you feel excited or scared. The brain wave patterns traced on an electroencephalogram (EEG) during hypnosis resemble the patterns that typically occur during the actual activities that the hypnotized person is imagining (participating in a chase, relaxing at the beach, playing a musical instrument, and so on).

You are no stranger to hypnosis. Dr. Griffith Williams describes spontaneous states of hypnosis (in Lecron 1952). Frequently, when you are concentrating on something of great interest to you, you enter hypnosis without any formal induction. Daydreaming is an hypnotic state. Long distance driving is highly conducive to hypnosis (and commonly results in amnesia for various parts of the trip). You may have entered hypnosis many times while attempting to remember a shopping list or a past sequence of events or while watching TV or feeling a strong emotion such as fear.

Every hypnotic trance includes the following elements:

1. Economy of action and relaxation. The hypnotized person experiences a reduction of muscular activity and energy output.

2. Limb catalepsy: a sort of rigidity in the muscles of the limbs, with a tendency for the arms and legs to stay in any position in which they are placed. This is sometimes described as the "lead pipe effect."

3. Understanding words at a literal level. If you ask a hypnotized person "Can you tell me your birthday?" he or she is likely to reply, "Yes."

4. Narrowing of attention.

5. Increased suggestibility. A hypnotized person who is told "Your arms are feeling very heavy" will actually feel a sensation of heaviness.

Optional benefits from hypnosis include:

1. The ability to produce anesthesia in any part of the body.

2. The ability to make posthypnotic suggestions to control painful symptoms, calm stressful emotions, change habits, and improve sleep, coping skills, and performance.

3. Control of some organic functions such as bleeding, heart rate, and so on.

4. Partial age regression: the experience of going back to relive something in the distant past, with all five senses operating to bring the physical sensations of the experience alive. These relived memories are frequently ones that are not available to the conscious mind.

5. Exceptional abilities of concentration: the capacity to learn and remember in enormous detail.

6. Time distortion: the capacity to compress a great deal of thinking and recall into a very short period of time.

7. Relaxation and calm can exist side by side with clearly focused and intense mental activity.

In this chapter you will learn to use self-hypnosis to experience positive thoughts and images of your own choosing for the purpose of relaxation and stress reduction.

You can learn self-hypnosis quickly and safely. There are no reported cases, even for the most inexperienced practitioners, of harm resulting from self-hypnosis. Since hypnosis is your experience of your own thoughts and images, hypnosis can only take place when your participation is active and voluntary. (This is true even when you are undergoing hypnotic induction by someone else.) You may decide to extend, modify, or cut short any of the hypnosis exercises in this chapter.

## Symptom Relief

Self-hypnosis has been clinically effective with symptoms of insomnia, minor chronic pain, headache, nervous tics and tremors, chronic muscular tension, and minor anxiety. It is a well-established treatment for chronic fatigue. You may also consider using self-hypnosis for any subjective experience which could be improved with positive words and images (for example, the rapid heart beat, cold sweaty palms, and knotted stomach associated with anticipatory anxiety).

## Counter Indications

Poor hypnotic candidates include people who are disoriented due to organic brain syndrome or psychosis, people who are severely mentally retarded, and people who are paranoid.

## Time for Mastery

Significant relaxation effects can be achieved within two days. To become proficient in the skill of self-hypnosis, practice the basic hypnotic induction twice a day for a week or once a day for two weeks. Then adapt the basic induction to your personal goals by adding specific hypnotic suggestions. Plan on practicing this modified induction until you no longer need it.

## Instructions

### Your Previous Experience With Hypnosis

The first step to learning how to use hypnosis for your own benefit is to take a few minutes to consider what being hypnotized means to you. Your previous experience with hypnosis may have colored your beliefs and feelings about it, thereby influencing how well you can make use of hypnosis now.

If you have had positive clinical experiences with hypnosis, you will find it very easy to enter hypnosis using the exercises in this chapter. If your only exposure to hypnosis has been stage hypnosis for entertainment, you may be worried that somehow you will be tricked into doing something foolish. Remember that people who get up on stage with a hypnotist during a show are choosing to be part of the entertainment for the audience. If you saw an old movie in which someone was hypnotized to perform some illegal or unethical deed, you might be concerned that you will commit some "villainous act while under the influence of hypnosis." Keep in mind that no case has ever been documented where a person under the influence of hypnosis committed a crime solely for the benefit of the hypnotist and not for the gain of the hypnotized person as well. When you are hypnotized by another person, you decide what you are willing to experience and do.

If you have heard that hypnosis can be used to unearth unconscious secrets, you may be worried that you will uncover some very disturbing memory from your distant past. Be aware that hypnosis is not a reliable method for accurately recalling forgotten memories and take any memories you do retrieve using hypnosis with a grain of salt. If you want to use hypnosis to look into your "forgotten past," it is best to do so with a trained professional.

If you are worried that you will blurt out something that you would prefer not to reveal, such as an affair or angry feelings towards another person, keep in mind that when you hypnotize yourself, you are in charge. Self-hypnosis puts you in the driver's seat. You choose what you want to think about, imagine, feel, and do.

## The Power of Suggestion

The second step in self-hypnosis is to learn the power of suggestion. Here are two simple exercises that can demonstrate the power of suggestion.

### Postural Sway

1. Stand up with your eyes closed and imagine holding a suitcase in your right hand.

2. Imagine bigger and bigger suitcases weighing down your right side, pulling you over.

3. After two or three minutes, open your eyes and notice any changes in your posture.

4. Again close your eyes and imagine that the north wind is blowing you, pushing you back on your heels. Feel the gusts. Notice if your weight is shifting in response to your imagination.

### Postural Suggestion

1. Stretch both arms in front of you at shoulder level. With eyes closed, imagine a weight being tied onto your right arm as it strains to stay up.

2. Imagine a second weight, and then a third. Feel the strain in your arm as it gets heavier and heavier . . . heavier and heavier.

3. Now imagine that a huge balloon filled with helium has been tied to your left arm and is tugging it up into the air . . . higher and higher . . . higher and higher.

4. Open your eyes and notice where your arms are relative to each other.

Most people who try these two exercises notice that their bodies move at least a little in response to these self-suggestions. If you do not notice any movement, practice the exercises a couple more times. If you still do not notice even the slightest amount of movement, hypnosis may not be for you.

## Personalized Self-Induction

The third step to self-hypnosis is to learn how to write a self-induction script. The following suggestions provide you with a basic outline for self-induction that you can adapt and change to suit your own particular style and purposes.

**Position.** If possible, sit in a reclining chair or comfortable high-backed chair with support for your arms, hands, neck, and head. Choose a comfortable position with your feet flat on the floor and your legs and arms uncrossed. Loosen your clothing. You may prefer to remove contact lenses and glasses. Set aside enough time to do this exercise without being interrupted.

**Key word or phrase.** You could choose something that is the opposite of your problem and hence the essence of the goal for which you are using hypnosis. For instance, if your problem is anxiety prior to giving a presentation, your goal and key phrase might be "Calm and clear" or "Relax now." You can repeat this statement slowly at the moment your eyes close and in your special place so that it becomes associated with deep relaxation. You could also use your favorite color, sound, or location. A meaningful key phrase may occur to you spontaneously when you experience being in your special place during hypnosis. With enough practice, this key word or phrase will be sufficient to quickly induce hypnosis.

**Breathing.**  After your eyes close, take several deep breaths. Breathe deeply all the way down into your abdomen and feel the spreading sense of relaxation as you exhale.

**Muscle relaxation.**  You will be relaxing your legs, arms, face, neck, shoulders, chest, and abdomen in that order. As you relax your legs and arms, the key phrase is "heavier and heavier, more and more deeply relaxed." As you relax your forehead and cheeks, the key phrase is "smooth and relaxed, letting go of tension." As you relax your jaw, the key phrase is "loose and relaxed." Your neck, too, becomes "loose and relaxed." Your shoulders are "relaxed and drooping." You relax your chest, abdomen, and back by taking a deep breath. As you exhale, you use the key phrase "calm and relaxed."

**Staircase or path to a special place.**  You will count each step going down to that peaceful place, and with each step you will become more and more deeply relaxed. Count slowly backwards from ten to zero. Each number you count is a step going down. Imagine that saying each number and taking each step help you feel more and more deeply relaxed. You can count backwards from ten to zero once, twice, or even three times. Each complete count will deepen your relaxation.

**Your special place.**  In this special place you feel total peace and complete safety. Your special place may be a meadow or a beach or the bedroom you grew up in. You will look around and notice the shapes and colors. You will listen to the sounds and smell the fragrances of your special place. You will also notice the temperature and how your body feels there.

It will be helpful for you to practice imagining your special place before attempting your first self-induction. Make sure that the image is detailed and evocative. If you are at the beach, make sure you can hear the waves crashing and hear the hiss of foam as the waves recede. See and hear the seagulls overhead. Notice the salty sea breeze, the warmth of the sun on your body, and the feel of the sand beneath you. Try to involve all your senses in building the scene: sight, sound, taste, smell, and touch.

**Deepening hypnosis.**  Use the following four key suggestions over and over, in varying orders and combinations, until you feel a deep sense of calm and letting go.

- *Drifting deeper and deeper, deeper and deeper*

- *Feeling more and more drowsy, peaceful, and calm*

- *Drifting and drowsy, drowsy and drifting*

- *Drifting down, down, down into total relaxation*

**Post-hypnotic suggestion.**  Once you've spent time relaxing in your special place, you may wish to give yourself post-hypnotic suggestions. Read the sections on "Hypnotic Suggestions" and on "Practice Writing Hypnotic Suggestions" later in this chapter for rules and techniques that will help you craft your own post-hypnotic suggestions.

**Coming out of hypnosis.** When it is time to end your trance, you can count back up from one to ten. In between numbers, tell yourself that you are becoming "more and more alert, refreshed, and wide awake." As you reach number nine, tell yourself that your eyes are opening. As you say the number ten, tell yourself that you are totally alert and wide awake.

Here is a summary of the key rules for a successful self induction.

1. Allow at least twenty minutes to enter and deepen the hypnotic state.

2. Don't worry about success or how you are doing. Hypnosis will get easier with practice.

3. Always allow time to relax your muscles and take deep breaths.

4. Use compelling instructions ("You are feeling more and more heaviness in your arms").

5. Use adjectives such as "drowsy, peaceful, comfortable" during self-induction.

6. Repeat everything until the suggestion begins to take hold.

7. Use creative imagery. For example, to induce heaviness, imagine your legs as lead pipes. For lightness, imagine helium-filled balloons pulling up your arm or floating on a cloud.

## Basic Self-Induction Script

The fourth step to self-hypnosis is to tape record the basic script below and play it back for your initial inductions.

When you read the induction aloud, speak in a monotone. Keep the tempo slow and monotonous. Pronounce one word after another with an even beat. Pause between each sentence. Speaking slowly, with little inflection, will help your mind drift and increase your relaxation and suggestibility. After some experience with this induction, you will be ready to write your own personalized self-induction.

*Sit in a comfortable position with your arms and legs uncrossed. Let your eyes focus gently on a point in front of you . . . and take a deep relaxing breath all the way down into your abdomen. Take another slow, deep, relaxing breath . . . and another. Even though your eyes are getting tired, keep them open a little longer and take another deep breath . . . and another. Your eyes become heavier and heavier . . . let them close, as you say to yourself . . .*

[Insert your key word or phrase here.]

*Now you can begin to relax the muscles in your body. Let your legs begin to relax . . . let your legs begin to feel heavy . . . heavier and heavier as they relax. Your legs are heavier and heavier as they let go of the last bit of muscular tension. Your legs are becoming more and more heavy and relaxed, heavy and relaxed. Your arms, too, are becoming more and more heavy . . . heavier and heavier as they let go of the last bit of muscular tension. You can feel gravity pulling them down. You feel your arms growing heavier and heavier, more and more deeply relaxed. Your arms letting go . . . letting go    . . . letting go of tension as they become heavier and heavier . . . more and more deeply relaxed. Your arms and legs feel heavy, heavy and relaxed. Your arms and legs feel totally relaxed as they let go of the last bit of muscular tension . . . more and more heavy and relaxed.*

*And your face, too, begins to relax. Your forehead is becoming smooth and relaxed. Your forehead is letting go of tension as it becomes more and more smooth and relaxed. And your cheeks too are becoming relaxed, smooth and relaxed. Your cheeks are relaxed and letting go of tension . . . your forehead and cheeks are totally relaxed . . . smooth and relaxed. And your jaw can now begin to relax . . . feeling more and more loose and relaxed. As your jaw becomes more and more deeply relaxed, feel the muscles letting go . . . and your lips beginning to part . . . and your jaw becoming more and more loose and relaxed.*

*And now your neck and shoulders can begin to relax. Your neck is loose and relaxed . . . your shoulders are relaxed and drooping. Feel your neck and shoulders becoming more and more deeply relaxed . . . so loose and relaxed.*

*Now, take another deep breath, and as you exhale let the relaxation spread into your chest and stomach and back. As you exhale, feel yourself becoming calm and relaxed . . . calm and relaxed. Take another deep breath . . . and as you exhale, feel your chest and stomach and back become calm and relaxed . . . calm and relaxed.*

*Feel yourself drifting deeper and deeper . . . deeper and deeper . . . becoming more and more drowsy, peaceful, and calm. Drifting and drowsy . . . drowsy and drifting . . . drifting down, down, down into total relaxation . . . drifting deeper and deeper . . . deeper and deeper . . . deeper and deeper.*

*Now it's time to go to your special place . . . a place of safety and peace. You can go down the stairway to your special place or down a path, and with each step you can count backwards from ten to zero . . . and with each step become more and more deeply relaxed. In ten steps you will be there . . . feeling peaceful and safe as you move toward your special place. Now you grow more and more relaxed with each step. Ten . . . nine . . . eight . . . seven . . . six . . . five . . . four . . . three . . . two . . . one . . . zero.*

[If you want to repeat this countdown two or even three times to deepen hypnosis, that's perfectly fine.]

*Now see the shapes and colors of your special place . . . hear the sounds . . . feel the feeling of your special place . . . smell the smells of your special place. See it . . . feel it . . . hear it . . . smell it. You can feel safe and calm in your special place, safe and calm.*

*Feel yourself drifting deeper and deeper, deeper and deeper . . . more and more drowsy, peaceful and calm. You feel drowsy and drifting, drifting and drowsy . . . drifting down, down, down into total relaxation. You are so relaxed, so calm, so peaceful.*

[Pause and spend time relaxing in your special place.]

*Now you know that you can . . .*

[Leave a blank space on the tape here for any post-hypnotic suggestion that you wish to use. Give yourself time to repeat the suggestion at least three times.]

*Now, when you are ready, it is time to come back up . . . to come all the way back, feeling alert, refreshed, and wide awake. Starting to come up now: one . . . two . . . three . . . four . . . more and more alert and aware . . . five . . . six . . . seven . . . more and more alert and awake . . . eight . . . nine . . . beginning to open your eyes . . . and ten . . . completely alert, refreshed, and wide awake. Alert, refreshed, and wide awake.*

## Abbreviated Inductions

An optional fifth step to self-hypnosis is to learn abbreviated inductions. These are shorthand techniques that can produce hypnosis in thirty seconds to two minutes. Here are some examples.

**Pendulum drop.**  To make a pendulum, tie an object such as a paper clip, pen, or ring to the end of a heavy thread ten inches long. Hold the thread in your dominant hand and let the pendulum dangle above the floor. Ask your subconscious for permission to go into hypnosis for two minutes. If the answer is yes, your eyes will want to close. As your eyes close, picture a candle flame. Take several deep breaths and allow yourself to slip deeper and deeper. Tell yourself that when you have entered hypnosis, your hand will relax and drop the pendulum. Count down slowly from ten to zero.

**Pencil drop.**  This technique is the same as the pendulum drop, except that you hold a pencil poised above a table. Pinch the point between your thumb and index finger.

**Yes repetition.**  Think the thought "yes" over and over, as you focus on an imagined candle flame. Go down the stairs or down a path while you continue to think "yes."

**Coin flip.**  Place a penny in your palm. Suggest to yourself that your hand will gradually begin to turn over. Just allow your hand to turn slowly, until the coin drops out. As the coin drops, permit your eyes to close and enter hypnosis.

**Eye fixation.**  Fix your eyes on a point slightly above your normal line of vision. Let your peripheral vision narrow and your eyes lose focus. Allow your eyes to close, accompanied by a feeling of drowsiness. To increase the drowsiness, roll your eyes up to the top of your head two or three times.

**Key word or phrase.**  Breathe deeply and slowly, and repeat the key word or phrase that you used on your self-induction talk. As you say the word or phrase, close your eyes and enter hypnosis.

These abbreviated methods are useful after you have become relatively proficient at self-hypnosis. Always remember to end an induction by suggesting that you will awaken refreshed and feeling good.

**Five finger exercise.**  The following exercise has been used very effectively for relaxation. Memorize the following steps. After you have gone through them, you can use the feeling of calm that follows to enter hypnosis.

1.  Touch your thumb to your index finger. As you do so, go back to a time when your body felt healthy fatigue. Imagine that you feel the way you feel right after you have just finished swimming or playing tennis or jogging or some other exhilarating physical activity.

2.  Touch your thumb to your middle finger. As you do so, go back to a time when you had a loving experience. You may choose to remember a moment of sexual fulfillment or a warm embrace or an intimate conversation.

3. Touch your thumb to your ring finger. As you do so, recall the nicest compliment you have ever received. Try to really accept it now. By accepting it, you are showing your high regard for the person who said it. You are really paying him or her a compliment in return.

4. Touch your thumb to your little finger. As you do so, go back to the most beautiful place you have ever been. Dwell there for awhile.

The five finger exercise takes less than ten minutes, but it pays off with increased vitality, inner peace, and self-esteem. It can be done at any time you feel tension.

## Hypnotic Suggestions

A very useful sixth step to self-hypnosis is to learn to give yourself positive suggestions for change. For best results, say these suggestions to yourself when you are in a relaxed and receptive frame of mind such as when you are in your special place during the basic self-induction. Or you may find that you prefer to intersperse suggestions throughout an induction.

Remember that autosuggestions are thoughts and images that influence your subjective experience. Here is a list of rules to keep in mind when you are creating suggestions for yourself.

1. Autosuggestions should be direct. Tell yourself, "I will be calm, confident, and in control."

2. Autosuggestions should be positive. Avoid wording suggestions in a negative way such as "I won't feel tired tonight."

3. Permissive suggestions sometimes meet with less resistance than firmer or more controlling ones. Try saying "I *can* feel relaxed and refreshed tonight" instead of "I *will* feel relaxed and refreshed." But note that some people do respond better to commands. You can experiment with both to find out which approach works best for you.

4. Make suggestions for the immediate future, not the present: "Soon the drowsiness is going to come."

5. Repeat all suggestions at least three times.

6. Attach a visual image to your suggestions. If you are trying to overcome a feeling of exhaustion, imagine yourself bouncing along with springs on your feet and see yourself looking athletic and happy.

7. Attach an emotion or sensation to your suggestions. If you are attempting to give up cigarettes, imagine how bad the first one tasted or think of the unpleasant burning in your lungs. If you are attempting to improve your confidence for a first date, imagine the feeling of closeness and belonging that you are looking for.

8. Never use the word "try" in any suggestion, since it implies doubt and the possibility of failure.

9. When working toward the control of unpleasant emotions or painful physical symptoms, start out by suggesting that the emotion or symptom is growing more intense. You might say, "My anger is getting bigger, I can feel the blood pushing at my veins, I'm getting hot, my muscles are tensing." Bring the feeling up to a peak and then tell yourself that the emotion or symptom is diminishing: "My anger is subsiding, my heart is slowing and beating normally, my flush is receding, my muscles are unknotting and beginning to relax." When an unpleasant emotion or symptom reaches its peak, it can only get better. Suggestion can rush that process of recovery. When you can turn your emotions and symptoms on and off during hypnosis, you will have gained enormous control over your life.

10. Write your suggestions out in advance, and then distill them to a catchword or phrase that you can easily remember when you are in the hypnotic state.

**Practice writing hypnotic suggestions.** Once hypnotized and relaxed, your subconscious mind is ready to believe what you tell it. Many of the symptoms that bother you, as well as your habitual tension responses to stress, were learned through suggestion. They can be unlearned through suggestion. For example, if you watched your father get angry every time he was forced to wait, and if on the first occasion when you delayed him he became angry at you, you may have learned by suggestion to respond exactly the same way. You can use hypnosis to learn new methods of coping with delay. Suggestions such as "Waiting is a chance to relax" and "I can let go of rushing" may undo the old habit.

In order to get the flavor of how suggestions can be written, write down hypnotic suggestions that you could use for the following problems:

1. Fear of coming into a dark house at night

2. Chronic fatigue

3. Obsessive and fearful thoughts about death

4. Fear of illness

5. Minor chronic head or back pain

6. Chronic anger and guilt

7. Self-criticism and worry about making mistakes

8. Low self-esteem

9. Lack of motivation

10. Feelings of insecurity and self-consciousness in the presence of other people

11. Anxiety about an upcoming evaluation or a test

12. Improving performance

13. Pain or muscle tension

14. Disease and injury

Now that you have written your own suggestions, examine these possible scripts for each of the fourteen problems.

1. Fear of coming into the house at night

   *I can come in tonight feeling relaxed and glad to be home, safe and secure.*

2. Chronic fatigue

   *I can waken refreshed and rested. I can enjoy the evening ahead. I can pace myself today so that I will accomplish my priorities. Whenever I feel my energy flagging, I can do* [the five finger exercise or other relaxation technique] *and then return to my daily activities relaxed and revitalized.*

3. Obsessive and fearful thoughts about death

   *I am full of life now. I will enjoy today. Very soon I can let go of these thoughts.* [Visualize a blackboard and see the date written there.]

4. Fear of illness

   *My body is feeling more and more healthy and strong. Each time I relax, my body becomes stronger.* [Visualize yourself as healthy, strong, and relaxed while doing a favorite activity.]

5. Minor chronic head or back pain

   *Soon my head will be cool and relaxed.* [Imagine cool images.] *Gradually I will feel the muscles in my back loosen.* [Imagine smooth, flowing, loosening images.] *In an hour, they will be completely relaxed. Whenever these symptoms come back, I will simply turn my ring a quarter turn to the right and the pain will relax away.*

6. Chronic anger and guilt

   *I can turn off anger and guilt because I am the one who turns it on.* [Practice turning up and turning down the unwanted emotion.] *I will relax my body and breathe deeply.*

7. Self-criticism and worry about making mistakes

   *When I catch myself being self-critical or worried, I can take a deep breath and let go. Breathe out negative tension and breathe in positive energy.* [Practice five finger exercise.]

8. Low self-esteem

   *Each day I will feel more capable and self-assured. I can do it. I can feel myself becoming more and more happy and successful every day. I can be kind to myself. I am liking myself more and more. I am an intelligent, creative, and talented person.*

9. Lack of motivation

   *I can feel confident that I will achieve my goals. I have the power within to change myself. I can see myself solving my problems and getting beyond them. The decisions I make are the right ones for now. I can put aside distractions and focus my attention on one goal. As I get into my project, I will get more and more interested in it. As I work toward my goal, step by step, new energy and enthusiasm will emerge. When I finish this, I will feel great! When I achieve my goal, I will reward myself with a weekend at the lake and a good dinner at the lodge. I deserve success. I can use my success in positive and worthwhile ways.*

10.  Feelings of insecurity and self-consciousness in the presence of other people

*The next time I see Ben, I can feel secure in myself. I can feel relaxed and at ease because I am perfectly all right. I can relax and enjoy the thought that there are people in my life who see me as a good friend, valuablm co-worker, and loving family member. I can respond to Ben in a firm and assertive manner. Whenever I lace my fingers together, I will feel confidence flowing throughout my entire body.*

11.  Anxiety about an upcoming evaluation or a test

*I can concentrate on my studies, absorbing and retaining everything I need to know. I feel confident that I will remember what I need to know at the time of the test. Whenever I feel nervous, I will remember to breathe deeply and say to myself, "alert and calm, alert and calm," and relax. My mind is becoming more and more calm and sharp. I will quickly and easily retrieve the correct information. When I successfully complete this test, I will reward myself with a whole day to myself and a trip to the record store. I can imagine myself getting an "A." Learning this material will let me finish this year with the best grades I've ever had.*

12.  Improving performance

*I can be calm and in control in response to stressful situations.* [Imagine yourself maintaining your cool and concentration in the face of specific pressures and fears.] *I can imagine myself playing a perfect game from start to finish. I can recall a time when I played a perfect game.* [Reflect on every perfect move and strategy.] *I will achieve my goal.* [Be specific about your objectives and visualize them in detail.]

13.  Pain or muscle tension

*I can see my pain as a saber of dry ice burning and stabbing me. Now I see the sun shining and I feel it warm my shoulders and stream down through my entire body. And the ice of the blade is steaming, melting away into a puddle in the warmth of the sun. Now I can feel my pain starting to flow, and as it flows it turns color into a warm, orange fluid moving slowly through my body toward my right arm, down my right arm, and into my clenched fist. When I am ready, I can let it go of it. I can just scoop my pain up and throw it away.* [Imagine a symbol that best represents your pain or tension. Have it interact with another symbol that eliminates the first symbol or transforms it into something more tolerable.]

14.  Disease and injury

*I can imagine a healing white light at the top of my head. I can see and feel it surrounding my entire body. I can feel it begin to move within my body, cleansing and healing as it slowly spreads throughout my entire body. I can imagine myself healthy, strong, and energetic doing what I want to do.*

## Self-Hypnotic Induction for a Specific Problem

An optional seventh step is to consider how self-hypnosis might fit into an over all plan to solve a problem in your life. The specific problem addressed here as an example is sleep disturbance. This section is adapted from Josie Hadley's and Carol Staudacher's *Hypnosis for Change*.

Before you are ready to begin hypnosis for a specific problem, there are number of issues that you need to address.

**Define your problem and your goal.** Do you have difficulty falling asleep, staying asleep, or waking up too early? Is your sleep restless? Do you have great difficulty waking up in the morning? Once you have clearly labeled your problem, you can easily define your goal in the form of a positive autosuggestion: "I can fall asleep quickly and easily" or "I will wake up refreshed and alert at the appropriate time" or "Soon I will be able to sleep deeply and continuously throughout the night."

**Identify and eliminate any possible external factors that may be contributing to your problem.** Ask yourself what might be interfering with getting a good night's sleep. Is your bedroom a comfortable place that invites sleep, or is it filled with clutter, noise, and light? Do you spend half the night coping with a restless bed partner and staring at a glowing clock face that keeps reminding you how much sleep you are losing? Are you consuming too many stimulants during the day? You need to address these problems before you use self-hypnosis for sleep, since you cannot expect self-hypnosis to solve these problems for you.

**Notice what you are telling yourself that may be contributing to your problem.** For example, people who have difficulty with sleep often focus on time. They say to themselves things like: "If I don't get to sleep by midnight, I know I won't be able to sleep at all." If you tend to worry, your mind can go wild when you turn off the light. "I really blew it today. Wait until my boss finds out!" "I know I didn't study enough for the test tomorrow." Do you use the quiet hours of the night to solve problems? "Until this question is answered, we can't go on!" "I'll tell her I didn't mean what I said, and then she'll say. . . ."

If part of your problem has to do with what you are telling yourself, you can use the chapters 13–15 on "Thought Stopping," "Refuting Irrational Ideas," and "Coping Skills" to help you identify and change the way you think. If you are being kept awake by your thoughts, here are some suggestions to calm your mind before you fall asleep.

- If you are a clock watcher, turn the clock to the wall, direct your thoughts away from time, and tell yourself, "As I rest, my mind will become calm and my body will relax."

- If you tend to dwell on the negative or on things that you cannot control, think about the positive things that you did during the day.

- If you are a night time problem solver, make an agreement with yourself to put aside your problems until tomorrow when you are at your sharpest and to save the night for restorative sleep.

When you create your own sleep induction, write in positive suggestions that incorporate these ideas so as to reinforce your new desired behavior.

**Record an induction tailored to your particular problem.** Begin by taping the basic induction up through the section leading to "your special place" and then add your own special suggestions. For sleep disturbance, you could choose to add the following script to the basic induction.

*And now just linger in your special place. There's no place to go, nothing to do. Just rest, just let yourself drift and float, drift and float into a sound and restful sleep. And as you drift deeper and deeper, imagine the positive things that you can think and do to allow yourself a sound and restful sleep. Your new positive thoughts are true. You have released negative thoughts and feelings. You have released stress and tension from your mind, body, and thoughts. Each new positive statement becomes stronger and stronger as you continue to drift deeper and deeper into relaxation. Just let yourself drift deeper and deeper into sleep. Just let those positive statements float in your mind as you drift into a sound and restful sleep.*

*And now become aware of how comfortable you feel, so relaxed, your head and shoulders are in just the right position, your back is supported, and you are becoming less aware of all the normal sounds of your surroundings, and as you drift deeper and deeper you may experience a negative thought or worry trying to surface in your mind, trying to disrupt your slumber, trying to disrupt your rest. Simply take that thought and sweep it up as you would sweep up the crumbs from the floor and place that thought or worry into the box. The box has a nice tight lid. Put the lid on the box and place the box on the top shelf of your closet. You can go back to that box at another time, a time that is more appropriate, a time that will not interfere with your sleep. And as these unwanted thoughts appear, sweep them up and place them in the box, put the lid on the box and place it on the top shelf of your closet and let them go. Let them go and continue to drift deeper and deeper into sleep.*

*Shift your thoughts back to your positive thoughts and positive statements. Just let these thoughts flow though your mind, thoughts such as "I am a worthwhile person."* [Pause.] *"I have accomplished many good things."* [Pause.] *"I have reached positive goals."* [Pause.] *Just let your own positive ideas flow though your mind. Let them flow and drift, becoming stronger and stronger as you drift deeper and deeper into sleep.*

*You may begin to see them slowly fade, slowly fade, as you become even more relaxed, more sleepy, more drowsy, more relaxed. Just imagine yourself in your peaceful and special place, smiling, feeling so good, so comfortable, so relaxed.* [Pause.] *And from your special place you can easily drift into a sound and restful sleep, a sound and restful sleep, undisturbed in a sound and restful sleep. You sleep through the night in a sound and restful sleep. If you should awaken you simply imagine your special place once again and drift easily back into a sound and restful sleep, a sound and restful sleep. Your breathing becomes so relaxed, your thoughts wind down, wind down, wind down and relax. You drift and float into a sound and restful sleep, undisturbed through out the night. You will awaken at your designated time feeling rested and refreshed.*

*Now there's nothing to do, nothing to think about, nothing to do but enjoy your special place, your special place that is so peaceful for you, so relaxing. Just imagine how it feels to relax in your special place. You may become aware of how clean and fresh your special place smells, or you may become aware of the different sounds of your special place, of the birds singing in the background or the water cascading over river rocks in a stream. Or you may become aware of how warm the sun feels as you lounge in a hammock or how cool the breeze feels from the ocean air. Or you may experience something else that is unique and wonderful in your special place. Just experience it, drift and float, all thought just fading, drifting into a sound and restful sleep. Just drift into a comfortable, cozy, restful sleep, your body feeling heavy and relaxed as you sink into your bed, so relaxed, just drifting into sleep . . . sleep . . . sleep. . . sleep . . . sleep . . . sleep. . .*

## Special Considerations

Do not practice an hypnotic induction in a car or in any other situation where your safety requires you to be fully alert and able to respond quickly. After an induction, always make sure that you are completely awake and alert before driving a car.

Some people, especially those who are sleep deprived, fall asleep during self-hypnosis. If sleep is not your goal and you have this problem, you may want to shorten the induction so that you are awake to hear the suggestions specifically geared to your goals. Keep in mind that many people who think that they are asleep during hypnosis are still able to hear and benefit from positive suggestions. If you are prone to fall asleep, use a timer to wake yourself up rather than worry about being late to your next activity.

You may find that as the symptom you are concerned about fades, you lose your motivation to continue practicing self-hypnosis. This is a typical experience and nothing to worry about. If your symptom returns at a latter time, you can use self-hypnosis again.

You can use your key phrase when you experience your symptom or any time you feel tense or uncomfortable in a stressful situation. Although you are unlikely to feel as relaxed as you do after a full self-hypnotic induction, you will still experience some measure of relief. In this way, your key phrase can also serve as a reminder that you do have a choice about how you respond to stress.

### Further Readings

Alman, Brian M., and Peter Lambrou. 1992. *Self-Hypnosis: The Complete Manual for Health and Self Change.* New York: Brunner-Mazel.

Fisher, Stanley. 1991. *Discovering the Power of Self-Hypnosis: A New Approach for Enabling Change and Promoting Health.* New York: Harper Collins.

Hadley, Josie, and Carol Staudacher. 1989. *Hypnosis for Change: A Manual of Proven Techniques.* 2nd ed. Oakland, CA: New Harbinger Publications.

Haley, Jay. 1993. *Uncommon Therapy: The Psychiatric Techniques of Milton Erickson.* New York: Norton.

Lecron, Leslie, ed. 1952. *Experimental Hypnosis.* New York: MacMillan.

———. 1988. *Self-Hypnosis: The Technique and Its Use in Daily Living.* New York: Signet.

Soskis, David A. 1986. *Self-Hypnosis: An Introductory Guide for Clinicians.* New York: W.W. Norton & Company.

## Audio Tapes

McKay, M., and P. Fanning. 1987. *Self-Hypnosis*. Oakland, CA: New Harbinger Publications.

Miller, E. 1980. *Letting Go of Stress*. Stanford, CA: Source.

# 9

# Autogenics

Autogenic Training (AT) is a systematic program that will teach your body and mind to respond quickly and effectively to your verbal commands to relax and return to a balanced, normal state. It is one of the most effective and comprehensive reducers of chronic stress.

In stress reduction and holistic health centers across the country AT is being increasingly used with biofeedback. Other health professionals use it as the treatment of choice to teach self-regulation of the autonomic nervous system.

When you do not have time to recuperate from emotionally and physically stressful events, your body chemistry becomes imbalanced and your mood is disturbed. In extreme cases, you may develop high blood pressure, hardening of the arteries, peptic ulcers, migraines, or rheumatoid arthritis. Feelings of anxiety and depression often acompany these psychosomatic diseases. In less extreme cases, you may experience the imbalance in the form of muscle tension, neck and backache, indigestion, or cold hands and feet. The goal of AT is to normalize your physical, mental and emotional processes which get out of balance due to stress.

AT has its origins in the research in hypnosis conducted by the famous brain physiologist Oskar Vogt. He worked at the Berlin Institute during the last decade of the 19th century. Vogt taught some of his experienced hypnotic subjects to put themselves in a trance that had the effect of reducing fatigue, tension, and painful symptoms such as headaches. It appeared to help the subjects deal more effectively with their everyday lives. The subjects usually reported that when their fatigue and tension lifted, they felt warm and heavy.

Johannes H. Schultz, a Berlin psychiatrist, became interested in Vogt's work. He found that you can create a state very much like an hypnotic trance just by thinking of heaviness and warmth in your extremities. Essentially, all you have to do is relax, undisturbed, in a comfortable position and concentrate passively on verbal formulas suggesting warmth and heaviness in your limbs. Schultz combined some of the autosuggestions of Vogt with some Yoga techniques and in 1932 published his new system in the book entitled *Autogenic Training*.

In its present form, AT not only provides you with the recuperative effects of traditional hypnosis, it also frees you from dependence on a hypnotist. You can learn to induce the feeling of warmth and heaviness whenever you choose.

Schultz's verbal formulas fall into three main kinds of exercises: the standard exercises concentrate on the body, the meditative exercises focus on the mind, and the special exercises are designed to normalize specific problems. This introductory chapter will cover only the standard exercises which deal with the general relaxation and normalization of the body.

The standard exercises are aimed at reversing the "fight or flight" or alarm states that occur when you experience physical or emotional stress. The first standard exercise includes the theme of heaviness. It promotes relaxation of the striped muscles in your body, the voluntary muscles used to move your arms and legs. The second standard exercise brings about peripheral vasodilation. That is, as you say, "My right hand is warm," the smooth muscles which control the diameter of the blood vessels in your hand relax so that more warming blood flows into your hand. This helps reverse the pooling of blood in the trunk and head that is a characteristic of the "fight or flight" reaction to stress.

The third standard exercise focuses on normalizing cardiac activity. It is simply "My heartbeat is calm." The fourth standard exercise regulates the respiratory system. The verbal formula is "It breathes me." The fifth standard exercise relaxes and warms the abdominal region, as you say, "My solar plexus is warm." The last standard exercise reduces the flow of blood to the head as you say, "My forehead is cool."

## Symptom Relief

AT has been found to be effective in the treatment of various disorders of the respiratory tract (hyperventilation and bronchial asthma), the gastrointestinal tract (constipation, diarrhea, gastritis, ulcers, and spasms), the circulatory system (racing heart, irregular heartbeat, high blood pressure, cold extremities, and headaches), and the endocrine system (thyroid problems). AT is also useful in reducing general anxiety, irritability, and fatigue. It can be employed to modify your reaction to pain, increase your resistance to stress, and reduce or eliminate sleeping disorders.

## Contraindications

AT is not recommended for children under five years old, persons who lack motivation, or individuals with severe mental or emotional disorders. Prior to beginning AT, it is advised that you have a physical exam and discuss with your medical doctor what physiological effects AT will be likely to have on you. Persons with serious diseases such as diabetes, hypoglycemic conditions, or heart conditions should be under the supervision of a medical doctor while in AT. Note that some trainees experience an increase in blood pressure and a few have a sharp drop in blood pressure when they do these exercises. Trainees with high or low blood pressure should check with their medical doctor to be sure that AT is regularizing it. If you feel very anxious or restless during or after AT exercises or experience recurring disquieting side effects, you should continue AT only under the supervision of a professional AT instructor.

# Time for Mastery

AT specialists recommend moving at a slow but sure pace in learning these exercises, taking from four to ten months to master all six exercises.

Begin with one and a half minutes sessions five to eight times a day. If you cannot find time for this, do 30 second sessions at least three times a day to get started. As you become more comfortable with AT, you can gradually increase the length of sessions to 30 to 40 minutes twice a day.

# Instructions

In doing these exercises, it is essential that you maintain an attitude of passive concentration. That is, experience whatever physical, mental or emotional response you have to the exercises without any expectations. Just let whatever happens happen. Passive concentration does not mean "spacing out" or going to sleep. You remain alert to your experience without analyzing it. This casual attitude is contrasted with active concentration, which occurs when you fix your attention on certain aspects of your experience and have an interest and goal-directed investment in it. Active concentration is essential for such things as preparing a new recipe or fixing a car. Passive concentration is required for relaxation.

Each exercise will introduce a verbal formula that you will keep in mind constantly as you passively concentrate on a particular part of your body. Repeat the formula over and over to yourself, keeping up a steady, silent, verbal stream.

It is very important to keep external stimuli to a minimum. Choose a quiet room where you won't be disturbed. Keep the room temperature at a moderately warm, comfortable level. Turn the lights down low. Wear loose clothing. Let your body be relaxed and your eyes closed before you begin these exercises.

There are three basic AT postures recommended:

1.  Sit in an armchair in which your head, back, and extremities are comfortably supported and you are as relaxed as possible.

2.  Sit on a stool, slightly stooped over, with your arms resting on your thighs and your hands draped between your knees.

3.  Lie down with your head supported, your legs about eight inches apart, your toes pointed slightly outward and your arms resting comfortably at your sides without touching them.

Scan your body to be sure that the position you choose is tension free. In particular, look for over-extension of limbs such as unsupported arms, head or legs, tightening of the limbs at the joints, or crooked spine.

There are six exercise themes, each with a particular verbal formula. The following is one suggested program for learning them. You may find that you need more or less time than is recommended, so adjust the program to your own pace. The most common mistake made by people just getting started is to become impatient and move too fast, not thoroughly learning

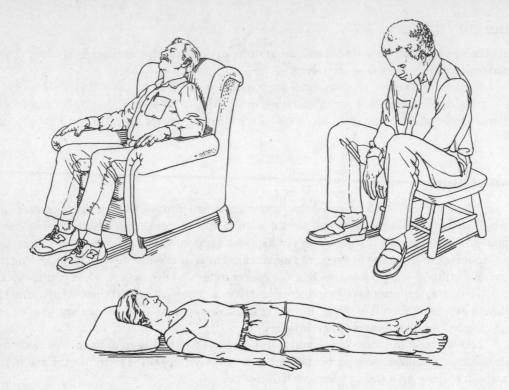

each theme. On the other hand, if your body is giving you consistent clear feedback that you are doing the exercise correctly and effectively, move on to the next exercise. If you feel stuck or are experiencing unpleasant side effects over a period of time, move on to the next exercise and postpone the difficult exercise to the end of your training. Perhaps ten percent of all trainees never experience the basic sensations of heaviness or warmth. This does not matter. The formula is used only to bring about a functional change in the body which you may or may not feel. Just focus on doing the exercise correctly.

You will not be able to maintain perfect passive concentration at first. Your mind will wander. That's OK. When you find this happening, just get back to the formula as soon as possible. In addition, you may experience some initial symptoms described as "autogenic discharges" which are normal but distracting. For example, you may sense a change in your weight or temperature, tingling, electric currents, involuntary movements, stiffness, some pain, anxiety, a desire to cry, irritability, headaches, nausea, or hallucinations. Whether the autogenic discharges you experience are pleasant or unpleasant, remember that they are transitory, that they are not the purpose of AT and that they will pass as you continue with the program.

When you are ready to stop an AT session, say to yourself, "When I open my eyes, I will feel refreshed and alert." Then open your eyes and breathe a few deep breaths as you stretch and flex your arms. Be sure that you are not still in a trance-like state when you go on to your regular activities.

# Standard Exercises for a 12-Week Program

## Heaviness Theme

**Week 1.** Repeat the following verbal formulas for one and a half minutes, five to eight sessions a day. Each time you say a formula, say it slowly, taking about five seconds, and then pause about three seconds. Repeat each formula about four times. Always start with your dominant arm. That is, if you write with your right hand, begin with your right arm. Repeat "My right arm is heavy" four times and then go on to the next phrase, "My left arm is heavy," and repeat it four times, and so on.

*My right arm is heavy.*

*My left arm is heavy.*

*Both of my arms are heavy.*

**Week 2.** Repeat the following verbal formulas for three minutes, four to seven times a day:

*My right arm is heavy.*

*My left arm is heavy.*

*Both of my arms are heavy.*

*My right leg is heavy.*

*My left leg is heavy.*

*Both of my legs are heavy.*

*My arms and legs are heavy.*

**Week 3.** Repeat the following for four minutes, four to seven times a day:

*My right arm is heavy.*

*Both of my arms are heavy.*

*Both of my legs are heavy.*

*My arms and legs are heavy.*

*Note:* If you have difficulty achieving a sensation of heaviness using the verbal formulas, you may want to add visual imagery. For example, you might imagine weights attached to your arms and legs gently pulling them down. Or you might want to think of your arms and legs as made of heavy lead sinking into the ground. Think of the heaviness along the entire arm from your shoulder down to the tips of your fingers.

## Warmth Theme

**Week 4.** Repeat the following for five minutes, four to seven times a day:

*My right arm is heavy.*

*My arms and legs are heavy.*

*My right arm is warm.*

*My left arm is warm.*

*Both of my arms are warm.*

**Week 5.**  Repeat the following for eight minutes, three to six times a day:

*My right arm is heavy.*

*My arms and legs are heavy.*

*My right arm is warm.*

*My left arm is warm.*

*My right leg is warm.*

*Both of my legs are warm.*

*My arms and legs are warm.*

**Week 6.**  Repeat the following for ten to fifteen minutes, three to six times a day:

*My right arm is heavy.*

*My arms and legs are heavy.*

*Both of my arms are warm.*

*Both of my legs are warm.*

*My arms and legs are warm.*

*My arms and legs are heavy and warm.*

**Week 7.**  Repeat the following for ten to twenty minutes, three to six times a day:

*My right arm is heavy.*

*My arms and legs are heavy.*

*My arms and legs are warm.*

*My arms and legs are heavy and warm.*

*Note:* If you have trouble experiencing a feeling of warmth using the verbal formulas, try visual imagery. For instance, imagine your right arm lying on a warm heating pad. Feel the warmth of the pad through your hand and arm. Imagine yourself in a nice warm shower or bath with the warmth of the water all around you. Imagine your hand submerged in a comfortably warm pan of water. Envision yourself sitting in the sunshine, with the sun falling warmly on your arms and legs. Think about holding a nice, comfortably warm mug of your favorite hot drink in your hand. Think about the blood flowing gently through the fingertips of your hands and through your toes.

Practice the rest of the exercises for ten to forty minutes, one to six times a day. Remember to move at your own pace.

**Week 8.  Heartbeat theme.**  If you have trouble becoming aware of your heartbeat, lie on your back with your right hand resting over your heart. If you experience any discomfort or distress while doing this exercise, move on to the next three themes and do this one in week eleven.

*My right arm is heavy.*

*My arms and legs are heavy and warm.*

*My heartbeat is calm and regular.*

**Week 9. Breathing theme.** This enhances the tendency of the previous themes to slow and deepen respiration.

*My right arm is heavy and warm.*

*My arms and legs are heavy and warm.*

*My heartbeat is calm and regular.*

*It breathes me.*

**Week 10. Solar plexus theme.** Skip this exercise if you have ulcers, diabetes, or any condition involving bleeding from abdominal organs.

*My right arm is heavy and warm.*

*My arms and legs are heavy and warm.*

*My heartbeat is calm and regular.*

*It breathes me.*

*My solar plexus is warm.*

**Week 11. Forehead theme.** It is best to do this exercise lying on your back, since it may cause dizziness.

*My right arm is heavy and warm.*

*My arms and legs are heavy and warm.*

*My heartbeat is calm and regular.*

*It breathes me.*

*My solar plexus is warm.*

*My forehead is cool.*

**Week 12. Special themes.** You can practice *autogenic modification* by making up what Schultz called "organ specific formulae" to deal with specific problems. For example, you can develop an indirect formula such as "My feet are warm" or "My shoulders are warm" each time you feel an embarrassing blush coming on. This exercise allows you to passively attend to something other than the problem. At the same time, you move some of the blood from your head that would contribute to the blushing. You might also use a direct formula such as, "My forehead is cool."

When you are troubled by a cough, you may want to use this formula: "My throat is cool, my chest is warm." To cope with asthma, use the same formula and add: "It breathes me, it breathes me calm and regular."

When you are in a very relaxed state toward the end of an AT session, you are highly suggestible. It is a good time to use what Schultz called "intentional formulae" to tell yourself to do things that you want to do and are having difficulty with. For example, if you want to stop smoking, say something over and over again such as, "Smoking is a dirty habit, I can do without it." If you want to eat less, say, "I have control over what I eat. I can eat less and be more attractive." The special intentional formulas should be believable, persuasive, and brief.

These additional formulas may be interspersed with the themes of the standard exercises, or said when you are finished saying the standard themes.

*I feel quite quiet*

*My whole body feels quiet, heavy, comfortable, and relaxed*

*My mind is quiet.*

*I withdraw my thoughts from the surroundings and I feel serene and still*

*My thoughts are turned inward and I am at ease*

*Deep within my mind, I can visualize and experience myself as relaxed and comfortable and still*

*I feel an inward quietness*

## Meditative Exercises

These exercises focus on mental rather than physical functions. They are intended to reinforce the effects of the standard exercises. Schultz reserved the meditative exercises for trainees who had mastered the standard exercises over a period of six to twelve months and who could prolong the autogenic state for 40 minutes without serious distracting effects.

Schultz's meditative exercises are similar to the methods of psychosynthesis, a program developed at about the same time by the Italian psychiatrist Roberto Assagioli. Both these western physicians sought to duplicate in a predictable way the physical and emotional benefits of eastern meditation without making use of its mystical and religious elements.

The meditative exercises stimulate the creative processes and mobilize the resources of both the body and mind toward greater self awareness, problem solving, and emotional and physiological health. They are effective because your mind affects your emotions and your body. If you turn your mental focus away from pain and problems, you will feel better emotionally and physically.

Practice the first stages of the meditative exercises twice a day for 20 minutes. When you begin the more complicated visualizations, you will probably want to spend up to an hour at a time. Spend a week on the color and movement exercises, then two to six weeks on the others in turn. Move at your own pace.

**Color and movement.**  Begin all exercises by assuming your favorite Autogenic posture and running quickly through the standard themes. Then, with your eyes still closed, roll your eyeballs upward. Imagine looking inward at the center of your forehead.

Visualize a static, uniform color filling your mind's eye. Experiment with blue, green, yellow, red, orange, and so on until you find a color that is easiest for you to hold in your imagination.

Let darker and lighter shades of your color form. Add movement by letting these vague areas of light and dark color drift around like clouds or shadows.

Add another color in a simple geometric shape. For example, if you have been visualizing blue, see a green triangle superimposed on the blue background. Add other shapes and colors gradually—a yellow square, an orange circle, and so on. Then try changing the color of the background.

Introduce movement by having the geometric shapes move up and down and sideways. Introduce depth by letting them grow larger and smaller. Imagine that the triangles are solid cones, the squares are cubes, and the circles are balls. Stack them up and roll them around.

This exercise gives you practice in forming, controlling, and holding vivid mental images.

**Objects.** Visualize and hold the image of a specific, unmoving object such as a face, mask, or statue. Let it be light in color against a dark background. Choose an object that comes easily to mind. Concentrate on its details.

If you have trouble getting a clear image or holding it, lengthen your practice sessions up to an hour. With these longer sessions you might need to rest in the middle, or interrupt a disturbing image. Use these cancellation phrases to take a break: "The images gradually recede . . . they have become less clear . . . they have completely disappeared . . . my legs are light . . . my arms are light . . . my heart and breathing normal . . . my forehead temperature normal." Stretch your arms, breathe deeply, and open your eyes. Take a break for a couple of minutes, then start your exercise over from the beginning.

**Concepts.** Pick an abstract concept such as happiness. Visualize the word printed on a page. Imagine hearing a voice saying "happiness" out loud. Give happiness a color and shape. Imagine a happy person in a fairy tale or a myth. Tell yourself the story or see it acted out as in a movie or a play. Allow your mind to bring up images, analogies, and associations connected to happiness.

Other abstractions to meditate on in this way are freedom, peace, justice, goodness, and so on.

**Fantasy scenes.** Put yourself in a fantasy scene: on top of a mountain, on the moon, seeing a sunrise, flying over clouds, looking out over the ocean, in a palace, or elsewhere. Concentrate on the details of sight, sound, touch, temperature, and movement. Notice if anyone else appears. What do they do or say? See the scene as a "filmstrip" in which you are an actor and an active participant.

You may encounter archetypal figures, religious themes, melodrama, or vivid sexual fantasies. Accept and observe whatever comes up. If it becomes disturbing, use your cancellation phrases and take a break.

**Real people.** Visualize real people. Start with someone like a store clerk or the mailman. It is easier to hold a clear image of someone you don't know well. Next easiest is someone you know and dislike. People you love will probably be the hardest to visualize clearly.

At this stage, the people you visualize may say or do anything, or you may have spontaneous insights about them. You have opened yourself up to messages from your unconscious self, a wellspring of valuable, interesting, and surprising information. What you get when you interrogate your unconscious self is unpredictable. Sometimes you may get images that are alarming. If you do, use the cancellation phrases to terminate the session.

## Further Reading

Coleman, D., and J. Green, eds. 1993. *Mind Body Medicine: How To Use Your Mind for Better Health.*Yonkers, NY: Consumer Reports Books.

Linden, W. 1990. *Autogenics: A Clinical Guide.* New York: Guilford Press.

Pelletier, Kenneth R. 1977. *Mind as Healer, Mind as Slayer.* New York: Delta.

———. 1984. *A Holistic Approach to Preventing Stress Disorders.* New York: P. Smith.

Peurifory, Reneau Z. 1992. *Anxiety, Phobias, and Panic: Taking Charge and Conquering Fear.* Citrus Heights, CA: Life Skills.

# 10

# Brief Combination Techniques

The relaxation exercises presented in this chapter are based on the work of many different therapists. They are creative blends of some of the techniques you have already learned about in this book. Learning several brief combination techniques can greatly benefit you for three reasons. First, when you put two or more relaxation approaches together, the combination can have a synergistic effect. This means that the sum relaxation effect of the combined techniques is far greater than what you would achieve if you did each relaxation procedure individually. As you experiment with the material presented in this chapter, you'll learn which techniques are best at activating each other and combining for the most powerful effect. The second reason that combination techniques are often more powerful is because the sequence is set up to draw you deeper into the relaxation experience. Each technique builds progressively upon the one before. For example, the relaxation you experience from visualizing a pleasant beach scene is more profound if you precede the visualization with some deep breathing. And if you follow the deep breathing and the beach scene with autogenic themes of heaviness and warmth, you have a sequence of techniques that build one upon the other toward a deeper relaxation response. The third advantage to using the combination techniques presented in this chapter is their brevity. You can easily do any of these combination sequences during a ten-minute coffee break. Any time you have a few minutes to spare, they can help you center yourself and regain a sense of calmness.

The combination techniques presented here are merely suggestions. While each one has been tested and proven useful, feel free to be inventive. Try your own unique combinations. Experiment with a different sequence. Since you are a unique person with unique needs and patterns of responses, it is important that you add, delete, and modify until you have a brief relaxation sequence that really works for you.

## Symptom Relief

The brief combination techniques presented here have been proven effective in the treatment of fight or flight symptoms and stress-induced physiological disorders. They are particularly helpful when stress is work-related and requires brief but frequent booster sessions during the day to cope with mounting tensions.

## Time for Mastery

If you have mastered the component techniques presented in earlier chapters of the book, these combination approaches can be immediately and effectively applied. Otherwise, allow one to two weeks to successfully use these combined approaches.

## Instructions

### 1. *Stretch and Relax*

A.  Take a big stretch. Tighten your arms and pull them back so that you stretch your chest and shoulders. Stretch and tighten your legs at the same time by first pulling your toes up toward you and then pushing them out straight.

B.  Place one hand on your abdomen, just above your belt. Inhale slowly and deeply through your nose into your abdomen. Push up your hand as much as feels comfortable. Take four more deep breaths using the same procedure.

C.  Suspend a pencil by its point over a desk or table or the floor. Tell yourself that when you are deeply relaxed the pencil will drop. The sound of the dropping pencil will be your signal to enter a healing, five-minute trance. (If you wish to omit the pencil, proceed with step C from here.) Close your eyes and say to yourself the key word or phrase that you have learned in self-hypnosis. Tell yourself that you will become more and more relaxed with each number as you count backwards from ten to zero. After the countdown, repeat to yourself these four phrases, over and over, in any order: "I am drifting deeper and deeper, deeper and deeper . . . I am more and more drowsy, peaceful, and calm . . . I am drifting and drowsy, drowsy and drifting . . . I am drifting down, down, down, into total relaxation." If your pencil has not already dropped by this time, let it go deliberately and remind yourself that you will now enjoy five minutes of peaceful self-hypnosis.

D.  While in trance, visit your special place and enjoy the uniquely relaxing qualities of that environment. Really experience the sights, sounds, and sensations of your special place. When it feels that you've been there long enough, count back from one to ten. Suggest that you are becoming more and more alert, refreshed, and wide awake as you count up.

### 2. *Autogenic Breathing*

A.  Begin by taking slow, deep breaths as described in 1B. Become aware of the growing feeling of relaxation as each deep breath expands your diaphragm.

B.  Visualize a beach. See the waves rolling up the sand, the seagulls wheeling overhead, a few puffs of fleecy clouds. Hear the roar of waves, and then the quiet. Hear the alternating roar, quiet, roar, quiet. Over the ocean sound you can hear the seagulls calling. Now feel the warm sand. Imagine it covering your body, warm and heavy. Really feel the weight of the sand on your arms and legs. Feel surrounded by warmth and comfort.

C.  While visualizing the sand, continue to breathe as deeply as feels comfortable. Notice the rhythm of your breath. As you breathe in, say the word "warm" to yourself. Try to feel the warmth of the sand around your body. As you breathe out, say the word "heavy." Experience the weight of the sand on your limbs. Continue your deep breathing, thinking "warm" as you inhale and "heavy" as you exhale. Continue for at least five minutes. (Note: If after a time you feel more comfortable shifting to shallower breathing, let yourself do so.)

## 3. *Stop and Breathe*

A.  Whenever you notice disturbing or anxiety-provoking thoughts, internally shout "stop" to yourself (see chapter 13 on "Thought Stopping"). Imagine hearing a voice with a great deal of sharpness and authority. If shouting "stop" to yourself doesn't interrupt the flow of thoughts, put a rubber band around your wrist and snap it as you shout "stop."

B.  Shift your attention to your breathing. Begin taking slow, deep breaths into your belly. Place a hand over your abdomen to make sure it is expanding with each breath.

C.  Now start counting your breaths. As you exhale, count one. As you exhale again, count two. Keep counting up to four. Each time you reach four, start over again at one. Try to keep your mind as empty as possible as you focus on counting each breath. Continue the procedure until you feel relaxed and repeat each time anxiety-provoking thoughts occur.

## 4. *Changing Channels*

A.  Use the same thought-stopping procedure described in 3A above.

B.  As soon as you have interrupted the stressful cognition, use a prerehearsed visualization to block the return of any unwanted thoughts. Make sure the visualization is something you can elicit easily without struggle. Use an exciting sexual fantasy, images of success from some important achievement, scenes from an anticipated vacation, or images of your special place. The common thread of all these suggestions is to see yourself doing something that feels really good, something you picture easily. (Helpful hint: try visualizing scenes you already use for daydreaming.)

C.  If visualization doesn't work, try these alternatives: turn on the radio, put a favorite tape in your Walkman, go out for a jog or some other strenuous aerobic exercise, start counting things (each Chevrolet you see, each person wearing a hat, how many families have children on your block), pick up a book or magazine, even sing or whistle. What matters is that the activity be arresting enough to divert attention away from stressful thoughts for a time.

**D.** Use a coping mantra. This is a reminder that you're basically safe and okay and can handle any stress that comes along. Some coping mantras are general affirmations such as "I am well . . . I am safe and calm . . . I trust my ability to cope . . . I am surrounded by support and love . . . I can relax my body and my mind . . . I can plan and decide later, now I'll relax." Other mantras require the development of a coping statement about a specific situation: "These are just stomach cramps and I'm not going to worry about them . . . Tests show my heart is strong and healthy . . . This is the same old neck pain, it always passes . . . I can always get a loan . . . I can set limits, I'll just tell her no . . . I can ask for help with _____ . . . I can make mistakes . . . I don't have to finish everything on time . . . I can disappoint _____ sometimes and we'll still love one another . . . I have a plan I can implement tomorrow . . . These are just fight or flight symptoms, they'll pass soon . . . I did the best I could, we'll see what happens." Use your coping mantra whenever the stressful thought threatens to take hold again. Repeat your mantra as often as necessary.

## 5. *I Am Grateful*

This exercise is particularly helpful as the day is wearing on and your sense of stress and frustration is rising. It is also an excellent sequence for relaxing and putting yourself in a pleasant frame of mind before you drift off to sleep.

**A.** Use the short form for progressive muscle relaxation outlined in the progressive relaxation chapter. (1. Curl fists, tighten biceps. 2. Wrinkle forehead, face like a walnut. 3. Arch back, take a deep breath. 4. Pull feet back, curl toes while tightening calves, thighs, buttocks.)

**B.** Reflect back over your day so far and select three things for which you feel grateful. These do not have to be major events. For example, you may be grateful for the warm shower you took this morning, a co-worker helping you, your child giving you a hug and telling you he loves you, a lovely sunrise, and so on. Take a moment to relive and enjoy these experiences.

**C.** Continue to think back over your day. Recall three things you did that you feel good about. Remember, these don't have to be major feats. For example, you may feel good about saying no to something you really didn't want to do, taking time for yourself to exercise or relax, or being supportive to someone you like. Take a moment to reexperience those positive moments.

## 6. *Deep Affirmation*

**A.** Put your hand over your abdomen and begin taking slow deep breaths as described in 1B.

**B.** Close your eyes and continue to breathe deeply as you scan your body for tension. Start with your toes and move up your body. Notice any tension in your calves, thighs, and buttocks. Explore areas of tension in your back, abdomen, or chest muscles. Notice your shoulders and neck, your jaw, cheeks, and forehead. Check for tension in your biceps, forearms, and hands. Whenever you discover a tense area, exaggerate the tension slightly so that you can become aware of it. Notice exactly which muscles in your body are tense and then say to yourself, "I am tensing my _____ . . . I am hurting myself . . . I am creating tension in my body . . . I will let go of that tension starting now."

**C.** Use the self-hypnosis exercise outlined in 1C.

**D.** Select an affirmation to use while in trance. The following is a list of suggested affirmations reprinted from *Visualization for Change* by Patrick Fanning.

*I can relax at will.*
*Tension is draining from my muscles.*
*I'm filled with peace, calm, and serenity.*
*I can turn my tension down like the volume on a radio.*
*Relaxation floods my body like healing, golden light.*
*I am in touch with my peaceful center.*
*I can look inward and find peace.*
*Relaxation is always within my grasp.*

When you have relaxed long enough, count back up from one to ten. Suggest as you count that you are feeling more and more refreshed, alert, and wide awake.

## 7. *The Tension Cutter*

**A.** Take four deep breaths as described in 1B.

**B.** Close your eyes. Visualize your tension by giving it a color or a shape. Now change the shape and color of your tension. Make it bigger or smaller, lighter or darker. Now see yourself picking it up. Look at it in your hands, toss it up and down once or twice like it was a ball. Now see yourself rearing back in slow motion to throw your tension away. Go ahead and throw it. See it slowly leave your hand and move further and further away. Watch until it disappears out of your awareness.

**C.** Now imagine your body filled with lights. See red lights for tension and blue lights for relaxation. Imagine the lights changing from red to blue in all the tension areas of your body. Be aware of any physical sensation you experience while you change to the blue light of relaxation. See all the lights in your body as blue and see that color blue becoming darker and darker. Feel yourself relaxing further with each shade of blue you experience.

**D.** Now it's time for a mini-vacation. Here are two itineraries.

*Vacation 1.* Picture yourself in a forest. The light is bright in places and mottled in others. You feel safe and comfortable, taking a long pleasant walk. The air around you is cool and refreshing. You enjoy the bright spots of sunshine on the ground where the sun has filtered down through the leaves. You are walking barefoot. The leaves and moss feel soft and cool on your feet. You hear the bird sounds and the soft rustle of wind through the trees. The sounds make you happy and comfortable. As you walk your muscles feel more and more loose, heavy, and relaxed. The forest carpet of leaves and moss feels so comfortable that you want to lie down and close your eyes to rest. Now you see a small stream making a soft, bubbly noise. And next to the stream is a patch of tall, soft grass, lit and warmed by sunlight. It's a lovely place to rest and you sink down to your knees and roll gently over onto the soft, warm grass. You hear the bubbling stream, the birds' song, and the gentle wind. You are so deeply relaxed that every part of your body from your toes to the top of your head is loose and heavy.

*Vacation 2.* Picture yourself alone in a beach house with a view of the sea. The first rays of sun light up the wall of your bedroom as you sink deeper into the warm, soft bed. You take a deep breath and notice how relaxed your muscles are. Outside you hear the sounds of seagulls and the rhythmic crashing of the waves. The waves roll in and out, in and out. Each wave makes you more and more deeply relaxed. In and out, in and out. Drowsy, heavy and calm. You can feel the cool salt air coming through the open window and you roll over to see the sand and the waves and the blue sky. You take deep breaths of the air and the relaxation deepens with each breath. You feel safe and yet very free, unhurried, aware that the day ahead is full of possibilities.

Use these examples as a model to create your own mini-vacations.

## 8. *Breath Counting*

**A.** Preselect a brief affirmation (see the list in 6D) or coping mantra (see the list in 4D). Try to make sure that the affirmation or coping reminder is no longer than seven or eight words. Make up a statement that feels right for you and your unique situation.

**B.** To begin the relaxation process, use the short form of progressive muscle relaxation found in 5A and the progressive relaxation chapter.

**C.** Take four deep breaths as described in 1B.

**D.** Now let your breathing go back to a normal rate. Focus on each breath, and as you exhale count the breath. When you get to the fourth breath, instead of counting four, say your affirmation or coping mantra. Here's a sample of what you might do. As you exhale you count one, two, three, "I can make mistakes and be okay," one, two, three, "I can make mistakes and be okay," and so on.

## 9. *Taking Control*

**A.** Get comfortable, close your eyes, and begin noticing your breathing. Try to notice each breath and nothing else. As you exhale, say to yourself the word "one." Keep saying "one" with each exhalation.

**B.** When you feel sufficiently relaxed, turn your attention from your breathing to a situation you find stressful or difficult. See yourself handling that stressful situation successfully, confidently. See yourself saying and doing the appropriate thing to succeed. See yourself smiling, standing or sitting erectly. Now visualize yourself hesitating or making a small error, uncertain for a moment. But then you go on, confidently finishing the task, looking satisfied. You remind yourself, "I can handle this, I'm in control."

## 10. *Accepting Yourself*

**A.** Use the body scanning procedure described in 6B.

**B.** Continue to relax by doing several minutes of autogenic breathing as described in 2C.

**C.** When you feel deeply relaxed, make these suggestions to yourself: "I let go of shoulds . . . I accept myself for all my humanness . . . I breathe, I feel, I do the best I can." Rewrite this mantra in any way that feels more authentic or true for you. Anything will work, as long as it carries the basic message that you accept yourself.

# 11

## Recording Your Own
## Relaxation Tape

One of the best ways to develop a complete relaxation regime is to make your own audio tape. A tape of twelve to twenty minutes can become a "relaxation workout" that incorporates many of the important techniques described in this book.

There are many relaxation tapes on the market, including five that are recommended for use with this book. But there are advantages to making your own. First, you can delete segments that don't work for you while retaining and emphasizing techniques that you find particularly effective. Second, you can combine as many or as few relaxation techniques as you want for a long, medium, or short relaxation workout. Third, you can be creative. You can develop your own unique approach, create special relaxation or coping mantras, or visualize images that you find uniquely peaceful or calming. Fourth, using your own voice can make the tape feel especially intimate and friendly. Finally, you may use any accompanying music or sound effects that you wish, or leave the background entirely silent.

Relaxation tapes are also a big help when you're feeling passive, when you want to be told what to do. It's a lot easier to put on a tape and follow instructions than it is to figure out each step of a relaxation procedure yourself.

## Symptom Relief

Tapes can be effective for almost any symptom of stress or stress-related illness. A taped relaxation procedure can be especially helpful when you are low in energy or motivation. If you commit yourself to play the tape at specific times during the day, you are more likely to follow your relaxation program consistently.

# Time for Mastery

You will probably need to make several relaxation tapes before your voice and phrasing and the techniques you've selected feel right to you. Let yourself experiment. Over the course of a week, you should be able to develop a tape that works sufficiently well for you to get real benefit. From then on, you may periodically change the tape, rewriting, adding, and deleting certain parts as ideas occur to you. Make an effort to listen to your tape at least twice a day, morning and evening.

# Instructions

The first thing to work on is your voice. Speak at normal volume, in a flat, almost monotonous tone. An uninflected voice on the tape will help keep your focus inward so that you can pay attention to your body and the exercise rather than to any distracting qualities of the voice. Speak slowly. Give yourself time to actually take a deep breath, tense or relax your arms, or form a visualization. Rushing through a relaxation tape defeats its purpose. When you wish to give special emphasis to an important word or instruction, simply say the words slower, drawing out the vowel sounds. "Your muscles are looose and relaxed . . . take a deeeeep breath . . . your forehead is smooooth as silk."

Many people enjoy hearing music in the background of a relaxation tape. There are two problems with adding your own musical background. First, you can't stop recording in order to fix mistakes. If you do, the background music will skip each time you stop the tape. Second, few rooms are acoustically suited for recording music. Your selection is apt to sound tinny or have a slight echo effect. But if music is important to you, go ahead and experiment. Try moving your microphone closer or farther away from the speaker; try different volumes for the music. If you enjoy New Age music, artists such as George Winston, Will Ackerman, Shadowfax, Steve Halpern, and Andreas Vollenweider can provide a very peaceful background. If you prefer classical music, the following pieces have been recommended by the Institute for Music and Imagery (Box 173, Fort Townsend, WA 94368).

> Respighi, *Fountains of Rome* ("The Fountain of Valle Giulia at Dawn," "The Villa Medici Fountain at Sunset")
> Debussy, *Danses Sacred and Profane*
> Bach, *Passacaglia and Fugue in C*
> Pachelbel, *Canon in D*
> Hadyn, *Cello Concerto in C* ("Adagio")
> Glinka, *Life of the Tsar* ("Susanin Aria")
> Sibelius, *Swan of Tuonela*
> Boccherini, *Cello Concerto in B* ("Adagio")

# Mantras and Affirmations

When you relax, you're in a suggestible state. Listening to your tape is an ideal time to remind yourself of important affirmations, coping strategies, and new attitudes that you are striving to remember. These affirmations and reminders may change daily. On the other hand, you may want to repeat an important basic truth each time you listen to the tape so that it gradually finds its way into your subconscious beliefs.

Here are some examples of helpful affirmations that you may wish to use while listening to the tape.

> *Each day I become more and more relaxed.*
> *I accept my body, every feeling, every sensation.*
> *I can relax away stress.*
> *I breathe deeply and calmly when I feel stress.*
> *I can be direct and clear with my boss.*
> *I am expressing my needs and feelings to my wife.*
> *I am responsible for making myself feel good.*
> *My stomach is loose and calm.*
> *The knots in my shoulders are dissolving.*
> *I am loving and good.*
> *I can stop unloving thoughts.*
> *I will succeed in my physics course.*
> *Whenever I feel stress, I'll fill my body with peaceful light.*

Affirmations can involve specific relaxation instructions, suggestions for behavioral change, imagery for healing, suggestions for improved self-esteem, mantras for success, reminders for attitudinal change, and assertions that everything, in the end, will turn out okay. If you want to change something, write an affirmation that will remind you to do so. Make the affirmation positive, and be certain it describes exactly what you want to achieve.

Mantras and affirmations work best if they are combined with an image, a mental picture of the change you want to create. If you want your stomach to be loose and calm, see braided strands untwisting. If you wish to express your needs and feelings to your wife, see yourself talking to her intimately and earnestly. If you wish to succeed in the physics course, see the report card with a B+ or an A.

## Constructing Your Relaxation Tape

The relaxation script below is divided into sections. Each section is a discrete component which can be included or deleted from your tape. Read through the entire script first and mark the sections that feel appropriate to include. Over the next few weeks you may rerecord your tape several times, adding or subtracting sections as you learn more about what works best for you.

## Relaxation Script

**Deep breathing.**   *Close your eyes. Put your hand over your abdomen (just above the belt). Take a deep breath, way down into your belly. (Pause.) Let go and hear the air whoosh out through your lips. (Pause.) And when you're ready, take another deep breath. You can feel your belly rise slowly as the air comes in. Let it out with a whooshing sound, like the wind, as you blow through your lips. Each breath leaves you more and more relaxed. Each breath purifies and relaxes your whole body and mind. Take another deep* *breath down into your belly. Feel your belly push out. As you relax, the air goes gently out your lips. Imagine with your next deep breath that clean, pure, white air is coming in through the soles of your feet. See it spread throughout your whole body, collecting the debris of tension and stress. The air gets darker as it takes the stress and tension from your body. Imagine the dark air being expelled through your lips, your whole body clean and fresh and relaxed. Now take a deep purifying breath and feel it cleaning your body of stress and tension. See the tension leaving your body with the breath. Relax and enjoy the feeling of peace and calm that has spread throughout your body with each deep breath. Imagine one more breath coming in through the soles of your feet, pure and white. It is removing the last bit of tension from your body. As you exhale you feel your body clean and relaxed, deeply relaxed.*

**Counting your breath.**    *Now let your breathing slow down and become automatic. Each breath continues to relax you. You are breathing quietly, peacefully. You're breathing in an easy and natural way. Each time you exhale, say silently to yourself, "one." Continue to breathe in and out, saying "one" each time you exhale. Whenever thoughts or perceptions take your attention away from your breathing, let go of them and return to saying "one." Breathe naturally, calmly, saying "one" as you exhale.* (Leave one to two minutes blank on the tape to really enjoy this exercise.)

**Progressive relaxation.**    *Now, while keeping the rest of your body relaxed, clench your right fist, tighter and tighter.* (Pause five seconds.) *Now relax. Notice the contrast between a tight muscle and a loose one. Notice a pleasant sort of burning that occurs when the muscle relaxes. Now try to relax your arm even more. Let the chair hold your arm up as you let go of the last bit of muscular tension. Now tighten your left fist, tighter and tighter.* (Pause five seconds.) *Relax and enjoy the feeling of looseness in your left arm. Really give yourself a chance to feel a difference between tension and relaxation.* (Pause.)

*Now bend your elbows and tense your biceps. Tense them as much as you can and observe the feeling of tautness.* (Pause five seconds.) *Relax, straighten out your arms. Let the relaxation develop and feel the difference.* (Pause.)

*Now turn your attention to your head and wrinkle up your forehead as tight as you can.* (Pause five seconds.) *Now relax and smooth it out. Let yourself imagine your entire forehead and scalp becoming smooth and relaxed.* (Pause.) *Now frown and notice the strain spreading throughout your forehead. Feel the tension and the tightness.* (Pause.) *Now let go, allow your brow to become smooth again. Notice the difference between tension and relaxation in your forehead.* (Pause.) *Now clench your jaw, bite hard, and notice the tension throughout your jaw.* (Pause five seconds.) *Relax your jaw. When the jaw is relaxed, your lips will begin to part. Really feel and appreciate the contrast between tension and relaxation in your jaw. Notice how it feels to relax your lips and tongue.*

*Now shrug your shoulders. Keep the tension as you hunch your head down between your shoulders.* (Pause five seconds.) *Relax. Drop your shoulders and feel the relaxation spreading through your neck, throat and shoulders. Pure relaxation, deeper and deeper. Feel how loose and easy your neck feels balanced on your shoulders.*

*Give your entire body a chance to relax. Feel the comfort and the heaviness. Take a deep breath and let it fill your abdomen.* (Pause.) *Now exhale, letting the air out with a whooshing sound. Continue relaxing, letting your breath come freely and gently. Now, tighten your stomach and hold. Note the tension.* (Pause five seconds.) *Relax. Place your hand on your stomach. Breathe deeply into your belly, pushing your hand up. Hold.* (Pause.) *And relax. Feel the contrast with the tension as the air rushes out.*

*Now concentrate on your back. Arch it very slightly, without straining. Focus on the tension in your lower back. Feel the tension.* (Pause) *And then relax. Imagine loosening the lower back and pelvic muscles, feel yourself sinking deeper into the chair or bed. Focus on letting go of all the tension in the muscles of your lower back and pelvis and abdomen. Feel yourself sinking heavier and heavier into the chair or bed as your abdomen and back relax more and more deeply.* (Pause.)

*Now tighten your buttocks and thighs. Hold the tension and notice how it feels.* (Pause five seconds.) *Relax and notice the contrast between tension and looseness. Really experience what it feels like to relax your buttocks and thighs.* (Pause.) *Now curl your toes downward, making your calves tense. Study the tension.* (Pause five seconds.) *Relax. Feel and enjoy the relaxation.* (Pause.) *Now bend your toes toward your face, creating tension in your shins.* (Pause five seconds.) *Relax again, enjoying the feeling of peace and heaviness that spreads everywhere in your legs.*

*Feel the heaviness in your body as the relaxation deepens. Feel yourself heavier and heavier, more and more deeply relaxed. More and more heavy, peaceful and calm.*

**Body awareness.** *Now you can scan your body for any last bit of tension. Let your arms become heavy and relaxed. Heavier and heavier, more and more deeply relaxed. Your arms are heavy, heavy, letting go of the last bit of muscle tension. More and more deeply relaxed. Letting go, letting go of all muscle tension.*

*And now your face too can relax. Your forehead becomes smooth as silk, smooth and relaxed, letting go of all the tension and the worry. Smooth and relaxed. Your cheeks become smooth and relaxed, completely free of tension. Your cheeks and forehead are smooth and relaxed. And your jaw too lets go of the last bit of tension. Your jaw hangs loose and relaxed, loose and relaxed. Your tongue and lips are relaxed. And as your jaw becomes completely loose and relaxed, your lips begin to part, very slightly. They begin to part as you let go of the last bit of muscle tension. Your jaw is loose and relaxed.*

*Your neck and shoulders can now let go. Your shoulders droop and relax, droop and relax. Your neck is loose and easy. Your neck and shoulders are relaxed, you feel safe and calm. Your shoulders droop and you let go of the last bit of muscle tension.*

*Now you can take another deep breath, way down into your belly. Your belly pushes up as you inhale.* (Pause.) *Let go now, making the whooshing noise with your lips. Feel the relaxation spread throughout your abdomen and chest and back. Take another deep breath, and as you do feel the air relax your chest and abdomen and back. Exhale with a whooshing noise, and feel the last bit of muscular tension leave your lower body.* (Pause.)

*Now focus on your legs. Let them become heavier and heavier, more and more deeply relaxed. Heavier and heavier, letting go of the last bit of muscular tension. Letting go, letting go of tension, more and more deeply relaxed as your legs become heavier and heavier. You can imagine your legs as lead pipes, so heavy and relaxed.*

*Now you feel a relaxation throughout your entire body. Every cell is relaxed, calm, and quiet. Your legs and arms are heavy and relaxed, your face is smooth and relaxed, your jaw hangs loosely, loosely. Your neck and shoulders are relaxed, your shoulders droop and relax. Take another deep breath.* (Pause.) *As you do, your entire body will be filled with peace, calm, and relaxation.*

**Special place.** *Now imagine a place where you feel peaceful, calm, and relaxed. A place where you are secure and safe. See whether it is outdoors or indoors, whether it is a place from your past or your present or a place you've never really seen. This is your special place, a retreat and a haven. You're going there now. You can see the shapes and colors of your special place. You see every detail like a picture.* (Pause.) *And now you can begin to hear the sounds of your special place. You can see and hear.* (Pause.) *And now you are able to feel your special place. You feeli can feel it against your skin. You feel bathed in peace and* *a deep sense of contentment in your special place. Take a deep breath as you let the peace and tranquility of your special place spread throughout your entire body. Enjoy your place for a while. Let it nourish and relax you.* (Pause one to two minutes.)

**Autogenics theme.** *Take a deep breath, way down into your belly. As you breathe in, say the word "warm" to yourself. And as you breathe out, say the word "heavy."* (Pause.) *Take another deep breath and think to yourself, "warm."* (Pause.) *Let it go and think, "heavy." Now breathe deeply, at your own pace, thinking "warm" on the in-breath and "heavy" on the out-breath. Feel the warmth and heaviness in your arms and legs. And with each breath let the feeling spread throughout your entire body, relaxing every muscle as you feel more and more heavy, warm, and relaxed.* (Pause 90 seconds.)

**Coping imagery.** *Notice the feeling of peace and relaxation. Imagine carrying this feeling into your everyday life. See yourself confident, relaxed, talking calmly. See yourself smiling with friends, co-workers, family. Your manner is easy as you state your needs and concerns. You see yourself standing comfortably and calmly with your boss, with people you barely know, with strangers. You see yourself smiling and enjoying the conversation. You are able to speak what is in your mind. You say what you feel and think clearly, in such a way that you are appreciated and understood. Your posture is relaxed yet straight. You feel strong and capable.*

**Affirmation.** *Now is the time to remember your affirmation. Say it to yourself slowly while focusing on any accompanying imagery. Give yourself time to let your affirmation really sink in, repeating as often as feels appropriate.* (Pause 20 seconds.)

**Anchoring.** *Now feel the relaxation in every part of your body. Notice the feeling of heaviness and peace in your arms and your legs. Feel the looseness in your jaw, the relaxation in your neck and shoulders. Take a deep breath, and as you exhale the last bit of tension will leave your body.* (Pause.) *Experience the feeling of being completely at rest.*

*Now, while staying very aware of what relaxation feels like in your body, place your right hand over your left wrist. Grasp your wrist gently, but firmly. Whenever you hold your wrist in this way it will be your cue to relax. Any time you hold your left wrist with your right hand you will recover the deep feelings of relaxation you have right now.*

*Take a deep breath. Feel it cleansing and refreshing your body. Feel the healing energy of relaxation flowing through your arms and throughout your body. When you link your hand and wrist, it completes a circuit so the healing energy flows freely and reaches every part of your body. From now on, whenever you wish to relax, you will hold your left wrist with your right hand.*

# Using Your Tape

Now it's time to try out your tape. As you experiment by including or omitting different segments, you will discover which procedures work best for you. You may want to try writing some of your own and including them on the tape. Certain breathing exercises, visualizations, or meditation procedures may be more effective for you than some of the techniques on this sample script. The only rule to follow is: Do what works.

"Do what works" applies not just to the omission or inclusion of techniques. It means that you should order the techniques in any sequence that feels good to you, experiment with your voice and inflection, and try recordings of wind chimes, waterfalls, babbling brooks, or any other background noises or sound effects that seem appropriate.

## Buying Tapes

If you prefer relaxation tapes based on a single specific technique, the following tapes were made to accompany this book and can be ordered from New Harbinger Publications: *Progressive Relaxation and Breathing; Body Awareness and Imagination; Autogenics and Meditation; Self-Hypnosis; and Thought Stopping.*

# 12

# Biofeedback

In a sense, all of the previous chapters in this book have talked about getting feedback from your body. As you practice body awareness and deep relaxation exercises, you increase your ability to recognize and control your personal physiological cues of tension and relaxation. You learn to notice that when you are tense, you experience cold hands and feet, tightness in your chest, shoulders, and jaw, or butterflies in your stomach. After relaxing, you notice that your hands and feet have warmed, muscles in your body have let go, and the butterflies are gone.

Biofeedback is the use of instruments to detect and amplify specific physical states in your body that you usually don't notice and to help bring them under your voluntary control. Biofeedback machines give you immediate information about such biological conditions as muscle tension, skin surface temperature, brain wave activity, skin conductivity (sweating), blood pressure, and heart rate. The feedback from the instruments provides you with instant and continuous information so that you can observe and modify your physical experience of stress.

Each of your body systems affects how you experience relaxation. If your muscles are relaxed and your skin temperature is warm, that doesn't mean you are completely stress free. Your heart rate might still be high, and an EEG might show high brain wave activity. Biofeedback helps you find out which components of your nervous system are and are not relaxed. It can enhance your awareness of what total relaxation feels like for you.

Biofeedback is often used as a supplement to many of the relaxation exercises in this book. For example, if you learn deep breathing and autogenics in order to relax, you can use biofeedback to find out just how relaxed your muscles are or how much you have lowered your heartbeats per minute.

After you've used biofeedback instruments to develop your ability to read the tension in your various body systems, you can continue without a machine. The goal is to learn to lower muscle tension or blood pressure or to increase hand temperature whenever you need to counter-

We wish to acknowledge Kathy Dale, LPT, Biofeedback Specialist, Kaiser Permanente Medical Center, San Jose, for her consultation and encouragement in the revision of this chapter.

act a stressful situation. You can identify subtle early signs of arousal and correct them before you become really stressed. If you catch your pattern of arousal at its earliest point, it's easier to reverse the direction of stress build-up.

Is biofeedback for you? If you are suffering symptoms of stress, it can be a very powerful treatment tool. However, if you start out thinking that biofeedback machines can magically erase tension from your body, you may end up very frustrated. That's because there are basically two steps in relaxation: first to identify when and where the tension is inside your body, and then to let go of it. The first step alone brings very little relief. You can become aware of stress cues inside your body via biofeedback, but you must also learn ways of letting go of physical tension. And that means finding stress reduction techniques that work for you.

The clinical application of biofeedback was pioneered by Alyce and Elmer Green of the Menninger Foundation in the late 1960s. Many other researchers have followed the Greens in exploring this promising treatment approach. By providing an objective measurement of bodily functions, biofeedback has given credibility to the whole field of stress reduction.

## Symptom Relief

The following symptoms can be treated with biofeedback:

| | |
|---|---|
| Tension headache | Attention deficit disorder |
| Migraine headache | Tinnitus |
| Hypertension | Pain management |
| Insomnia | Raynaud's syndrome |
| Spastic colon | Panic attacks |
| Muscle spasms | Some tics and tremors |
| Anxiety | Gastrointestinal disorders |
| Phobic reactions | Decreased blood glucose levels |
| Asthma | Stress incontinence |
| Stuttering | Painful intercourse |
| Teeth grinding | Painful menstrual cramps |
| Epilepsy | Increased vaginal muscle tone |

## How Biofeedback Works

You cannot consciously will the tension out of your body, but you can learn to let yourself relax. Biofeedback teaches you what this process feels like. It does so by providing a mirror that reflects what is going on in your body as you practice deep relaxation techniques. It provides evidence that you are making small, but objectively measurable progress. When you combine relaxation techniques with biofeedback, you can learn to deepen your relaxation response. Soon you will be able to apply your increased awareness of subtle cues of tension to your daily life. When you feel a sign of tension building, you can tell yourself exactly what you need to do to relax.

Biofeedback does this by allowing you to become aware of and modify body functions regulated by both your voluntary or *somatic* nervous system and your involuntary or *autonomic* nervous system. The voluntary nervous system controls the skeletal muscles that are employed in deliberate or consciously controlled movement, such as leg, arm, or hand movement. The involuntary nervous system governs the heart, blood vessels, breathing, stomach, endocrine glands, and all functions which have traditionally been considered outside of your control. Biofeedback technology gives you the ability to tune into and regulate these functions.

A biofeedback system usually consists of four parts: a transducer, an amplifier, a signal reducer, and a signal display. A transducer receives signals from the individual and converts them into a form measurable by instruments. Examples include skin electrodes and temperature probes. An amplifier converts the minute electrical signal into an electrically manageable quantity by amplifying it. The signal reducer extracts the significant part of the information. Finally, the signal display converts the energy of the reduced signal into a form that has meaning to the individual, such as a moving tracer on a graph or an auditory tone.

# How biofeedback works

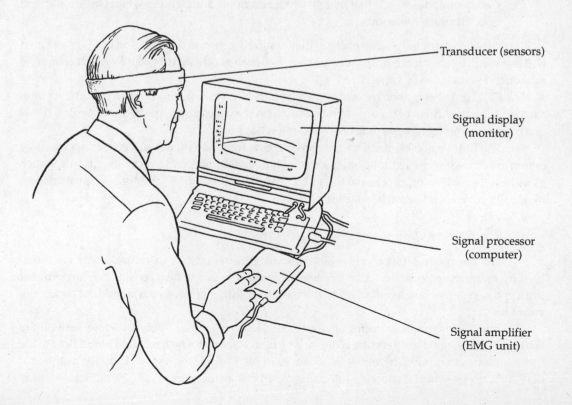

Transducer (sensors)

Signal display
(monitor)

Signal processor
(computer)

Signal amplifier
(EMG unit)

A biofeedback loop begins as the trainee produces the original signals that are picked up, processed, and fed back to him. He perceives and processes the feedback from the signal display and then reacts to the feedback, continuing the loop as he generates more signals.

In this chapter we discuss the five main ways that biofeedback measures important body functions. Although these five standard modalities are the ones most commonly used, biofeedback principles and practice allow any physiological function to be measured and trained: gut tonus, acid and enzyme secretion, sexual response, blood pressure, cardiac functions, and so on. Eventually the ability to monitor any physiological function in the laboratory will be made available for clinical use.

## Electromyogram (EMG) Training

An EMG machine monitors skeletal muscle tension, which is part of the voluntary nervous system. Almost any muscle can be monitored, but the following three muscles are most commonly used:

1. *Frontalis:* the muscle in your forehead that makes you frown and tightens when you are worried or under pressure.

2. *Masseter:* the muscle that tightens your jaw and stays clenched when you are frustrated or angry.

3. *Trapezius:* the muscle that hunches your shoulders and tightens when you are alarmed or chronically anxious.

These muscles are chosen because they typically respond to stress and can be measured without much interference from other muscles. They are a good starting point from which muscle relaxation training can be generalized.

EMG training is done by placing two sensors (electrodes) at a convenient distance from each other on the skin over the appropriate muscle. A third electrode is placed on a neutral tissue (such as over a bone) to serve as an electrical reference point.

The EMG is the biofeedback instrument most frequently used. It has been successfully employed to treat muscular tension, insomnia, and anxiety, and psychosomatic disorders such as asthma, hypertension, ulcers, colitis, and menstrual distress. EMG training has proven to be highly effective with tension headaches.

## Thermograph (Temperature) Training

The thermograph monitors minute fluctuations in body temperature. These are measured by monitoring finger, hand, or foot temperature. A sensor (a heat sensitive semiconductor in an epoxy bead) is usually attached to the middle or little finger of your dominant hand or to your foot.

The thermograph is useful because your skin temperature goes down when you are anxious. This lowered temperature is due to *peripheral vasoconstriction*, reduced blood flow to the tiny capillaries that nourish your skin. Changes in blood flow are regulated by the autonomic nervous system, which responds to stress (sympathetic arousal) by taking blood from the skin and sending it to the skeletal muscles. It is accordingly believed that voluntarily raising skin temperature will produce an anti-stress effect.

Temperature training has been very successful with migraine headaches and vascular problems often associated with cold hands and feet. Controlling body temperature is one way of monitoring and controlling the whole autonomic nervous system. The ability to raise the temperature of your hands appears to be a good indicator of whether the autonomic nervous system is relaxed. When the autonomic nervous system is relaxed, headaches usually subside or can be prevented from occurring. The thermograph and the EMG machine are often used together to monitor tension in both nervous systems.

## Galvanic Skin Response (GSR) Training

A feedback dermograph measures the electrical conductance or electrical potential in your skin. This instrument can monitor tiny changes in the concentration of salt and water in your sweat gland ducts. An imperceptible electric current is run through your skin. As your sweat glands become more active, the machine registers your skin's increased ability to conduct electricity. Some feedback dermographs also measure electrical potential in your skin. The natural metabolism of cells produces a slight voltage (actually millivolts) which varies as sweat gland activity varies. The lower the measurable voltage, the less sweat gland activity there is. Historically, the GSR has been used in lie detectors as a measure of emotional arousal.

The sympathetic branch of your autonomic nervous system controls sweating. By monitoring the activity of your sweat glands, GSR training helps you gain control over your autonomic nervous system. It is often used in the treatment of excessive sweating *(hyperhidrosis)*, phobia, and anxiety states. GSR training usually takes place in conjunction with EMG and temperature training.

## Electroencephalogram (EEG) Training

EEG training is a method of monitoring brain waves. Brain waves have been classified into four states: beta (wide awake and thinking), alpha (associated with a state of calm relaxation), theta (deep reverie or light sleep), and delta (deep sleep). EEG equipment lets you know which brain wave state you are in. EEG training is used in the treatment of insomnia.

"Alpha training" was popular for several years as a way of teaching people to relax. Through monitoring their brain waves, participants were trained to become aware of a subjective state associated with relaxation (the "alpha state") and eventually to duplicate the feelings that went along with this state. Alpha training is now less often used by professional biofeedback trainers, as it has been found that people can achieve the alpha state without necessarily relaxing other body systems. Alpha training alone is not effective with insomnia or epilepsy, as was previously thought, and should only be used in conjunction with other biofeedback modalities.

Researchers have since developed a new EEG machine called a *neuroanalyzer*. Based on the suggestion that certain kinds of electrical activity in the sensory motor strip (the part of the brain controlling motor activity) are better indicators of relaxation, the neuroanalyzer is used to monitor and feed back the sensory motor rhythm. The idea is to shape your brain wave activity so that you have:

1.  Less beta activity (problem-solving mode)

2.  Less delta activity (total sleep)

3.  More sensory motor rhythm intensity

4.  Less muscle tension

Research suggests that sensory motor rhythm feedback has been clinically effective with insomnia and epilepsy.

### Heart Rate Training

A heart rate monitor measures beats-per-minute and gives immediate feedback on how relaxation efforts are affecting heart rate. Since your heart rate changes in response to stress and speeds up when fight-or-flight messages are sent from the autonomic nervous system, a lowered heart rate is an important component of the relaxation response.

There are also biofeedback machines that give readings of blood pressure. People using these machines can find out which thoughts and attitudes raise or lower their blood pressure. They can also observe the effect of relaxation exercises on blood pressure.

## Personal Biofeedback

If you are interested in gaining some experience with biofeedback without investing a lot of time and money, here are a few simple suggestions to try before, during, and after you practice relaxation exercises.

1.  Put your hand to your face to measure the skin temperature of your hands.

2.  Monitor your pulse in your wrist or the carotid artery in your neck to measure your heart rate.

3.  Pay attention to your rate of breathing.

4.  Notice muscle tension or discomfort that you typically experience.

5.  Hold a food thermometer between your index finger and thumb while relaxing. (An indoor-outdoor thermometer or the thermometer from your fish tank will work as well).

The biofeedback industry has developed inexpensive monitoring equipment for home use. Some people have bought machines that measure only temperature, only heart rate, or only alpha activity. The problem is that these instruments only give feedback on a single system. The more systems you measure, the better your awareness is of what it takes for *you* to get relaxed. Just lowering your heart rate or just raising your skin temperature usually isn't enough for total relaxation. At the very least you should be measuring skin temperature, skin conductivity, and heart rate.

Levels of quality in home training equipment vary. You can find wrist watches that measure heart beats-per-minute and inexpensive temperature monitors such as heat sensitive

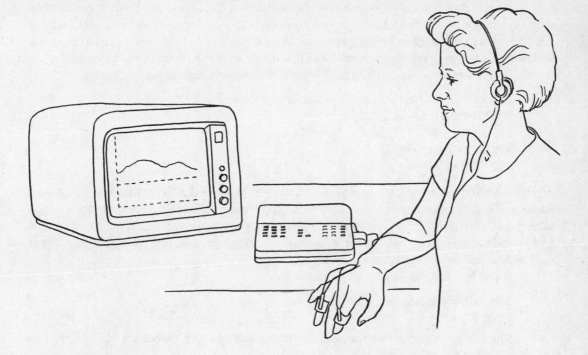

dots and stress control cards that change color. Some companies have developed handheld GSR trainers. These gadgets do provide a gross measure of certain body activities. Unfortunately, there is also usually interference from systems unrelated to the system that you want to measure. Measures are broadly calibrated and not very accurate. Heat sensitive dots, for example, usually indicate gross temperature changes of 2.5 degrees or so, where a sophisticated thermograph will measure a fluctuation of one-hundredth of a degree.

Some companies make moderately expensive home trainer components and systems. A complete system should have a GSR, a thermograph, and an EMG trainer. You should also pick up an inexpensive pulse monitor.

The EMG is the most expensive of the home trainer components (but also the easiest to learn). If you can't afford one, explore the possibility of renting one or at least acquire the GSR, temperature, and heart rate components.

Alpha home trainers are rarely used now, since they are too inaccurate to effectively train you to relax. A sophisticated machine is needed to measure brain waves, and alpha trainers simply don't do the job. Furthermore, alpha training is harder to learn than EMG or GSR training. Since you often get alpha waves as a side effect of training from these other systems, an alpha trainer is actually unnecessary.

If you own a personal computer, you may already have the heart of a personal biofeedback system. The latest home training systems consist of EMG, temperature, GSR, and other sensors that plug into your personal computer. The readings are interpreted and displayed on the screen by a special program. These home trainers are available for both IBM PC and Apple applications.

You can teach yourself to relax with home trainers, but always use them in conjunction with other relaxation techniques. In general, working with a professional will probably be more effective than practicing biofeedback at home. He or she will have high-quality equipment and will be trained at overcoming the roadblocks that might otherwise interrupt your progress.

To get a directory of certified biofeedback practitioners in your area, write to:

Association for Applied Psychophysiology & Biofeedback
10200 West 44th Avenue
Suite 304
Wheat Ridge, CO 80033
(303) 422-8436

Also at the same address and phone number is the Biofeedback Certification Institute of America. The association maintains a membership list and a registry of the biofeedback practitioners that it certifies. Most large cities now have a Biofeedback Institute that trains professionals and provides biofeedback training for individuals wishing to pursue this technique. Most large universities also make biofeedback training available.

If you live in California, you can also call:

Biofeedback Society of California
1-800-272-6966

The following companies specialize in the manufacture of biofeedback equipment.

Thought Technology Ltd.
RR 1
Route 9 North
Box 380
West Chazy, NY 12992
1-800-361-3651

J&J Engineering
797 Holgar Court, N.E.
Poulsbo, WA 98370
(206) 779-3853

The Stens Corporation
6451 Oakwood Drive
Oakland, CA 94611
(510) 339-9053
(213) 389-6223
1-800-25-STENS outside California
*(The Stens Corporation also provides training.)*

Biofeedback Research Institute, Inc.
6399 Wilshire Blvd.
Suite 1010
Los Angeles, CA 90048
(213) 933-9451

Self Regulation Systems
14770 NE 95th Street
Redmond, WA 98052
(206) 882-1101
1-800-345-5642

## Further Reading

Basmajjan, J. B. 1989. *Principals and Practice for Clinicians.* 3rd ed. Baltimore: Williams & Wilkins.

Schwartz, M. S., et al. 1987. *Biofeedback: A Practitioner's Guide.* New York: Gilford Press.

Shellenberger, R., and J. Green. 1986. *From the Ghost in the Box to Successful Biofeedback Training.* Greeley, Colorado: Health Psychology Publishers.

# 13

# Thought Stopping

Thought stopping can help you overcome the nagging worry and doubt which stands in the way of relaxation. Thought stopping was first introduced by Bain in 1928 in his book *Thought Control in Everyday Life*. In the late 1950's, it was adapted by Joseph Wolpe and other behavior therapists for the treatment of obsessive and phobic thoughts. Obsessions are repetitive and intrusive trains of thought that are unrealistic, unproductive and often anxiety provoking. A "worry wart" is an example of an obsessive person. Obsessions may take the form of self doubt: "I will never be able to do this job right" or "I'm too plain to get a date." Obsessions may also take the form of fear: "I wonder if something is wrong with my heart" or "If they raise the rent, I'll have to move." Phobias are specific objects or situations which are so frightening that they are avoided if at all possible. Phobic thoughts are also anxiety producing, and may preoccupy the affected individual.

Thought stopping involves concentrating on the unwanted thoughts and, after a short time, suddenly stopping and emptying your mind. The command "stop" or a loud noise is generally used to interrupt the unpleasant thoughts. There are three explanations for the success of thought stopping: (1) The command "stop" serves as a punishment, and behavior which is consistently punished is likely to be inhibited. (2) The command "stop" acts as a distractor, and the imperative self-instruction is incompatible with obsessive phobic thoughts. (3) Thought stopping is an assertive response and can be followed by thought substitutions of reassuring or self-accepting statements. For example, you say, "These big 747's are awfully safe" instead of "Look at that wing shake, I bet it's ready to come off."

It has been well documented that negative and frightening thoughts invariably *precede* negative and frightening emotions. If the thoughts can be controlled, overall stress levels can be significantly reduced.

## Symptom Relief

Thought stopping has proved effective with a wide variety of obsessive and phobic thought processes: color naming, sexual preoccupation, hypochondriasis, obsessive thoughts of failure, sexual inadequacy, obsessive memories and frightening reoccurring impulses leading to chronic tension and anxiety attacks. While thought stopping is only effective in approximately 20 percent of cases involving compulsive ritual behavior, it is more than 70 percent effective against phobias such as fear of snakes, driving, the dark, elevators, someone lurking in the house at night, fear of insanity, and so on. Thought stopping is recommended when the problem behavior is primarily cognitive, rather than acted out. It is indicated when specific thoughts or images are repeatedly experienced as painful or leading to unpleasant emotional states.

## Time for Mastery

For effective mastery, thought stopping must be practiced conscientiously throughout the day for three days to one week.

## Instructions

### 1. *Explore and List Your Stressful Thoughts*

Use the following stressful thoughts inventory to help you assess which recurrent thoughts are the most painful and intrusive.

**Stressful Thoughts Inventory**

Put a check mark after each item that applies to you. For items that you check, rate them in column A from 1 to 5, based on these statements:

1. *Sensible.* This is quite a sensible and reasonable thing for me to think.

2. *Habit.* This is just a habit. I think it automatically, without really worrying about it.

3. *Not necessary.* I often realize that this thought is not really necessary, but I don't try to stop it.

4. *Try to stop.* I know this thought is not necessary. It bothers me, and I try to stop it.

5. *Try very hard to stop.* This thought upsets me a great deal, and I try very hard to stop it.

For items that you check, rate them in column B from 1 to 4, based on the following statements:

1. *No interference.* This thought does not interfere with other activities.

2. *Interferes a little.* This thought interferes a little with other activities, or wastes a little of my time.

3. *Interferes moderately.* This thought interferes with other activities, or wastes some of my time.

4. *Interferes a great deal.* This thought stops me from doing a lot of things, and wastes a lot of time every day.

| Stressful Thought | Check here if your answer is yes | A<br>If yes, rate from 1 to 5 | B<br>Rate from 1 to 4 |
|---|---|---|---|
| Do you worry about being on time? | ☐ | _____ | _____ |
| Do you worry about leaving the lights or the gas on, or whether the doors are locked? | ☐ | _____ | _____ |
| Do you worry about keeping the house always clean and tidy? | ☐ | _____ | _____ |
| Do you worry about keeping things in their right place? | ☐ | _____ | _____ |
| Do you worry about your physical health? | ☐ | _____ | _____ |
| Do you worry about doing things in their right order? | ☐ | _____ | _____ |
| Do you ever have to count things several times or go through numbers in your mind? | ☐ | _____ | _____ |
| Are you a person who often has a guilty conscience over quite ordinary things? | ☐ | _____ | _____ |
| Do unpleasant or frightening thoughts or words ever keep going over and over in your mind? | ☐ | _____ | _____ |
| Have you ever been troubled by certain thoughts of harming yourself or others—thoughts which come and go without any particular reason? | ☐ | _____ | _____ |
| Do you worry about household things that might chip or splinter if they were to be knocked over or broken? | ☐ | _____ | _____ |
| Do you ever have persistent ideas that someone you know might be having an accident or that something might have happened to them? | ☐ | _____ | _____ |
| Are you preoccupied with the fear of being raped or assaulted? | ☐ | _____ | _____ |
| Do you go back and think about a task you have already completed, wondering how you could have done it better? | ☐ | _____ | _____ |
| Do you find yourself concerned with germs? | ☐ | _____ | _____ |
| Do you have to turn things over and over in your mind before being able to decide about what to do? | ☐ | _____ | _____ |
| Do you ask yourself questions or have doubts about a lot of things that you do? | ☐ | _____ | _____ |
| Are there any particular things that you try to keep away from or that you avoid doing, because you know that you would be upset by them? | ☐ | _____ | _____ |

| Stressful Thought | Check here if your answer is yes | A<br>*If yes, rate from 1 to 5* | B<br>*Rate from 1 to 4* |
|---|---|---|---|
| Do you worry about money a lot? | ☐ | _____ | _____ |
| Do you frequently think that things will not get better and may, in fact, get worse? | ☐ | _____ | _____ |
| Do you become preoccupied with angry or irritated thoughts when people don't do things carefully or correctly? | ☐ | _____ | _____ |
| Do you ruminate about details? | ☐ | _____ | _____ |
| Do guilt-tinged memories return to you over and over? | ☐ | _____ | _____ |
| Do you have recurring feelings of jealousy, or fear of being left? | ☐ | _____ | _____ |
| Do you feel nervous about heights? | ☐ | _____ | _____ |
| Are you at times preoccupied with desire for things you cannot have? | ☐ | _____ | _____ |
| Do you worry about auto accidents? | ☐ | _____ | _____ |
| Do you find yourself returning to thoughts about your faults? | ☐ | _____ | _____ |
| Do you worry about growing old? | ☐ | _____ | _____ |
| Do you feel nervous when thinking about being alone? | ☐ | _____ | _____ |
| Do you worry about dirt and/or dirty things? | ☐ | _____ | _____ |
| Do you tend to worry a bit about personal cleanliness or tidiness? | ☐ | _____ | _____ |
| Does a negative feature of your appearance or makeup preoccupy you at times? | ☐ | _____ | _____ |
| Do you worry about getting trapped in crowds, on bridges, elevators, and so on? | ☐ | _____ | _____ |
| Do you think again and again about your failures? | ☐ | _____ | _____ |
| Sometimes do you think about your home burning? | ☐ | _____ | _____ |
| Do you think frequently of certain things of which you are ashamed? | ☐ | _____ | _____ |
| Are you preoccupied with uncomfortable thoughts about sex or sexual adequacy? | ☐ | _____ | _____ |

(Adapted from the Leyton Scale)

Ask yourself these questions about each stressful thought you checked: Is the thought realistic or unrealistic? Is the thought productive or counter-productive? Is the thought neutral or self-defeating? Is the thought easy or hard to control?

Thought stopping requires consistent motivation. Decide now if you really want to eliminate any of the stressful thoughts you have listed. Select a thought that you feel strongly committed to extinguishing. Column A is the *discomfort* rating for each thought, while column B is the *interference* rating for how disruptive it is to your life. Any thought that has a discomfort rating above three, or an interference rating above two may warrant thought stopping procedures.

## 2. *Imagine the Thought*

Close your eyes and bring into imagination a situation in which the stressful thought is likely to occur. Try to include normal as well as obsessive thinking. In this way, you can interrupt the stressful thoughts while allowing a continuing flow of healthy thinking.

## 3. *Thought Interruption*

Thought interruption can be accomplished initially by using one of two "startler" techniques:

Set an egg timer or alarm clock for three minutes. Look away, close your eyes, and ruminate on your stressful thought as described above in step two. When you hear the ring, shout "Stop!" You may also want to raise your hand, snap your fingers or stand up. Let your mind empty of all but the neutral and nonanxious thoughts. Set a goal of about 30 seconds after the stop, during which your mind remains blank. If the upsetting thought returns during that time, shout "Stop!" again.

Tape record yourself loudly exclaiming "Stop!" at intermittent intervals (e.g. three minutes, two minutes, three minutes, one minute). You may find it useful to repeat the taped stop messages several times at five second intervals. Proceed the same way as with the egg timer or alarm clock. The tape recording shapes and strengthens your thought control.

## 4. *Unaided Thought Interruption*

Now take control of the thought stopping cue, without the timer or tape recorder. While ruminating on the unwanted thought, shout "Stop!"

When you succeed in extinguishing the thought on several occasions with the shouted command, begin interrupting the thought with "Stop!" said in a normal voice.

After succeeding in stopping the thought by using your normal speaking voice, start interrupting the thought with "Stop!" verbalized in a whisper.

When the whisper is sufficient to interrupt stressful thoughts, use the sub-vocal command "stop." Imagine hearing "Stop!" shouted inside your mind. Tighten your vocal chords and move your tongue as if you were saying "Stop!" out loud. Success at this stage means that you can stop thoughts alone or in public, without making a sound or calling attention to yourself.

### 5. *Thought Substitution*

The last phase of thought stopping involves thought substitution. In place of the obsessive thought, make up some positive, assertive statements that are appropriate in the target situation. For example, if you are afraid of flying, you might say to yourself, "This is a fantastically beautiful view from way up here." Develop several alternative assertive statements to say to yourself, since the same response may lose its power through repetition.

## Example of Successful Thought Stopping

A business executive who did a great deal of traveling developed a fear of sleeping in strange places. He was aware that his obsessive worrying about having to take overnight trips had begun about the time of his divorce. When preparing for bed in the motel, he would think about people entering the room by passkey while he slept. While planning his next business trip at home, he would become very tense anticipating the anxiety he would feel in the strange motel.

Utilizing thought stopping techniques, he allowed himself to visualize unpacking in a strange motel, thinking about plans for the next day, anticipating going to bed. He imagined lying in darkness with the feeling that the door might be swinging slightly ajar. In the middle of these thoughts the egg timer went off—he shouted "Stop!" and simultaneously snapped his fingers. If the thought recurred before 30 seconds were up, he shouted "Stop!" again.

After succeeding with the shout, he began saying "Stop!" in a normal voice, and then a whisper. Finally, he was able to shout "Stop!" silently inside his head. He noted that he had repeated each phrase five or ten times before feeling that he could go on to the next one. During the next three days, he shouted "Stop!" sub-audibly at the very beginning of each phobic thought. Occasionally he reinforced the command by snapping a rubber band which he kept around his wrist. The thoughts decreased in frequency and only lasted a few moments when they occurred. He had markedly decreased stress on his next trip. He took his tape recorder and set it to say "Stop!" at intervals of five, ten, three, and eight minutes during the time he was preparing for bed. By the end of the trip, he was aware that he wasn't thinking about the terrors of sleeping in strange places, but was much more focused on the challenges of his business.

## Special Considerations

1. Failure with your first attempt at thought stopping may mean that you have selected a thought that is very difficult to extinguish. In this situation, select an unwanted thought that is either less intrusive or less frightening than your initial choice. It is helpful to become proficient at the technique before tackling the more stressful obsessive or phobic thoughts.

2. If the sub-vocalized "Stop!" is not successful for you, and you find it embarrassing to say "Stop!" aloud in public, you can substitute one of these techniques: Keep a rubber band unobtrusively around your wrist, and when unwanted thoughts occur,

snap it. Or pinch yourself when the unwanted thoughts occur. Or finally, you might try pressing your finger nails into the palms of your hands to stop unwanted thoughts.

3.  You should be aware that stopping a thought takes time. The thought will return and you will have to interrupt it again. The main effort is to stifle each thought just as it begins, and to concentrate on something else. The thoughts will return less and less readily in most cases, and eventually cease to be a problem.

4. See chapter 10 on "Brief Combination Techniques" for two variations on thought stopping: "Stop and Breathe" and "Changing Channels."

## Further Reading

Nelson, J. 1988. *Understanding*. Rocklin, CA: Prime Publishing.

Wolpe, J. 1969. *The Practice of Behavior Therapy*. Oxford: Pergamon Press.

# 14

# Refuting Irrational Ideas

*"Man is not disturbed by events, but by the view he takes of them."*

—Epictetus

Almost every minute of your conscious life you are engaging in self-talk, your internal thought language. These are the sentences with which you describe and interpret the world. If the self-talk is accurate and in touch with reality, you function well. If it is irrational and untrue, then you experience stress and emotional disturbance. This sentence is an example of irrational self-talk: "I can't bear to be alone." No physically healthy person has ever died merely from being alone. Being alone may be uncomfortable, undesirable, and frustrating, but you can live with it and live through it.

More irrational self-talk: "I should never be cruel to my wife. If I am, I know I'm a rotten person." The words "should never" allow no possibility of flaw or failure. When the inevitable fight occurs, you indict yourself as entirely rotten—all on the basis of a single incident.

Irrational ideas may be based on outright misperceptions ("When the airplane's wing shakes, I know it's going to fall off") or perfectionistic shoulds, oughts, and musts ("I ought to keep quiet rather than upset anyone"). Inaccurate self-talk such as "I need love" is emotionally dangerous compared to the more realistic "I want love very much, but I don't absolutely need it, and can survive and feel reasonably happy without it." "How terrible to be rejected" is fear-producing in comparison to "I find it unpleasant and momentarily awkward, and feel regretful when I am rejected." Imperatives such as "I've got to be more helpful around the house" can be converted to more rational statements, such as "There would probably be more peace and compatibility if I did a greater share of the work."

# Feedback Loop

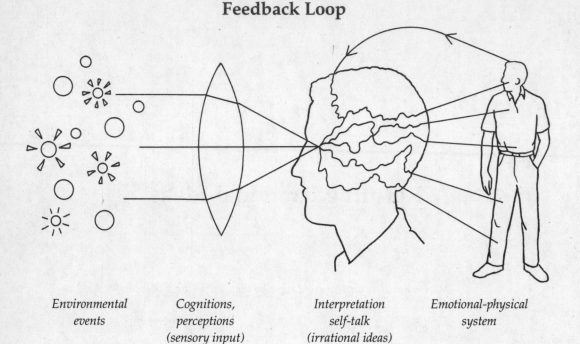

| Environmental events | Cognitions, perceptions (sensory input) | Interpretation self-talk (irrational ideas) | Emotional-physical system |

Albert Ellis developed a system to attack irrational ideas or beliefs and replace them with realistic statements about the world. He called his system Rational Emotive Therapy and introduced it first in *A Guide to Rational Living* with co-author Harper in 1961. Ellis' basic thesis is that emotions have nothing to do with actual events. In between the event and the emotion is realistic or unrealistic self-talk. It is the self-talk that produces the emotions. Your own thoughts, directed and controlled by you, are what create anxiety, anger, and depression. The chart above shows how it works.

## Example

### A. Facts and events

A mechanic replaces a fuel pump he honestly believed was malfunctioning, but the car's performance doesn't improve. The customer is very upset and demands that he put the old fuel pump back.

### B. Mechanic's self-talk

"He's just a grouch—nothing would please him."

"Why the hell do I get all the tough jobs?"

"I ought to have figured this out by now."

"I'm not much of a mechanic."

### C. Emotions

Anger and resentment

Depression

The mechanic may later say to himself, "That guy really made me mad." But it is not the customer or anything that the customer has done which produces the anger—it is the mechanic's own self-talk, his interpretation of reality. This irrational self-talk can be changed, and the stressful emotions changed with it.

## Symptom Relief

Rimm and Litvak (1969) found that negative self-talk produced substantial physiological arousal. In other words, your body tenses and becomes stressed when you use such irrational syllogisms as:

People seem to ignore me at parties.
It's obvious that I'm either boring or unattractive to them.
How terrible!

The emotional results of irrational self-talk are anxiety, depression, rage, guilt, and a sense of worthlessness. Rational Emotive Therapy has been shown effective in decreasing the frequency and intensity of these emotions.

## Time for Mastery

Assessment of your irrational beliefs, plus homework sufficient to refute one of these beliefs, can take approximately twenty minutes a day for two weeks. Rational Emotive Imagery, the process by which you work directly on changing your emotions, also takes about two weeks if you practice ten minutes a day.

## Directions—Rational Emotive Therapy

### Assessment

This Beliefs Inventory is designed to uncover particular irrational ideas which contribute to unhappiness and stress. Take the test now. Score it and note the sections where your scores are highest.

Note that it is not necessary to think over any item very long. Mark your answer quickly and go on to the next statement. Be sure to mark how you actually think about the statement, *not* how you think you *should* think.

## Beliefs Inventory

| Agree | Disagree | Score | Belief |
|-------|----------|-------|--------|
| • ☐ | ☐ | _____ | 1. It is important to me that others approve of me. |
| • ☐ | ☐ | _____ | 2. I hate to fail at anything. |
| • ☐ | ☐ | _____ | 3. People who do wrong deserve what they get. |
| •• ☐ | ☐ | _____ | 4. I usually accept what happens philosophically. |
| •• ☐ | ☐ | _____ | 5. If a person wants to, he can be happy under almost any circumstances. |
| • ☐ | ☐ | _____ | 6. I have a fear of some things that often bothers me. |
| • ☐ | ☐ | _____ | 7. I usually put off important decisions. |
| • ☐ | ☐ | _____ | 8. Everyone needs someone he can depend on for help and advice. |
| • ☐ | ☐ | _____ | 9. "A zebra cannot change his stripes." |
| • ☐ | ☐ | _____ | 10. I prefer quiet leisure above all things. |
| •• ☐ | ☐ | _____ | 11. I like the respect of others, but I don't have to have it. |
| • ☐ | ☐ | _____ | 12. I avoid things I cannot do well. |
| • ☐ | ☐ | _____ | 13. Too many evil persons escape the punishment they deserve. |
| •• ☐ | ☐ | _____ | 14. Frustrations don't upset me. |
| •• ☐ | ☐ | _____ | 15. People are disturbed not by situations but by the view they take of them. |
| •• ☐ | ☐ | _____ | 16. I feel little anxiety over unexpected dangers or future events. |
| •• ☐ | ☐ | _____ | 17. I try to go ahead and get irksome tasks behind me when they come up. |
| • ☐ | ☐ | _____ | 18. I try to consult an authority on important decisions. |
| • ☐ | ☐ | _____ | 19. It is almost impossible to overcome the influences of the past. |
| •• ☐ | ☐ | _____ | 20. I like to have a lot of irons in the fire. |
| • ☐ | ☐ | _____ | 21. I want everyone to like me. |
| •• ☐ | ☐ | _____ | 22. I don't mind competing in activities in which others are better than I. |

| Agree | Disagree | Score | Belief |
|---|---|---|---|
| • ☐ | ☐ | _____ | 23. Those who do wrong deserve to be blamed. |
| • ☐ | ☐ | _____ | 24. Things should be different from the way they are. |
| •• ☐ | ☐ | _____ | 25. I cause my own moods. |
| • ☐ | ☐ | _____ | 26. I often can't get my mind off some concern. |
| • ☐ | ☐ | _____ | 27. I avoid facing my problems. |
| • ☐ | ☐ | _____ | 28. People need a source of strength outside themselves. |
| •• ☐ | ☐ | _____ | 29. Just because something once affects your life strongly doesn't mean it need do so in the future. |
| •• ☐ | ☐ | _____ | 30. I'm most fulfilled when I have lots to do. |
| •• ☐ | ☐ | _____ | 31. I can like myself even when many others don't. |
| •• ☐ | ☐ | _____ | 32. I like to succeed at something, but I don't feel I have to. |
| • ☐ | ☐ | _____ | 33. Immorality should be strongly punished. |
| • ☐ | ☐ | _____ | 34. I often get disturbed over situations I don't like. |
| •• ☐ | ☐ | _____ | 35. People who are miserable have usually made themselves that way. |
| •• ☐ | ☐ | _____ | 36. If I can't keep something from happening, I don't worry about it. |
| •• ☐ | ☐ | _____ | 37. I usually make decisions as promptly as I can. |
| • ☐ | ☐ | _____ | 38. There are certain people whom I depend on greatly. |
| •• ☐ | ☐ | _____ | 39. People overvalue the influence of the past. |
| •• ☐ | ☐ | _____ | 40. I most enjoy throwing myself into a creative project. |
| •• ☐ | ☐ | _____ | 41. If others dislike me, that's their problem, not mine. |
| • ☐ | ☐ | _____ | 42. It is highly important to me to be successful in everything I do. |
| •• ☐ | ☐ | _____ | 43. I seldom blame people for their wrongdoings. |
| •• ☐ | ☐ | _____ | 44. I usually accept things the way they are, even if I don't like them. |
| •• ☐ | ☐ | _____ | 45. A person won't stay angry or blue long unless he keeps himself that way. |
| • ☐ | ☐ | _____ | 46. I can't stand to take chances. |

| Agree | Disagree | Score | Belief |
|---|---|---|---|
| • ☐ | ☐ | _____ | 47. Life is too short to spend it doing unpleasant tasks. |
| •• ☐ | ☐ | _____ | 48. I like to stand on my own two feet. |
| • ☐ | ☐ | _____ | 49. If I had had different experiences I could be more like I want to be. |
| • ☐ | ☐ | _____ | 50. I'd like to retire and quit working entirely. |
| • ☐ | ☐ | _____ | 51. I find it hard to go against what others think. |
| •• ☐ | ☐ | _____ | 52. I enjoy activities for their own sake, no matter how good I am at them. |
| • ☐ | ☐ | _____ | 53. The fear of punishment helps people be good. |
| •• ☐ | ☐ | _____ | 54. If things annoy me, I just ignore them. |
| • ☐ | ☐ | _____ | 55. The more problems a person has, the less happy he will be. |
| •• ☐ | ☐ | _____ | 56. I am seldom anxious over the future. |
| •• ☐ | ☐ | _____ | 57. I seldom put things off. |
| •• ☐ | ☐ | _____ | 58. I am the only one who can really understand and face my problems. |
| •• ☐ | ☐ | _____ | 59. I seldom think of past experiences as affecting me now. |
| •• ☐ | ☐ | _____ | 60. Too much leisure time is boring. |
| •• ☐ | ☐ | _____ | 61. Although I like approval, it's not a real need for me. |
| • ☐ | ☐ | _____ | 62. It bothers me when others are better than I am at something. |
| • ☐ | ☐ | _____ | 63. Everyone is basically good. |
| •• ☐ | ☐ | _____ | 64. I do what I can to get what I want and then don't worry about it. |
| •• ☐ | ☐ | _____ | 65. Nothing is upsetting in itself—only in the way you interpret it. |
| • ☐ | ☐ | _____ | 66. I worry a lot about certain things in the future. |
| • ☐ | ☐ | _____ | 67. It is difficult for me to do unpleasant chores. |
| •• ☐ | ☐ | _____ | 68. I dislike having others make my decisions for me. |
| • ☐ | ☐ | _____ | 69. We are slaves to our personal histories. |

| Agree | Disagree | Score | Belief |
|---|---|---|---|
| • ☐ | ☐ | _____ | 70. I sometimes wish I could go to a tropical island and just lie on the beach forever. |
| • ☐ | ☐ | _____ | 71. I often worry about how much people approve of and accept me. |
| • ☐ | ☐ | _____ | 72. It upsets me to make mistakes. |
| • ☐ | ☐ | _____ | 73. It's unfair that "the rain falls on both the just and the unjust." |
| •• ☐ | ☐ | _____ | 74. I am fairly easygoing about life. |
| • ☐ | ☐ | _____ | 75. More people should face up to the unpleasantness of life. |
| • ☐ | ☐ | _____ | 76. Sometimes I can't get a fear off my mind. |
| •• ☐ | ☐ | _____ | 77. A life of ease is seldom very rewarding. |
| • ☐ | ☐ | _____ | 78. I find it easy to seek advice. |
| • ☐ | ☐ | _____ | 79. Once something strongly affects your life, it always will. |
| • ☐ | ☐ | _____ | 80. I love to lie around. |
| • ☐ | ☐ | _____ | 81. I have considerable concern with what people are feeling about me. |
| • ☐ | ☐ | _____ | 82. I often become quite annoyed over little things. |
| •• ☐ | ☐ | _____ | 83. I usually give someone who has wronged me a second chance. |
| • ☐ | ☐ | _____ | 84. People are happiest when they have challenges and problems to overcome. |
| •• ☐ | ☐ | _____ | 85. There is never any reason to remain sorrowful for very long. |
| •• ☐ | ☐ | _____ | 86. I hardly ever think of such things as death or atomic war. |
| •• ☐ | ☐ | _____ | 87. I dislike responsibility. |
| •• ☐ | ☐ | _____ | 88. I dislike having to depend on others. |
| • ☐ | ☐ | _____ | 89. People never change basically. |
| • ☐ | ☐ | _____ | 90. Most people work too hard and don't get enough rest. |
| •• ☐ | ☐ | _____ | 91. It is annoying but not upsetting to be criticized. |

| Agree | Disagree | Score | Belief |
|---|---|---|---|
| •• ☐ | ☐ | _____ | 92. I'm not afraid to do things which I cannot do well. |
| •• ☐ | ☐ | _____ | 93. No one is evil, even though his deeds may be. |
| •• ☐ | ☐ | _____ | 94. I seldom become upset over the mistakes of others. |
| •• ☐ | ☐ | _____ | 95. Man makes his own hell within himself. |
| • ☐ | ☐ | _____ | 96. I often find myself planning what I would do in different dangerous situations. |
| •• ☐ | ☐ | _____ | 97. If something is necessary, I do it even if it is unpleasant. |
| •• ☐ | ☐ | _____ | 98. I've learned not to expect someone else to be very concerned about my welfare. |
| •• ☐ | ☐ | _____ | 99. I don't look upon the past with any regrets. |
| • ☐ | ☐ | _____ | 100. I can't feel really content unless I'm relaxed and doing nothing. |

## Scoring the Beliefs Inventory

### A. Single dot items

If the item has one dot (•) and you checked the "agree" box, give yourself one point in the space provided next to the item.

### B. Double dot items

If the item has two dots (••) and you checked the "disagree" box, give yourself a point in the space provided next to the item.

### C. Add up your points for items:

1, 11, 21, 31, 41, 51, 61, 71, 81, and 91, and enter the total here: _____. The higher the total, the greater your agreement with the irrational idea that *it is an absolute necessity for an adult to have love and approval from peers, family, and friends.*

2, 12, 22, 32, 42, 52, 62, 72, 82, and 92, and enter the total here: _____. The higher the total, the greater your agreement with the irrational idea that *you must be unfailingly competent and almost perfect in all you undertake.*

3, 13, 23, 33, 43, 53, 63, 73, 83, and 93, and enter the total here: _____. The higher the total, the greater your agreement with the irrational idea that *certain people are evil, wicked, and villainous, and should be punished.*

4, 14, 24, 34, 44, 54, 64, 74, 84, and 94, and enter the total here: _____. The higher the total, the greater your agreement with the irrational idea that *it is horrible when things are not the way you would like them to be.*

5, 15, 25, 35, 45, 55, 65, 75, 85, and 95, and enter the total here: _____. The higher the total, the greater your agreement with the irrational idea that *external events cause most human misery—people simply react as events trigger their emotions.*

6, 16, 26, 36, 46, 56, 66, 76, 86, and 96, and enter the total here: _____. The higher the total, the greater your agreement with the irrational idea that *you should feel fear or anxiety about anything that is unknown, uncertain, or potentially dangerous.*

7, 17, 27, 37, 47, 57, 67, 77, 87, and 97, and enter the total here: _____. The higher the total, the greater your agreement with the irrational idea that *it is easier to avoid than face life's difficulties and responsibilities.*

8, 18, 28, 38, 48, 58, 68, 78, 88, and 98, and enter the total here: _____. The higher the total, the greater your agreement with the irrational idea that *you need something other or stronger or greater than yourself to rely on.*

9, 19, 29, 39, 49, 59, 69, 79, 89, and 99, and enter the total here: _____. The higher the total, the greater your agreement with the irrational idea that *the past has a lot to do with determining the present.*

10, 20, 30, 40, 50, 60, 70, 80, 90, and 100, and enter the total here: _____. The higher the total, the greater your agreement with the irrational idea that *happiness can be achieved by inaction, passivity, and endless leisure.*

## Irrational Ideas

At the root of all irrational thinking is the assumption that things are done to you: "That really got me down . . . She makes me nervous . . . Places like that scare me . . . Being lied to makes me see red." Nothing is done to you. Events happen in the world. You experience those events (*A*), engage in self-talk (*B*), and then experience an emotion (*C*) resulting from the self-talk. *A* does not cause *C*—*B* causes *C*. If your self-talk is irrational and unrealistic, you create unpleasant emotions.

Two common forms of irrational self-talk are statements that "awfulize" and "absolutize." You awfulize by making catastrophic, nightmarish interpretations of your experience. A momentary chest pain is a heart attack, the grumpy boss intends to fire you, your mate takes a night job and the thought of being alone is unthinkably terrible. The emotions that follow awfulizing self-talk tend themselves to be awful—you are responding to your own description of the world.

Irrational self statements that "absolutize" often include words such as "should, must, ought, always, and never." The idea is that things have to be a certain way, or you have to be a certain way. Any deviation from that particular value or standard is bad. The person who fails to live up to the standard is bad. In reality, it is the standard that is bad, because it is irrational.

Albert Ellis has suggested ten basic irrational ideas, which are listed below. To these we have added some additional common self-statements which are highly unrealistic. Based on your scores on the Beliefs Inventory, and your knowledge of the situations in which you characteristically experience stress, check the ones that seem to apply to you.

☐ **1. It is an absolute necessity for an adult to have love and approval from peers, family and friends.**

In fact, it is impossible to please all the people in your life. Even those who basically like and approve of you will be turned off by some behaviors and qualities. This irrational belief is probably the single greatest cause of unhappiness.

☐ **2. You must be unfailingly competent and almost perfect in all you undertake.**

The results of believing that you must behave perfectly are self blame for inevitable failure, lowered self esteem, perfectionistic standards applied to mate and friends, and paralysis and fear at attempting anything.

☐ **3. Certain people are evil, wicked, and villainous, and should be punished.**

A more realistic position is that they are behaving in ways which are antisocial or inappropriate. They are perhaps stupid, ignorant, or neurotic, and it would be well if their behavior could be changed.

☐ **4. It is horrible when people and things are not the way you would like them to be.**

This might be described as the spoiled child syndrome. As soon as the tire goes flat the self-talk starts: "Why does this happen to me? Damn, I can't take this. It's awful, I'll get all filthy." Any inconvenience, problem, or failure to get your way is likely to be met with such awfulizing self-statements. The result is intense irritation and stress.

☐ **5. External events cause most human misery—people simply react as events trigger their emotions.**

A logical extension of this belief is that you must control the external events in order to create happiness or avoid sorrow. Since such control has limitations and we are at a loss to completely manipulate the wills of others, a sense of helplessness and chronic anxiety results. Ascribing unhappiness to events is a way of avoiding reality. Self-statements *interpreting* the event caused the unhappiness. While you may have only limited control over others, you have enormous control over your emotions.

☐ **6. You should feel fear or anxiety about anything that is unknown, uncertain, or potentially dangerous.**

Many describe this as "a little bell that goes off and I think I ought to start worrying." They begin to rehearse their scenarios of catastrophe. Increasing the fear or anxiety in the face of uncertainty makes coping more difficult and adds to stress. Saving the fear response for actual, perceived danger allows you to enjoy uncertainty as a novel and exciting experience.

☐ **7. It is easier to avoid than to face life's difficulties and responsibilities.**
There are many ways of ducking responsibilities: "I should tell him I'm no longer interested—but not tonight . . . I'd like to get another job, but I'm just too tired on my days off to look . . . A leaky faucet won't hurt anything . . . We could shop today, but the car is making a sort of funny sound." If you have checked this idea, please add your standard excuses to avoid responsibility here:

*Area of responsibility*                    *Method of avoidance*

_____    _____

_____    _____

_____    _____

_____    _____

_____    _____

☐ **8. You need something other or stronger or greater than yourself to rely on.**
This belief becomes a psychological trap in which your independent judgment and your awareness of your particular needs are undermined by a reliance on higher authority.

☐ **9. The past has a lot to do with determining the present.**
Just because you were once strongly affected by something, does not mean that you must continue the habits you formed to cope with the original situation. Those old patterns and ways of responding are just decisions made so many times they have become nearly automatic. You can identify those old decisions and start changing them *right now*. You can learn from past experience, but you don't have to be overly attached to it.

☐ **10. Happiness can be achieved by inaction, passivity, and endless leisure.**
This is called the Elysian Fields syndrome. There is more to happiness than perfect relaxation.

**Other irrational ideas**

☐ **11. You are helpless and have no control over what you experience or feel.**
This belief is at the heart of much depression and anxiety. The truth is we not only exercise considerable control over interpersonal situations, but also control how we interpret and emotionally respond to each life event.

☐ **12. People are fragile and should never be hurt.**
This irrational belief results in failure to openly communicate important feelings, and in self sacrifice that gives up what is nourishing and pleasurable (Farquhar and Lowe 1974). Since everything you need or want seems to hurt or deprive

someone else, you feel frustration, helplessness, and depression. Relationships become full of dead space where conflicts developed and nothing was said.

☐ **13. Good relationships are based on mutual sacrifice and a focus on giving.**

This belief rests on the assumption that it is better to give than to receive. It is expressed in a reluctance to ask for things and the anticipation that your hidden needs will be divined and provided for. Unfortunately, constant self-denial usually results in bitterness and withdrawal.

☐ **14. If you don't go to great lengths to please others, they will abandon or reject you.**

This belief is a by-product of low self-esteem. You usually run less risk of rejection if you offer others your true unembellished self. They can take it or leave it. But if they respond to the real you, you don't have to worry about slacking off, letting down your guard, and being rejected later.

☐ **15. When people disapprove of you, it invariably means you are wrong or bad.**

This extremely crippling belief sparks chronic anxiety in most interpersonal situations (Farquhar and Lowe 1974). The irrationality is contained in the generalization of one specific fault or unattractive feature to a total indictment of the self.

☐ **16. Happiness, pleasure, and fulfillment can only occur in the presence of others, and being alone is horrible.**

Pleasure, self worth, and fulfillment can be experienced alone as well as with others (Farquhar and Lowe 1974). Being alone is growth-producing and desirable at times.

☐ **17. There is a perfect love, and a perfect relationship.**

Subscribers to this belief often feel resentful of one close relationship after another. Nothing is quite right because they are waiting for the perfect fit. It never comes.

☐ **18. You shouldn't have to feel pain; you are entitled to a good life.**

The realistic position is that pain is an inevitable part of human life. It frequently accompanies tough, healthy decisions and the process of growth. Life is not fair, and sometimes you will suffer no matter what you do.

☐ **19. Your worth as a person depends on how much you achieve and produce.**

A more rational assessment of your real worth would depend on such things as your capacity to be fully alive, feeling everything it means to be human (Farquhar and Lowe 1974).

☐ **20. Anger is automatically bad and destructive.**

Anger is frequently cleansing. It can be an honest communication of current feelings, without attacking the personal worth and security of others (Farquhar and Lowe 1974).

☐ **21. It is bad or wrong to be selfish.**

The truth is that no one knows your needs and wants better than you, and no one else has as great an interest in seeing them fulfilled. Your happiness is your responsibility. Being selfish means you are accepting that responsibility.

It is quite probable that you could add other irrational ideas to this list. Please do. The best way to uncover your own irrational ideas is to think of situations in which you experience anxiety, depression, anger, guilt, or a sense of worthlessness. Behind each of these emotions, particularly if they are chronic, is irrational self-talk.

**Your other irrational ideas:** _____

_____

_____

Much of the difficulty in uncovering irrational self-talk results from the speed and invisibility of thoughts. They may be lightning quick and barely on the edge of awareness. You will rarely be conscious of a complete sentence, as in the irrational statements above. Because self-talk has a reflexive, automatic quality, it is easy to keep the illusion that feelings arise spontaneously from events. However, once the thoughts are slowed down like a slow motion film, frame by frame, the millisecond it takes to say "I'm falling apart" is exposed for its malignant influence. The thoughts that create your emotions may frequently appear in a kind of shorthand: "No good . . . crazy . . . feeling sick . . . dumb," and so on. That shorthand has to be stretched out into the original sentence from which it was extracted. The sentence can then be challenged with methods you'll learn in the section on refuting irrational ideas.

## Rules to Promote Rational Thinking

Evaluate your self-statements against these six rules or guidelines for rational thinking (from David Goodman's *Emotional Well Being Through Rational Behavior Training.*)

**It doesn't do anything to me.**
The situation doesn't make me anxious or afraid. I say things to myself that produce anxiety and fear.

**Everything is exactly the way it should be.**
The conditions for things or people to be otherwise don't exist. To say that things should be other than what they are is to believe in magic. They are what they are because of a long series of causal events, including interpretations, responses from irrational self-talk, and so on. To say that things should be different is to throw out causality.

**All humans are fallible creatures.**
This is inescapable. If you haven't set reasonable quotas of failure for yourself and others, you increase the prospects for disappointment and unhappiness. It becomes all too easy to attack yourself and others as worthless, bad, and so on.

**It takes two to have a conflict.**
Before beginning a course of accusation and blame, consider the 30 percent rule. Any party to a conflict is contributing at least 30 percent of the fuel to keep it going.

**The original cause is lost in antiquity.**
It is a waste of time to try to discover who did what first. The search for the original cause

of chronic painful emotions is extremely difficult. The best strategy is to make decisions to change your behavior *now*.

**We feel the way we think.**

This is the positively stated principle behind the first statement in this list. It reinforces the idea that events don't cause emotions—our interpretations of events cause emotions.

## Refuting Irrational Ideas

There are five steps (A through E) to disputing and eliminating irrational ideas. Start by selecting a situation that consistently generates stressful emotions in you.

A. **Write down the facts** of the event as they occurred at the time you were upset. Be certain to include only the *objective* facts, not conjecture, subjective impressions, or value judgments.

B. **Write down your self-talk** about the event. State all your subjective value judgments, assumptions, beliefs, predictions, and worries. Note which self-statements have been previously described as irrational ideas.

C. **Focus on your emotional response.** Make a clear one or two word label such as angry, depressed, felt worthless, afraid, and so on.

D. **Dispute and change the irrational self-talk** identified at step B. Here's how it is done, according to Ellis:

1. **Select the irrational idea** that you wish to dispute. As an illustration, we will use the irrational idea, "It's not fair that I have to suffer with such a problem."'

2. **Is there any rational support for this idea?** Since everything is as it should be, given long chains of cause and effect, the answer is no. The problem must be endured and dealt with because it happened. It happened because all the conditions existed necessary to make it happen.

3. **What evidence exists for the falseness of this idea?**

   a. There are no laws of the universe that say I shouldn't have pain or problems. I can experience any problem for which the necessary conditions exist.

   b. Life is not fair. Life is just a sequence of events, some of which bring pleasure and some of which are inconvenient and painful.

   c. If problems occur, it is up to me to solve them.

   d. Trying to keep a problem from developing is adaptive, but resenting and not facing it once it exists is a dangerous strategy.

   e. No one is special. Some go through life with relatively less pain than I do. This is due to one of two things: Luck of the draw, or decisions I have made that contributed to the necessary conditions for my problems.

    f.  Just because I have a problem doesn't mean I have to suffer. I can take pride in the challenge of a creative solution. This may be an opportunity to increase my self-esteem.

4.  **Does any evidence exist for the truth of this idea?**  No, my suffering is due to my self-talk, how I have interpreted this event. I have convinced myself that I should be unhappy.

5.  **What is the worst thing that could happen to me** if what I want to happen doesn't, or what I don't want to happen does?

    a.  I could be deprived of various pleasures while I deal with the problem.

    b.  I might feel inconvenienced.

    c.  I might never solve the problem and experience myself as ineffective in this particular area.

    d.  I might have to accept the consequences of failure.

    e.  Others might not approve of how I am behaving or I might be rejected as incompetent.

    f.  I might feel more stress, tension, and a sense of being up against it.

6.  **What good things might occur** if what you want to happen doesn't, or what you don't want to happen does?

    a.  I might learn to tolerate frustration better.

    b.  I might improve my coping skills.

    c.  I might become more responsible.

E.  **Substitute alternative self-talk,** now that you have clearly examined the irrational idea and compared it with rational thinking.

    1.  There's nothing special about me. I can accept painful situations when they emerge.

    2.  Facing the problem is more adaptive than resenting it or running away from it.

    3.  I feel what I think. If I don't think negative thoughts, I won't feel stressful emotions. At worst I will experience inconvenience, regret, and annoyance—not anxiety, depression, and rage.

## Homework

To succeed in your war against irrational ideas, you need a daily commitment to homework. Use the homework sheet below as a model. Fill out one at least once a day.

Here is an example of a homework sheet completed by a woman who had a date with a friend cancelled:

# Homework Sheet

**A. Activating event:**

*A friend canceled a date with me.*

**B. Rational ideas:**

*I know he's under a lot of time pressure right now . . . I'll do something by myself.*

**Irrational ideas:**

*I'll feel terribly alone tonight . . . The emptiness is setting in . . . He doesn't really care for me . . . No one really wants to spend time with me . . . I'm falling apart.*

**C. Consequences of the irrational ideas:**

*I was depressed . . . I was moderately anxious.*

**D. Disputing and challenging the irrational ideas:**

**1. Select the irrational idea:**

*I'll feel terribly alone tonight . . . I'm falling apart.*

**2. Is there any rational support for this idea?**

*No.*

**3. What evidence exists for the falseness of the idea?**

*Being alone is not as pleasurable as having a date, but I can find pleasure in an alternative activity.*

*I usually enjoy being alone, and I will tonight as soon as I face the disappointment.*

*I'm mislabelling frustration and disappointment as "falling apart."*

**4. Does any evidence exist for the truth of the idea?**

*No, only that I've talked myself into feeling depressed.*

**5. What is the worst thing that could happen to me?**

*I could continue to feel disappointed and not find anything really pleasurable to do tonight.*

**6. What good things might occur?**

*I might feel more self reliant, and realize that I do have inner resources.*

**E. Alternative thoughts:**

*I'm OK. I'll get out my detective novel. I'll treat myself to a good Chinese dinner. I'm good at being alone.*

**Alternative emotions:**

*I feel quiet, a little disappointed, but I'm anticipating a good meal and a good book.*

# Homework Sheet

A.  Activating event:

_____

_____

B.  Rational ideas:

_____

_____

Irrational ideas:

_____

_____

C.  Consequences of the irrational ideas:

_____

_____

D.  Disputing and challenging the irrational ideas:
   1.  Select the irrational idea:

   _____

   _____

   2.  Is there any rational support for this idea?

   _____

   _____

   3.  What evidence exists for the falseness of the idea?

   _____

   _____

   4.  Does any evidence exist for the truth of the idea?

   _____

   _____

   5.  What is the worst thing that could happen to me?

   _____

   _____

   6.  What good things might occur?

   _____

   _____

E.  Alternative thoughts:

_____

_____

Alternative emotions:

_____

_____

Use this format with all the stressful events you experience. Spend at least twenty minutes a day on the homework. When possible, do the homework right after the event has occurred. Use a separate sheet for each event, and save them as a record of your growth.

# Special Considerations

If you have difficulty making headway with Rational Emotive Therapy, one of three factors may be at influence:

1. You remain unconvinced that thoughts cause emotions. If this is the case, confine your work initially to the following technique of Rational Emotive Imagery. If you then find that changes in your self-talk can push you toward less stressful emotions, the assumption that thoughts cause emotions may become more believable.

2. Your irrational ideas and self-talk are so lightning swift that you have difficulty catching them. You need to keep a journal while undergoing intense emotions. Put down everything that flows through your mind: scenes, images, single words, vague half-formed thoughts, names, sounds, sentences, and so on.

3. You have difficulty remembering your thoughts. If this is the case, don't wait till after the fact. Use a journal to write everything down just as it is happening.

## Rational Emotive Imagery

Dr. Maxie Maultsby (1971) introduced Rational Emotive Imagery in an article entitled "Systematic Written Homework in Psychotherapy." It will help you develop strategies to change stressful emotions. The technique works as follows:

1. Imagine an event that is stressful and usually accompanied by unpleasant emotions. Notice all the details of the situation: sight, smell, sound, how you are dressed, what is being said.

2. As you clearly imagine the event, let yourself feel uncomfortable. Let in the emotions of anger, anxiety, depression, worthlessness, or shame. Don't try to avoid the emotion—go ahead and feel it.

3. After experiencing the stressful emotion, *push* yourself to change it. You can fundamentally alter this emotion so that anxiety, depression, rage, and guilt can be replaced by keenly felt concern, disappointment, annoyance, or regret. If you think you can't do this, you are only fooling yourself. Everybody can push themselves to change a feeling, if only for a few moments.

4. Having contacted the stressful feeling and pushed it, however briefly, into a more appropriate emotion, you can examine how you did it. What happened inside your head that altered your original depression, anxiety, rage, and so on? You told yourself something different about yourself, or others, or the situation.

5. Instead of saying, "I can't handle this . . . This will drive me crazy," you might now be saying, "I've dealt successfully with situations like this before." You have changed your beliefs, your interpretations of experience. Once you know how you changed the stressful emotion to a more appropriate one, you can substitute the new, adaptive beliefs any time you want. Become deeply aware of how the new beliefs lead you away from stress and produce more bearable emotions.

**Example.** Rational Emotive Imagery was practiced by a housewife who became depressed whenever her husband turned on the television in the evening. During the day, she conjured the situation up in her imagination: her husband wiping his mouth, getting up from the table, taking the plates to the sink, and leaving the room. She could imagine a few moments later the sound of the television coming on, the changing of channels, voices from his favorite situation comedy. As she went through the sequence, she sank into despondency.

After becoming fully in contact with the stressful emotion, she pushed herself to change the feeling into one of disappointment and irritation. It felt like shoving a huge rock, and it took fifteen minutes of effort before she could get even momentary contact with the more appropriate emotions. Practicing at hourly intervals, she was soon able to push the depression into irritation or disappointment for several minutes.

She was ready to examine how she had changed her thoughts (self-talk) in order to change her emotions. She found she could change depression into irritation by saying, "I don't have to feel helpless. If he wants to spend his time with TV, I can do something that feels good to me." Other thoughts included: "It's his life. He can waste it if he wants to. I'm not going to waste mine. There are people that I don't visit because I think I should stay home with him. I'm going to take care of myself. He may be displeased if I don't stay home, but this is not fulfilling for me."

## Developing Alternative Emotional Responses

Here is a list of sample situations and alternative emotional responses:

| Situation | Stressful Emotion | Appropriate Emotion |
|---|---|---|
| Fight with mate | Rage | Annoyance, irritation |
| Failure to meet work deadline | Anxiety | Concern |
| Cruelty toward your child | Intense guilt | Regret |
| Something you enjoy very much is canceled | Depression | Disappointment |
| Criticized | Worthless | Annoyance, concern |
| A public mistake | Shame | Irritation |

Now fill in your own stressful situations, including the stressful emotions you feel, and the more appropriate emotions you would like to feel.

*Situation*                          *Stressful Emotion*          *Appropriate Emotion*

_____    _____    _____

_____    _____    _____

_____    _____    _____

_____    _____    _____

_____    _____    _____

_____    _____    _____

_____    _____    _____

You can use Rational Emotive Imagery in each of these situations. If the stressful emotions do not change right away, let yourself keep feeling them until they do change. It is an absolute certainty that you can alter these emotions by merely pushing yourself to do so. Afterwards, you will isolate the key thoughts and phrases that made the new, more appropriate emotion possible. Changing your self-talk to include these more adaptive thoughts, beliefs, and ideas will make it increasingly easy to change the emotion. For best results, practice this technique ten minutes a day for at least two weeks.

## Insight

It is important to recognize that there are three levels of insight necessary to change:

1. Knowledge that you have a problem, and awareness of some of the events that may have caused the problem.

2. Seeing clearly that the irrational ideas which you acquired early in life are creating the emotional climate you live in now, and that consciously or unconsciously you work fairly hard to perpetuate them.

3. The strong belief that after discovering these two insights, you will still find no way of eliminating the problem other than steadily, persistently, and vigorously working to change your irrational ideas.

Without a commitment to this last insight, it will be very difficult to alter your habitual emotional responses.

If you think this technique could be useful to you, but you are unable to master it, contact a rational emotive therapist or center for consultation.

### Further Reading

Beck, A. T. 1979. "Cognitive Therapy: Nature and Relation to Behavior Therapy." In *Behavior Therapy.* New York: NAL/Dutton.

———. 1989. *Love Is Never Enough: How Couples Can Overcome Misunderstandings, Resolve Conflict, And Solve Relationship Problems With Cognitive Therapy.* New York: Harper-Collins.

Burns, D. D. 1989. *Feeling Good Handbook.* New York: NAL/Dutton.

Ellis, A. 1980. *Growth Through Reason.* Palo Alto, CA: Science and Behavior Books.

Ellis, A. *A New Guide to Rational Living.* North Hollywood, California: Wilshire Books, 1975.

———. 1985. *Anger: How To Live With and Without It.* New York: Carol Publishing Group.

———. 1988. *Anger: How To Stubbornly Refuse To Make Yourself Miserable about Anything—Yes, Anything.* New York: Carol Publishing Group.

Farquhar, W., and J. Lowe. 1974. "A List of Irrational Ideas." In Tosi, D. J. *Youth Toward Personal Growth, a Rational Emotive Approach.* Columbus, OH: Charles E. Merrill.

Lazarus, A. A. 1971. *Behavior Therapy and Beyond.* New York: McGraw Hill.

Maultsby, M. 1971. "Rational Emotive Imagery." *Rational Living* 6:16-23.

# 15

# Coping Skills Training

Coping skills training teaches you to relax away anxiety and stress reactions. It gives you more self-control in the particular situation that you find anxiety provoking. The basic procedures were formulated by Marvin Goldried in 1973 and by Suinn and Richardson in 1971 as outgrowths of Wolpe's work with deep muscle relaxation and systematic desensitization. These techniques were later expanded by Meichenbaum and Cameron in 1974 in a treatment program they called "stress inoculation."

It is not necessary, just because you are in a stressful situation, to feel nervous and upset. You have merely *learned* to react that way. Coping skills training involves learning, instead, to relax using progressive muscle relaxation, so that whenever or wherever you are experiencing stress, you can let go of the tension. The first step is to construct a personal list of stressful situations and arrange the list vertically from the least anxious to most anxious situation. Using your imagination, you can call up each of those situations and learn to relax away any stress you feel. The second step is the creation of a private arsenal of stress-coping remarks. These will be used to get you through the periods when you are saying to yourself, "I can't do this . . . I'm not strong enough . . . They seem so much smarter than I am," and so on.

Coping skills training provides rehearsal in imagination for the real life events you find distressing. You learn to relax in the imagined scenes and are thereafter prepared to relax away tension when under fire, when facing deadlines, when problem solving, and so on. Eventually, self-relaxation procedures and stress-coping thoughts become automatic in any stressful situation.

## Symptom Relief

Coping skills training has been shown to be effective in the reduction of general anxiety, as well as interview, speech, and test anxiety. It appears to be useful in the treatment of phobias, particularly the fear of heights. The control of specific and generalized anxiety has long-term effects: Two year follow-ups of hypertense, post-cardiac patients showed that 89 percent were still able to achieve general relaxation using coping skills training, 79 percent could still generally control tension, and 79 percent were able to fall asleep sooner and sleep more deeply.

## Time for Mastery

Assuming you have already learned progressive relaxation, which takes one to two weeks, initial mastery of coping skills training can be achieved in approximately one week. Once you are able to relax away tension in situations conjured up in the imagination, it is a matter of putting the skill to work during actual stressful events. This is a *habit* that takes time and practice, and the time very much depends on the amount of practice and commitment.

## Instructions

### Learning to Relax Efficiently

The foundation stone of coping skills training is knowing how to relax. First, you need to have learned progressive relaxation (see chapter 4) sufficiently well so that deep muscle relaxation can be achieved in a minute or two. This relaxation procedure should be "over learned" so it can be done almost automatically, at a moment's notice. The sequences of tensing and relaxing muscles can then be gone through with the same unconscious coordination with which you drive a car or tie your shoelaces.

The second component of relaxation is diaphragmatic or abdominal breathing, sometimes called "belly breathing." To achieve deep breathing, place both hands on your abdomen, just above the pubic area. Breathe in so that the air expands your belly and pushes your hands. Direct all the air downward into your abdomen to push your hands as much as feels comfortable. Let each breath be deep, at a rhythm that feels right to you, and let it gently push your hands. Exhale with a sigh, and imagine that the tension is flowing out of your body as you let go of each breath. (For a more detailed explanation, see chapter 3 on breathing.)

### Making a Stressful Events Hierarchy

You are now ready to make a list of all your current life situations which trigger anxiety. Include any stressful event that you are likely to encounter in the relatively near future. Be specific, including the setting and the persons involved. Get as close to 20 items on your list as possible, and let them run the full gamut from very mild discomfort to your most dreaded experiences.

Your list can be turned into a hierarchy by ranking the stressful experiences in order, from the least to the most anxiety producing. Each item on the list should represent an increase in stress over the last item, and the increases should be in approximately equal increments. To accomplish this, Wolpe has devised a rating system based on *Subjective Units of Distress* (SUDS). Total relaxation is zero SUDS, while the most stressful situation on your hierarchy is rated at 100 SUDS. All the other items fall somewhere in between, and are assigned SUDS scores based on your subjective impression of where each situation falls relative to your most relaxed or most anxious states. For example, if the most stressful item on your hierarchy, "making conversation with attractive members of the opposite sex," is ranked at 100 SUDS, then "working right up to a deadline" might be ranked 65 SUDS, and "speech at PTA meeting" might fall down around 35 SUDS. You are the expert on how you react to each situation, and you therefore must decide

| Rank | Item | SUDS (Subjective Units of Distress) |
|---|---|---|
| 1 | Running cub scouts meeting Wednesday afternoons | 5 |
| 2 | Rushing to get son to violin lesson | 10 |
| 3 | Routine doctor's appointment | 15 |
| 4 | Gynecological exam | 20 |
| 5 | Yard duty in cold weather | 25 |
| 6 | Catching up on Saturday with housework and bills and correcting papers | 30 |
| 7 | Fatigued at end of day, but still needing to shop and cook | 35 |
| 8 | Disagreement with husband over bills, spending on dresses, etc. | 40 |
| 9 | Deadline for written evaluation of student teacher, problem child, etc. | 45 |
| 10 | Preparing house for social occasion | 50 |
| 11 | Having to work late at school and going home after dark | 55 |
| 12 | Extra work assignment when tired: hall displays, report to school psychologist | 60 |
| 13 | Preparation for observation by principal | 65 |
| 14 | Being alone at night because husband is working late | 70 |
| 15 | Evening consultation meetings with parents | 75 |
| 16 | Principal criticizes something in which a lot of work has been invested | 80 |
| 17 | Complaints from parents | 85 |
| 18 | Husband announces a business trip | 90 |
| 19 | Fit of worrying about health brought on by intense menstrual symptoms | 95 |
| 20 | Asthmatic son sick at home while working | 100 |

where each stressful event fits, relative to the others. It is advisable, on a list of 20 items, to separate them by increments of five SUDS. In that way, the items will progress in relatively equal steps from one to twenty. The following sample hierarchy was constructed by a school teacher:

A good hierarchy is a mixture of many different concerns. Its focus is not limited to one particular fear or problem in your life. The described situations are succinct, but clear enough to reconstruct the scene in imagination.

## Applying Relaxation Techniques to Your Hierarchy

Your hierarchy can now be used for learning how to relax while experiencing stress. Start with the first scene (lowest SUDS) and build a clear picture of the situation in your imagination. Hold onto the stressful image for 30 to 40 seconds. Notice the beginning of any tension in your body, any sense of anxiety. Use the sensation of tension as a signal for deep muscle relaxation and deep breathing. Tightening in your body is like an early warning system of what later will be real emotional discomfort. You can relax away this tension, even as you imagine the stressful situations.

When you have twice imagined a particular scene without tension or anxiety, holding the clear image 20 seconds each time, go on to the next item in your hierarchy. In the next few days, move through your entire hierarchy of stressful situations using this same procedure, progressing from the least to most difficult. At the end, you will have a more profound awareness of how and where tension builds in your body. You will welcome early signs of tension as your signal to relax. Mastery of those items with the highest SUDS provides a degree of confidence that stress reduction is possible, even in the most threatening situations.

Learning relaxation in the face of fear requires that each scene be vivid and real to you. Make an effort to call up the sounds, smells, sights, and textures of the situation. The first few times you may not feel "in it" at all. However, the more you practice putting yourself in the picture, letting the scene touch each of your senses, the easier it will be to really feel what it's like to be there. If you have trouble evoking the scene, describe it vividly and completely into a tape recorder. Play it back with eyes closed, letting the words call up the sense impressions of your problem situation. Include on the tape all dialogues and statements by others that you find distressing and describe your body movements. As soon as you are successful at visualizing the scene, notice any physical tension and begin the relaxation response. Rather than a signal for anxiety, physical tension is now your signal to relax.

The first day you begin practicing relaxation with your hierarchy, don't push much beyond three or four scenes. Stop before you get tired or turned off by the procedure. By the end of four days, you should have made it through your entire hierarchy. After you have relaxed your way through the list two or three times, you may expect a feeling of greater confidence when confronting the same problem situations in real life.

## Stress-Coping Thoughts

Having mastered relaxation skills using the hierarchy, you are ready to create a personal list of stress-coping thoughts. Stress-coping thoughts can short circuit painful emotions. To understand how they work, you must consider the four components of an emotional response:

1. **The stimulus situation:** Your supervisor has just gotten angry at you for forgetting an appointment.

2. **Physical reactions:** Your autonomic nervous system produces symptoms such as hand tremor, tightness in the stomach, sweating, palpitations, light headedness, and so on.

3. **Behavioral response:** You attempt to deal with the situation by apologizing and getting away as quickly as possible.

4. **Thoughts:** Your interpretations of the situation, predictions, and self-evaluations are what create emotions. If, at this point, you say to yourself, "I can't stand this . . . It's too much for me . . . I'm falling apart," then the emotional response will be fear. If your self statements are, "I've had it with him riding me all the time . . . He's a real jerk," then your emotional response is likely to be anger.

Your interpretation of the incident, how you imagine it will affect the future, and what you say to yourself about your own worth are the ways you select and intensify the emotions you will feel.

If you say to yourself, "I'm going to fail (prediction), I'm too nervous and disorganized for this kind of job (self-evaluation), I know he wants to get rid of me (interpretation)," then your physiological response will probably be sweating, tremor, and a knot in your stomach. Noticing the physical reactions, you might then think, "I'm panicking, I can't do this anymore, I've got to go home." These self-statements in turn increase the physiological symptoms and the tendency to make poor decisions. The feedback loop from thoughts to physical reactions to behavioral choices to more negative thoughts can continue unbroken into a state of chronic stress.

Your thoughts don't have to intensify fear. Instead, they can act as tranquilizers for a tense stomach, calming you and pushing away panic. The feedback loop can work for you as well as against you. Stress-coping thoughts tell your body there is no need for arousal—it can relax. In the middle of any stressful situation, you can begin saying to yourself a series of fear-conquering statements such as, "Stay calm . . . You've dealt with this before . . . Relax now . . . He can't really hurt me."

The more attention you give to your coping monologue, the quicker will come relief from physiological arousal and what was described in chapter 1 as the "fight or flight" reaction. Make your own list of stress-coping thoughts and memorize them. Meichenbaum and Cameron's stress inoculation program suggested the following categories for stress coping statements:

1. **Preparation**

   There's nothing to worry about.
   I'm going to be all right.
   I've succeeded with this before.
   What exactly do I have to do?
   I know I can do each one of these tasks.
   It's easier once you get started.
   I'll jump in and be all right.

Tomorrow I'll be through it.
Don't let negative thoughts creep in.

### 2. Confronting the stressful situation

Stay organized.
Take it step by step, don't rush.
I can do this, I'm doing it now.
I can only do my best.
Any tension I feel is a signal to use my coping exercises.
I can get help if I need it.
If I don't think about fear, I won't be afraid.
If I get tense, I'll take a breather and relax.
It's OK to make mistakes.

### 3. Coping with fear

Relax now!
Just breathe deeply.
There's an end to it.
Keep my mind on right now, on the task at hand.
I can keep this within limits I can handle.
I can always call ___.
I am only afraid because I decided to be. I can decide not to be.
I've survived this and worse before.
Being active will lessen the fear.

### 4. Reinforcing success

I did it!
I did all right. I did well.
Next time I won't have to worry so much.
I am able to relax away anxiety.
I've got to tell ___ about this.
It's possible not to be scared. All I have to do is stop thinking I'm scared.

Adapted from "The Clinical Potential of Modifying What Clients Say to Themselves" by D. Meichenbaum and R. Cameron. In M. J. Mahoney and C. E. Thoresen, *Self-Control: Power to the Person.* Copyright © 1974 by Wadsworth, Inc. Reprinted by permission.

Some of these stress-coping thoughts may work for you, but your best ones will probably be those you write yourself. Memorize a number of them for each of the four stages of coping: preparation for stress, facing the challenge, feeling the rising fear, and self-congratulation. Make the coping statements meaningful to *you*, and change them if they begin to lose their power. Keep the list handy: scotchtape some of the most useful stress-coping thoughts on your nightstand, over the kitchen sink, on the inside flap of your briefcase. Slip them inside the cellophane of your cigarettes. Let them become second nature.

A note of caution: some people are afraid to tempt fate by congratulating themselves for any achievement. They harbor the superstition that self-praise *causes* disaster. What this really means is that something else, such as fate or luck, is also given credit for their successes. Taking credit for coping means that *you* are responsible for how things turn out, and you have power to limit painful emotions.

### Coping "In Vivo"

The final step in the training is applying coping skills in real life situations. When encountering stress, body tension is used as a cue to relax away tightness. At the same time, stress-coping thoughts flow in a constant stream as you prepare for and confront the situation, limit the fear, and praise yourself for meeting the challenge.

It is expected that using coping skills in vivo will be more difficult than relaxing away stress in the imagined scenes. Some setbacks are inevitable. Practice, however, will make relaxation and stress-coping thoughts so natural that they will automatically begin at the first clutch of tension.

## Example

A kitchen remodeling contractor, who felt shy and worried excessively about his business, made the following hierarchy:

| Rank | Item | SUDS (Subjective Units of Distress) |
|:---:|---|:---:|
| 1 | Attempting to figure out the bills | 5 |
| 2 | Repair or maintenance of the car | 10 |
| 3 | Reading about falling construction market and tight money. Concerned about drop in business | 15 |
| 4 | Going camping to Yosemite alone | 20 |
| 5 | Waking up Saturday morning with absolutely no planned activities for the weekend | 25 |
| 6 | Measurement is off and produces a noticeably poor fit | 30 |
| 7 | Dental visit | 35 |
| 8 | Having a small group over to the apartment for dinner. Friends from the singles group | 40 |
| 9 | Past 2:00 a.m. and still not able to sleep | 45 |
| 10 | Construction materials on order do not arrive, delaying work | 50 |

| Rank | Item | SUDS Subjective Units of Distress) |
|------|------|------|
| 11 | Going to dinner party including new woman friend's sister and ex-roommate from college. Strangers | 55 |
| 12 | Bouts of worry during layoff period between jobs | 60 |
| 13 | Striking up a conversation at a party for singles | 65 |
| 14 | First evening with a new woman friend. Dinner, dancing | 70 |
| 15 | Required to make presentation of remodeling options to a prospective customer | 75 |
| 16 | First sexual overtures to a new woman friend | 80 |
| 17 | Coldly turned down for a date | 85 |
| 18 | Customer is quite displeased with kitchen cabinets, workmanship, etc. | 90 |
| 19 | Visit to father, whose worsening heart condition leaves him observedly more frail | 95 |
| 20 | Cost of a job is running over the original bid to do the work | 100 |

Following mastery of relaxation procedures and construction of the hierarchy, an attempt was made to call into imagination the first stressful situation (5 SUDS). He had difficulty, however, visualizing the scene. Bills were usually made out in a small den, furnished with desk and easy chair. He went to the den and wrote down his sense impressions: "Window looking out on lamp pole and street, green desk blotter, hum of fluorescent light, squeak of swivel chair, rustle of shuffling papers, aftertaste from licking stamps and envelopes." The elements of the scene were tape-recorded and played back. He repeated the tape until he could construct a vivid image of the setting in imagination. The effort invested in sharpening his imagination in the first scene paid off with the others. They were easier, and he knew he could tape-record a vivid picture if there was any difficulty.

Moving through the hierarchy, he learned to watch for the first signs of tension—usually in his diaphragm and upper abdomen. These became the signal to relax away stress. Holding the image of a scene for 30-40 seconds, he "listened" to his body, focusing on deep breathing and progressive relaxation. After visualizing a scene twice, for at least 20 seconds each time, without tension or anxiety, he proceeded to the next item on the hierarchy. Sometimes, he would have to visualize a situation six or more times before the image held no anxiety.

Practice was scheduled mornings and evenings for 15 minutes. He was able to successfully relax away tension in four to five scenes per day, and within five days he completed the hierarchy. The hierarchy was then repeated, start to finish, one additional time.

During this same period, he had also been working on writing his list of stress-coping thoughts. They were as follows:

1. **Preparation**

   I've done this before.
   This is a good time to make a definite plan.
   Turn off the worry and *do* something.
   Stay focused on what I have to do.
   It can't ruin me worse things have happened.
   Embarrassment is just throwing away my self-acceptance.

2. **Confronting**

   No fear thoughts.
   It doesn't matter what others think; do it.
   I'll take care of myself.
   It only lasts a little while.
   I'll feel very good when this goes well.
   I have a specific proposal for solving this problem.

3. **Coping with fear**

   How much fear do I feel? Watch it go down as I relax.
   Deep breathing really works.
   Concentrate on breathing.
   I can keep my stomach tension free.
   It will be pleasant later at home.
   If I think of what I have to do, I can crowd out fear thoughts.

4. **Reinforcing success**

   I dealt with that and felt a lot more comfortable than usual.
   I'm getting healthier.
   I can really relax now.
   It's easier to turn off worry.
   Problems don't have to flatten me anymore.

He typed a file card with the phrase "Turn off the worry and *do* something" and taped it to the inside of the front door. Other signs went on the shaving mirror, the truck dash, and so on. In each real life stressful situation, he began to apply the relaxing skills and to select appropriate stress-coping thoughts. For the first two weeks, he was plagued by the problem of forgetting his training and sometimes became overwhelmed by the intensity of the situation. After a time, he developed the capacity to spot stress coming and to start tuning into any physical tension. The process of "checking in" with his body and starting coping skills was becoming automatic.

**Further Reading**

Godfried, M. R. 1973. "Reduction of Generalized Anxiety Through a Variant of Systematic Desensitization." In *Behavior Change Through Self-Control*, edited by M. R. Goldried and M. Merbaum. New York: Holt, Rinehart and Winston.

Meichenbaum, D. 1974. "Self Instructional Methods." In *Helping People Change*, edited by F. K. Kanfur, and A. P. Goldstein. New York: Pergamon Press.

Meichenbaum, D. and R. Cameron. 1974. "Modifying What Clients Say to Themselves." In *Self-Control: Power to the Person*, by M. J. Mahoney and C. E. Thoresen. Monterey, CA: Brooks/Cole.

Suinn, R. M., and F. Richardson 1971. "Anxiety Management Training: A Non-specific Behavior Therapy Program for Anxiety Control." *Behavior Therapy* 2:498-510.

# 16

# Goal Setting and Time Management

Most people approach the subject of time management with one major question: "How can I get more done in less time?" If you are one of these people, you are probably wondering how you are going to fit some of the exercises described in the other chapters of this book into your already overloaded schedule. You may feel so pressured to take care of the demands and details in your life that you rarely have guilt-free time to do as you please. Or you may have loads of free time, yet never get around to doing the things that would give you the most satisfaction. Other problems associated with ineffective time management time include:

- Constant rushing
- Frequent lateness
- Low productivity, energy, and motivation
- Frustration
- Impatience
- Chronic vacillation between alternatives
- Difficulty setting and achieving goals
- Procrastination

How is it that while we all have 24 hours in a day, some of us feel like we have no time at all, while others manage to get their work done and still have enough time left over to enjoy themselves? People who effectively manage their time have learned to structure their lives so that they focus most of their time and energy on what is most important to them and minimize the time they spend on activities that they do not value. They realize that the quality of their lives is enhanced when they are able to do a few things well, instead of trying to find time to do a little of everything.

If you are thinking, "All of my responsibilities are important; I can't simply drop some of them to do what I please," consider the *80-20 principle*. Vilfredo Pareto, an Italian economist, noted that 20 percent of what we do yields 80 percent of the results. Conversely, 80 percent of what we do yields 20 percent of the results. It is possible to apply this principle to many areas of life. For example, about 20 percent of the newspaper is worth your while to read. You are better off just skimming the rest of it. A good 80 percent of most people's mail is junk and best not read at all. Just about 80 percent of your housework can wait almost indefinitely, while 20 percent of it, if not done, would soon make your home uninhabitable.

This chapter will help you clarify your values, define your goals, and develop a plan for reaching them. Exercises will help you to realize how you are actually spending your time and then choose ways to bring your life into closer alignment with your priorities. You will also learn how to combat procrastination and more efficiently organize your time.

## Symptom Relief

Effective time management has been used in minimizing deadline anxiety, procrastination, and job fatigue.

## Time for Mastery

You can begin to clarify what is most important in your life in as little as an hour and then return to this important task as additional ideas occur to you. Take at least a few more hours to define your goals. You can create an action plan for one of your goals in an hour. You will need at least three days to complete the time log. Take at least a few hours to compare how you are actually spending your time with your priorities and goals and to decide how you want to change the way you are spending your time so that it more closely matches your ideals and goals. While you can put the tips to combat procrastination and organize your time more efficiently into practice in a week, it will probably take you several months of conscious effort before these techniques become habitual. If all this seems like a big investment, consider that the time you spend now will give you more free time in the future.

## Instructions

In this chapter you will be asked to do six tasks:

1. Clarify your values.

2. Set goals.

3. Develop an action plan.

4. Evaluate how you spend your time.

5. Combat procrastination.

6. Organize your time.

Since each step builds on the previous steps, start with the first step and work your way through to the last.

# Clarifying Your Values

The first step toward effective time management is deciding what is most worthwhile or desirable to you. People typically have priorities involving such things as career, health, home, family, spirituality, finances, leisure, learning, creativity, happiness, peace of mind, and communication. Knowing what is most valuable to you gives you direction in life. You can focus the majority of your time and energy on these values, rather than on things that are less important to you. When you have to choose between alternatives, you can look to your priorities to help you make your decision.

## *Identify Your Highest Priorities*

The two brief guided fantasies that follow will help you identify your highest priorities.

1. Close your eyes, take a few deep breaths, and relax. Imagine yourself in a favorite place where you can take a few minutes to think. The time is many years from now. You have lived a long and full life. Reflect upon your life from this mature vantage point. What did you most enjoy experiencing and doing? What did you most appreciate accomplishing or having? Write your answers in this space or on a separate piece of paper.

    _____

    _____

    _____

    _____

    _____

2. Return to your relaxed position and imagine yourself again in your favorite place. This time, you are still your current age. You have just learned that you have a rare illness that has no symptoms but will kill you in six months. Given only half a year to live, what do you want to experience, do, accomplish, and have? Write your answers in this space or on another piece of paper.

    _____

    _____

    _____

    _____

    _____

Compare your two sets of answers. Are they the same or different? Most people actually faced with a life-threatening illness find that their priorities change. Things one thought to be crucial seem less important, and things once overlooked take on new meaning.

## Order Your Values

Take the list that you have developed and order your values from the most to the least important for you. You will find that this list will come in handy when you have difficulty choosing between two or more alternatives.

Here's how Alice, a single working parent, listed her values in order of importance.

| | |
|---|---|
| 1. Family | 5. Nice home |
| 2. Financial security | 6. Friends |
| 3. Health | 7. Travel |
| 4. Creativity | 8. Honesty |

Alice was troubled because her bosses pressured her to sign off on incomplete drafts of her designs. When she refused, they simply bypassed her signature. She vacillated between reporting her company's infractions to a government regulatory agency and remaining silent to avoid reprisal. In examining her values, she realized that not speaking out was a form of dishonesty. But she also realized that while honesty was important to her, it had the lowest priority of all her values, and that all her other values were being successfully fulfilled by her job. With this insight, she stopped criticizing herself and waited until she had found a job in another company to report her former employer's misconduct so that she did not jeopardize the other important aspects of her life.

Rank your own values from the most to least important for you.

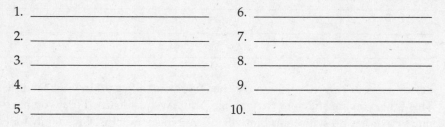

1. _____    6. _____

2. _____    7. _____

3. _____    8. _____

4. _____    9. _____

5. _____   10. _____

# Setting Goals

The second step to effective time management involves setting goals. Values are ideals. They are the things, experiences, qualities, and principles that you would most like to have in your life. Goals are real and specific. Goals are objectives that you want to achieve, given the constraints of your time and other resources. Your fondest hope might be to become a champion race car driver. Your goal might be to cross the Indianapolis 500 finish line first three years from now. To bring your life into closer alignment with what you consider most worthwhile, use your list of values to guide you in defining your goals.

## Designing Effective Goals

Here are five crucial questions to ask yourself when designing effective goals.

1. **Is this a goal that you really want to devote a lot of time and energy to accomplish?** Or is it simply a dream of what you would like to have fall in your lap, but are not willing to work for? Many people think that they would like to travel around the world, but are not willing to save the money it would take.

2. **Is this goal consistent with your highest values?**  One reason that you may not accomplish a goal is because it does not fit in with what is most important to you. If you value education and your goal is to finish college in the next year, but your highest priorities are family and socializing with friends, you may want to give yourself more time to complete this goal so that you won't have to neglect your family and friends.

3. **Is this goal achievable?**  Is it specific enough so that you will know when you have achieved it? Is it achievable within a definite time frame that you can set for yourself? Do you have access to the resources necessary to achieve it? Rather than saying that you want to "retire on a comfortable income," you may want to set a date for retirement and specify an amount of money that you know you can realistically earn and save to support the lifestyle that you want to have. You can modify your goals as you get more information.

4. **Is this goal positive?**  You are more likely to achieve goals that you are moving toward, rather than away from. Instead of setting yourself the negative goal of no longer overeating, give yourself the positive objective of eating three sensible, nutritious meals a day.

5. **Are your goals in balance?**  Do most of your goals involve career and finances, while almost none of them have to do with health, relationships, or fun? Lack of balance is a major source of stress. If you spend your workday alone in front of a computer terminal, a short-term goal might be to get regular exercise out of doors with other people.

## *Balancing Your Goals*

Do you have about an equal number of short-term, medium-term, and long-term goals? Some people plan on waiting until they retire to live their lives the way they really want to. Others can enjoy the here and now, but are handicapped when it comes to achieving goals that involve delayed gratification. A mixture of short-term, medium-term, and long-term goals can provide you with satisfaction in the here and now, as well as offering you objectives that you find meaningful to work toward over a lifetime.

Are your short-term and medium-term goals compatible with your long-term goals? If you want to live to a ripe old age to travel the world with old friends, your short-term and medium-term goals need to include taking care of your health, cultivating friendships, and making money.

Do you periodically reassess your goals to make sure that they are still what you want? As you work toward your goals, you get new information and insights. Part of balancing your goals involves adapting them to changes taking place in your life. Be flexible.

Here's how Eric, a 41-year-old manager in an electronics firm, used his list of values to guide him in setting his life goals. First he listed his values:

1. *Family:* To enjoy, take care of, and provide for them.

2. *Health:* To preserve the good health I have into my eighties.

3. *Financial security:* To have enough money to take care of family, leisure, travel dreams, and retirement.

4. *Professional success:* To become a vice president with my company.

5. *Nature:* To spend time in the wilderness every year; to learn more about animal behavior.

6. *Friends:* To enjoy them and help out.

7. *Spiritual:* To maintain my connection with my higher power and give my children an opportunity for this also.

8. *Travel:* To go as often and as far as time and money permit.

9. *Communication:* To be open and honest with others and feel that they are with me.

Here are the goals that Eric developed, based on his list of values.

*Long-term goals* (over five years):

1. Own and live in a house on the lake where I spent my summers as a child.

2. Optimize my health with regular exercise, diet, rest, and medical checkups.

3. Raise my three children and provide them with an education.

4. Save and invest enough money so that I can retire at 55 years old, live at the lake, and travel.

5. Publish a book on tracking based on my wilderness experience.

*Medium-term goals:*

1. Become a vice president for the company in four years.

2. Buy a new house to accommodate our growing family within two years.

3. Find a church that the whole family can agree on and become an active participant.

4. Listen to audiotapes on personal financial planning and investing when commuting.

5. Go on a backpacking trip with friends to the Lost Coast a year and a half from now.

*Short-term goals:*

1. Go camping with my wife alone for a long weekend in the next month.

2. Set up a weekly family night starting this Thursday.

3. Have a fun evening with friends at least once a week.

4. Jog three mornings and take a hike with family and friends at least once a month.

5. Meditate for fifteen minutes before leaving the office for home.

6. Remember to take a few deep breaths and relax my muscles when faced with a stressful event.

Write down one or more specific goals for each of your priorities. You may find it helpful to list your various goals under the following three categories:

1. Your long-term goals (goals that will take you over five years to accomplish).

_____

_____

_____

_____

_____

2. Your medium-term goals (goals that will take you from one to five years).

_____

_____

_____

_____

_____

3. Your short-term goals (goals that will take from one week to less than one year).

_____

_____

_____

_____

_____

# Developing an Action Plan

Your third step is to identify the specific steps that you need to take in order to achieve each of your goals. The most common reason that people do not attain their objectives is that they do not have an action plan that describes step by step how they are going to get from where they are now all the way to their goal. Without an action plan, your goal may seem too big and too remote. Without knowing what to do first, you never get beyond the dreaming stage.

An effective action plan includes:

• A well thought-out and specific goal

• A description of all the resources that you will need and how you will access them

- Each step you must take in the correct order
- How you will monitor your progress
- The most likely reasons why you might procrastinate and how you will deal with this
- What rewards you will use to motivate yourself

You can use two strategies to create an action plan.

**1. Imagine that you have already achieved your goal.** How would you feel, look, behave, and sound? How would people around you respond to you? Once you have a clear picture of what you want and are in touch with the good feelings that picture generates for you, begin to work backwards from that fantasized image. Ask yourself what steps you must have taken to achieve your objective. Notice which resources you used. Did you need to develop new skills? Did you use outside resources or simply rely on your personal ones? How much time did it take? How did you deal with obstacles such as your fears and excuses and other people's demands on your time? How did you motivate yourself to keep going? Run a mental movie from where you are now all the way through to achieving your goal. Write down in order the steps you took.

Tom, a student in a college English class, used this approach. His goal was to receive an "A" on a paper for his creative writing class. First he visualized getting his paper back from his professor with an "A" on its cover. After relishing his pleasure and excitement and enjoying the imaginary congratulations of his friends, he went on to think through the steps he could have taken to reach that goal. Here's the original list of steps that he generated:

1. I take a walk by myself just to come up with a topic for my paper.

2. While walking, I come up with a great idea about writing a short story about salmon fishing in Alaska, which is how I earned extra money last summer. I reminisce about my experiences. I get excited about writing the paper.

3. I write an outline of my story.

4. I write a rough draft of my story.

5. I look over the rough draft and write a more polished version.

6. I have my friend read my paper. I am encouraged by her positive comments.

7. I review and incorporate many of my friend's suggestions.

8. I make the final copy of my paper.

9. I turn my paper in on time.

After thinking about his action plan, Tom realized that it didn't really deal with one familiar obstacle: his own tendency to get sidetracked by his family and friends. He decided that his best strategy would be to reward himself with some time off once he had written a rough draft and then bring himself back to the project by again visualizing accomplishing his goal.

**2. Brainstorm.** A second way to create an action plan is to write your goal at the top of a blank sheet of paper and then randomly ask yourself questions about everything you need to know and do in order to achieve your objective. When you are finished brainstorming, rewrite the specific steps you need to take from where you are now all the way through to your goal.

Angela's goal was to establish an ongoing aerobic exercise program. She started by asking herself these questions:

*Why do I want to exercise?*

I want to feel and look healthy, fit, trim, and strong. One of my long-term goals is to be healthy into my old age.

*How often and how long do I need to exercise aerobically to get the results I want?*

I need to read more about exercise to answer these questions. I can talk to my friends about their experiences with exercise. I want to start out gradually and set more challenging goals as I become stronger.

*What kind of exercise do I like? What kind am I capable of doing and have the time and resources to do?*

Walking, swimming, jogging, biking, and working out to an aerobic dance videotape are all good candidates.

*What do I need in order to exercise safely and have a hassle free time?*

I need an exercise that I can do without getting in my car and having to deal with traffic. (That lets out swimming and biking!) There's a safe trail near my house. I have a VCR and I can buy an aerobic dance tape. Except for shoes, I already have plenty of clothes I can dance, walk, and jog in.

*Which tape should I buy?*

I can ask my friends for recommendations, or rent some tapes and see which I like best. I can go to the book, record, or video store and buy the ones I like best.

*What kind of shoes? And where do I find these shoes?*

Go to the local sports shoe store and ask the salesperson for help. I could read up on shoes, but I'd rather talk to my friends.

*When am I going to exercise?*

After work, when I first come home, before I do anything else.

*How am I going to motivate myself to stick with this program?*

I can jog with a friend. I can participate in local races. I can notice how much better I feel and look when I have been exercising regularly for a while. I can reward myself with new exercise clothes and tapes and gold stars. I can always do aerobic dance, even when the weather is bad or it's dark outside.

*How am I going to monitor my progress?*

I will keep track of my progress by reviewing the gold stars on my calendar every other week with my friend Stacey who knows what I am trying to accomplish and is very supportive of me.

Here's the action plan that Angela developed after she had read through and reorganized her answers:

1. Define my specific exercise goal and keep in mind my purpose in exercising regularly.

2. Read more about aerobic exercise to find out how often and how long I need to exercise.

3. Talk to my friends about jogging, proper shoes, and aerobic dance tapes.

4. Find a jogging partner. (An optional step: not essential for me to start my program.)

5. Consult with salesperson at local sport shoe store and buy a comfortable pair of shoes to fit my needs.

6. Try out aerobic tapes by renting or borrowing them first.

7. Buy favorite aerobic tapes at local record, book, or video store.

8. Jog or do an aerobic dance tape when I first come home from work.

9. Monitor my progress by putting a gold star on the days of the week I exercise. I'll use the calendar in my kitchen, since I look at it every day.

10. Evaluate my progress with my boyfriend Zack. He's a jock and very supportive of me becoming more active.

11. Reward myself by buying new exercise clothes, participating in local races, buying new tapes. I can look and feel great!

## Evaluating Your Progress

Identifying a way to keep track of your progress should be a part of your action plan. One powerful approach is to plan to go over what you have accomplished toward your goal with a support person every couple of weeks. Choose a support person who understands and appreciates what you are trying to do. This person should be able to give you positive suggestions and encouragement, as well as point out when you are fooling yourself.

By the time of your second two-week progress evaluation, you should begin to see some positive results. Success can serve as a powerful reinforcer to continue your program, but don't let your first gains trick you into slacking off. Old habits don't die easily, and it can take three months to develop new ones.

If you are not seeing positive results, or you catch yourself making excuses for not following through on your plan, don't be too hard on yourself. Instead, reassess your original goal. Is this what you really want? If not, modify your goal. If it is something you want, consider how you can modify your action plan so that you can get moving toward your goal.

## Writing a Self-Contract

You can formalize your goals and your action plan by writing a contract for yourself. In the contract, spell out your goals clearly and precisely. Include the details of how and when you are going to achieve them and how you plan to reward yourself for your efforts. Sign and date your contract. To ensure that you follow through on your self-contract, show it to the support

---

### Sample Contract Form

I, _____ , am going to do _____
          *(your name)*                                                          *(activity or goal)*

for or by _____ . I will monitor my progress by
                    *(how long, how often, by when)*

_____ . I will evaluate my progress every
              *(the method you will use)*

_____ with my support person _____
          *(how often)*                                                          *(name)*

I will reward myself with _____ .
                                        *(something that will motivate you)*

---

person you have asked to sit down with you every other week for the next three months to evaluate your progress.

Here's the self-contract that Angela wrote out for her exercise goal.

*I, Angela Sanchez, am going to walk, jog, or exercise to an aerobic dance tape forty minutes per day four days a week starting this week. I will monitor my progress by giving myself a gold star every day that I exercise and by participating in local races. I will reward myself with a new T-shirt or shorts or aerobic tape at the end of each month I stick with my goal and I know I will be feeling and looking great. I will evaluate my progress every two weeks for the next three months with my boyfriend by reviewing the gold stars on my calendar and discussing what it's like for me to be exercising regularly.*

*Angela Sanchez*
*June 1st*

## Evaluating How You Spend Your Time

Now you can begin the fourth step toward effective time management by keeping a daily log of your time. It is best to do this in real time, rather than trying to estimate how much time you spent on the various activities that fill your day. Most people tend to grossly underestimate how long it takes to do things and to overlook or forget the unplanned activities that pop up during the day. If you really want to learn something new about yourself, stop once an hour during your waking day to record how long it took you to do each activity that you were involved in during that hour. At the very least, get out your notebook after lunch and dinner and before bed and write down every activity you engaged in. Note the amount of time each one took. When you're through, the total amount of time for all activities should be fairly close to the total number of hours you were awake.

Keep this time inventory for at least three days. Categories of activities at work might include: paperwork, work-related and personal phone calls, socializing face-to-face, meetings, low-priority work, productive work, routine work, eating, and daydreaming. Typical activities not related to work are: personal hygiene, grooming, dressing, cooking, eating, naps, daydreaming, child care and parenting, shopping, household chores and maintenance, commuting, travel for errands, telephone calls, face-to-face conversations, television, hobbies, reading, participating in sports, exercising, and other recreation. Modify or add categories to suit yourself. Keep in mind that this time log is designed to help you break down and examine as carefully as you need to the various ways that you use your time, so that later you can decide if you want to spend more or less time engaged in each of these activities.

Samantha, a radio public affairs interviewer, kept the following record on the first day of her three-day time assessment.

## Samantha's Time Log

| Activity | Time |
| --- | --- |
| Waking through lunch | |
|     Lying in bed trying to get up | 20 minutes |
|     Shower | 20 minutes |
|     Grooming and dressing | 25 minutes |
|     Cooking breakfast | 5 minutes |
|     Eating breakfast and reading paper | 10 minutes |
|     Phone call (family) | 10 minutes |
|     Commute and listen to news | 45 minutes |
|     Morning staff meeting (10 minutes late) | 40 minutes |
|     Routine work - review and respond to:<br>        Phone messages<br>        Electronic mail<br>        Written memos<br>        Mail | 60 minutes |
| Daydreaming | 5 minutes |
| Socializing (friend) | 15 minutes |
| Meeting (15 minutes late) | 45 minutes |
| Productive work (preparing for interview) | 40 minutes |
| Lunch with friend (15 minutes late) | 75 minutes |

| Activity | Time |
|---|---|
| After lunch through dinner | |
|     Productive work (preparing for interview) | 95 minutes |
|     Phone call (friend) | 5 minutes |
|     Daydreaming | 10 minutes |
|     Low-priority work (helping co-worker) | 65 minutes |
|     Socializing with co-worker | 15 minutes |
|     Phone call (work related) | 30 minutes |
|     Commute | 45 minutes |
|     Shopping | 40 minutes |
|     Mail | 10 minutes |
|     Phone call (personal) | 25 minutes |
|     Neighbor visits | 20 minutes |
|     Phone (work related) | 30 minutes |
|     Cook while listening to news on TV | 60 minutes |
|     Eat | 20 minutes |
| After dinner until sleep | |
|     Clean up kitchen | 15 minutes |
|     Phone call (personal) | 10 minutes |
|     Television (documentary) | 60 minutes |
|     Reading novel | 25 minutes |
|         Turn off light (30 minutes late) | |

## Evaluating Your Time Log

Now that you know how you are actually spending your time, you are ready to compare the inventory you made with your real priorities. From there, you'll be able to go on to decide what changes you want to make to bring your current schedule into closer alignment with your most important values and goals. Here are some questions to guide you in making this comparison.

1. **Which of the activities on your daily log are in line with your values and goals?** Mark these activities with a star.

## Sample Time Log

| Activity | Time |
|---|---|
| Waking through lunch | |
| | |
| | |
| | |
| | |
| | |
| | |
| | |
| After lunch through dinner | |
| | |
| | |
| | |
| | |
| | |
| | |
| After dinner until sleep | |
| | |
| | |
| | |
| | |
| | |
| | |

Samantha starred reading the paper and listening and watching the news, since these activities reflected her priority of "staying current with the news." She starred her productive time at work preparing for radio interviews because this reflected her priority to be a "successful radio interviewer." She starred "phone calls with friends" since one of her priorities was to spend time with friends.

**2. Which of the activities on your daily log are not in line with your values and goals?** Circle these activities.

Samantha was amazed to find that on this day she had spent three hours and fifteen minutes preparing, eating, and cleaning up after meals. She felt that over two hours on the phone and reading memos and mail for work was excessive. She also realized that she had wasted a half hour in the morning with extra time in bed and a long shower. She recognized that she allowed unexpected calls and socializing to get in the way of being on time. When she analyzed her work patterns, it became obvious that her most productive hours were at midday—and that lunch was a big interruption right in the middle of this time.

Look at the circled items on your list and write down how you how you would be willing to reschedule, reduce, or eliminate low priority activities in your day.

_____

_____

_____

_____

_____

**3. Are any of your values being violated by any of the activities on your daily log?** Mark these activities with an "X."

Engaging in activities that run counter to your values can make you feel guilty, ashamed, anxious, depressed, resentful, or exhausted. Samantha's problem with tardiness ran counter to her priorities of "peace of mind" and "being a successful radio interviewer." She felt rushed, anxious, guilty, and embarrassed when she arrived at meetings late.

Look at the items that you have marked with an X and write down how you would be willing to change your behavior so that it no longer violated your values.

_____

_____

_____

_____

_____

**4. Are some of your values and goals being neglected or ignored?**  Activities that reflect these neglected values and goals may be the very ones that you need to expand or increase in order to bring balance to your life. On the other hand, these neglected values may actually have a lower priority at this time in your life than your other values, and you may realize that you feel okay about postponing activities associated with them.

Samantha noticed that her priorities having to do with friends, family, and health were underrepresented in how she spent her time. Except for brief phone calls, she didn't talk with her family. Since her parents and sisters lived in another state and she had recently visited them, this limited contact was okay with her for right now. She did want to spend more time with friends and to take better care of herself physically. Her sedentary life style and eating habits had caused her to gain weight.

Write down how you would be willing to change your behavior so that it would be consistent with the values and goals that you have been neglecting.

Samantha decided that she was willing to make the following immediate changes in her use of time.

1. Eat a quick breakfast that does not require cooking.

2. Give "being on time" priority over unexpected phone calls and other low priority activities.

3. Limit lunch to an hour and take it later in the day to take advantage of most productive time of day.

4. Prepare simple dinners in half an hour.

5. Limit most work related calls to ten minutes.

6. Skim written communication for "must know" and "must respond" information.

7. Give "going to sleep on time" priority over TV and reading.

8. Get up with the alarm and limit shower to ten minutes.

9. Go the gym and work out with my friends four nights a week.

While it is unlikely that you would want to try to do something that reflects each one of your values and goals every single day, you can integrate all of your values and most of your goals into your activities if you plan your time on a weekly or even monthly basis. Continue using the tools you learned earlier in this chapter to clearly define your goals and prepare an action plan that lets you evaluate and reward yourself for the progress you have made.

## Combating Procrastination

The fifth step toward effective time management is to get yourself unstuck. You have already learned several ways to combat procrastination in this chapter. What distasteful activity are you avoiding? Compare it with your values. Does it violate one of your priorities? If it does, are you ready to take a stand and declare that you are not going to do it? If not, what can you do to change your circumstances in the future so that you will no longer be violating one of your values? If you are avoiding an activity that is tied to one of your goals, review the section in this chapter on setting effective goals. If you don't know where to start, create an action plan. If you simply need to get better organized, refer to the sixth and final step in this chapter.

Here are ten additional suggestions to use when you find yourself procrastinating.

**1. Stop worrying.** You probably spend more time worrying about chores that you do not want to do than you would spend by simply doing them. To illustrate this point to yourself, keep track of how much time it takes for you to complete each distasteful task.

**2. Start small.** Once you start doing an unpleasant task, you may find that it isn't as bad as you anticipated. So lead yourself into the cold water with a small but related task. If you have to mow the lawn, decide to go as far as filling the gas tank on the mower and wheeling it out to the edge of the lawn.

**3. Count the cost.** Make a list of all the unpleasant aspects of doing the activity that you are avoiding and then make a second list of the consequences of putting it off. Look squarely at the costs and risks of delay and ask yourself which list contains the greater amount of unpleasantness. Use this information to create enthusiasm for getting the job done.

**4. Look for the hidden rewards.** Look for any payoffs that you may be receiving for *not* getting the distasteful job done. For example, by procrastinating you may be avoiding feeling anxious or facing the possibility of failure. Also examine the advantages of avoiding whatever changes might follow from completing the task. For example, success might mean that you lose the attention that you now get from people who nag you or sympathize with your predicament.

**5. Confront negative beliefs.** Read chapter 14 on "Refuting Irrational Ideas" to confront beliefs that may be interfering with doing what you need to do. You may be making statements to yourself like "No way am I going to do this, it just isn't fair" or "I must do it perfectly" or "Life should be easy" or "I can't stand the thought of giving a speech in front of a group of strangers" or "What if I succeed? They'll expect even more out of me" or "I'll fail, so why try?"

**6. Double your resistance.** Exaggerate and intensify whatever you are doing that is putting off beginning a task. If you are staring at yourself in the mirror in the morning instead of getting to work, draw that stare out. Really study all your pores and go over each quadrant of your face minutely. Keep it up until you are really bored and getting to work seems like a more attractive alternative.

**7. Take responsibility for each delay.** You are the one wasting your own precious time. Make a list of each procrastination or escape activity and note how long it took. Add up the total and list all the positive things you could have done with that time if you'd simply finished the job to begin with.

**8. Tie a distasteful activity to an activity that you know you will do.** Find a gym you can go to on your way home from work or plan to exercise by walking to lunch in a restaurant twenty minutes from your office.

9.  **Reward yourself for doing activities that are unpleasant to you.**

10. **Finish things.** Avoid beginning a new task until you have completed a specific segment of your current task. The experience of finishing something is itself a great reward.

## Organizing Your Time

The sixth and final step toward more effective time management is to get better organized. Here are twelve suggestions to structure your time and focus your attention on creating the life of your choice.

1.  **Purchase an organizer.** Find one that includes a daily, weekly, and monthly calendar and use it.

2.  **Post copies of your written values, goals, action plans, and self-contracts in places where you will often be reminded of them.** Use brightly colored paper and ink to catch your eye. Try keeping a copy in your organizer or on a wall calendar or your bathroom mirror or any other place that you look at frequently.

3.  **Make sure that your list of daily goals and your calendar reflect your long-term, medium-term, and short-term goals.** If you want to be physically fit and relaxed, schedule time each day for exercise and for practicing relaxation techniques. If spending quality time with a loved one is high priority, block off regular time on your calendar to do this and include that time on your daily "to do" list. If you arrange your schedule of activities on a weekly or even monthly basis, you will find that you have time to work on all of your important goals.

4.  **Plan for efficiency.** Combine activities that can be done at the same time, such as watching your favorite TV show while exercising, ironing, or washing dishes. Sequence activities to save time. Match tasks to your varying energy levels. Although you can usually predict your energy level at different points during the day and plan accordingly, occasionally you will run out of steam earlier than anticipated. If so, you may want to reschedule activities that require energy and alertness to a time when you can perform them with maximum efficiency.

5.  **Minimize time wasters.** Cut back on TV, telephone interruptions, drop-in visitors, unproductive meetings, ineffective delegation of responsibilities, crises, activities that lack direction, and overly ambitious goals. Plan ways to avoid as many predictable time wasters as possible, but be realistic enough to schedule some time for unexpected interruptions.

6.  **Learn to say no.** Set limits on how much you are willing to do for others. If you have difficulty with this, see chapter 17 on "Assertiveness Training."

7.  **Make a list of things to do when you're waiting.** Good candidates include doing a relaxation exercise, planning tomorrow's list of goals, reviewing your priorities and goals, reading a book, or filing your nails.

8.  **Set aside several short periods each day for quiet time.** Use this time to practice your deep relaxation techniques. This will help you stay in touch with what is most important to you, rather than rushing faster and faster in response to others' demands.

**9. When you are performing a high-priority activity, focus your full attention on it.** Make a list of your usual distractions and plan how you can block each one of them. For instance, if you often find yourself daydreaming when you should be working, schedule in a visualization session or some other way of using your imagination during one of your quiet times.

**10. Arrange your environment to support your values and goals.** If your priorities require focus and concentration, make sure that you have a quiet room or corner available for reading, writing, practicing deep relaxation, or just thinking through your plans.

**11. Don't waste time on decisions that involve equally attractive or inconsequential alternatives.** If you find yourself in a quandary over choices like this, just flip a coin and go with the winning call.

**12. Reward yourself for improving your time management.** One of the greatest rewards of effective time management comes from not having to rush to accomplish the important things in your life. By prioritizing and planning your activities, you can choose to move through your day at a more leisurely pace.

## Organizing Your Day

Managing your time on a daily basis requires setting immediate priorities and sticking to them. At the beginning of each day, develop a "to-do" list that reflects your goals as well as necessary tasks. Each day's list should be prioritized by sorting activities into the following categories:

1. *Top drawer.* These are the most essential and most desired items.

2. *Middle drawer.* You could put these activities off for a while, but they are still important.

3. *Bottom drawer.* You can easily put these tasks off indefinitely with no harm done.

Go through your list and mark each item TD, MD, or BD according to its status. Now, as you start your day, you have a blueprint for how to apportion your time. Start with the top-drawer items first and work your way down the list. Only move on to the middle drawer when ALL of your top-drawer items have been completed. If you have too many top-drawer tasks to finish in a day, then you've given too many things a high priority. Only assign top-drawer status to tasks that absolutely cannot be put off and would result in negative consequences if they were.

Banish the bottom-drawer items from consideration, unless you have completed all your higher priority items for the day. The definition of bottom-drawer items is that they can wait. Unless it's your boss who's asking, keep away from commitments that force you to spend time in the bottom drawer. Be prepared to say "I don't have the time" to these requests. If circumstances force you to take on a bottom- drawer task, try to delegate it. Give it to your secretary, your housecleaner, your mother-in-law.

As you move through your day, stay focused on the high-priority tasks and make sure that you limit your opportunities for procrastination. Block off any escape routes that turn up by scheduling daydreaming for a later time, putting off socializing until a chunk of work is done, avoiding getting caught up in busywork or less important errands, and resisting the impulse to run out for ice cream or other tempting indulgences.

At the end of the day, review your to-do list. Check off the items that you completed as planned and give yourself a mental pat on the back. Add anything you did that was not on your original list. Note whether items that you allowed yourself to be seduced into doing were high-priority items, unavoidable interruptions, or low-priority items. Important things you did not finish can be moved to the next day. A good time to prepare a day's list of goals is the preceding evening or first thing in the morning. Either way, you start out fresh, on top of things, and in tune with your own priorities.

## Further Reading

Brinkman, R. 1993. *Life by Design: Making Lifestyle Choices That Contribute to Better Physical and Emotional Health.* Boulder, CO: Career Track Publications. *(An audiotape and workbook set.)*

Epstein-Shepherd, B. 1993. *Creating More Time in Your Life.* Boulder, CO: Career Track Publications. *(An audiotape set.)*

Scott, D. 1981. *How To Put More Time in Your Life.* New York: New American Library.

Stautberg, S. S., and M. L. Worthing. 1992. *Balancing Acts! Juggling Love, Work, Family, and Recreation.* New York: Master Midea.

# 17

# Assertiveness Training

How you interact with others can be a source of considerable stress in your life. Assertiveness training can reduce that stress by teaching you to stand up for your legitimate rights, without bullying others or letting them bully you.

Before reading any further, it will be useful to write down how you would typically respond to the following problem situations:

1. You buy your favorite beverage in the market, and after you walk out you discover that the change is a dollar short.

   *I would* _____

   _____

   _____

2. You order a steak rare and it arrives medium-well.

   *I would* _____

   _____

   _____

3. You're giving a friend a lift to a meeting. The friend keeps puttering around for half an hour so that you will arrive late.

   *I would* _____

   _____

   _____

4.  You ask for $5 worth of gas at a service station. The attendant fills up your tank and asks you for $9.50.

    *I would* _____

    _____

    _____

5.  You are relaxing with the paper after a long day. Your spouse pops in, list in hand, and says, "I never thought you'd get here. Quick, pick these up from the store."

    *I would* _____

    _____

    _____

6.  While you wait for the clerk to finish with the customer ahead of you, another customer comes in and the clerk waits on him before you.

    *I would* _____

    _____

    _____

After you have written down what you would do in these problem situations, set your responses aside. They will be put to use shortly.

Assertiveness was initially described as a personality trait by Andrew Salter in 1949. It was thought that some people had it, and some people didn't, just like extroversion or stinginess. But Wolpe (1958) and Lazarus (1966) redefined assertiveness as "expressing personal rights and feelings." They found that nearly everybody could be assertive in some situations, and yet be totally ineffectual in others. The goal of assertiveness training is to increase the number and variety of situations in which assertive behavior is possible, and decrease occasions of passive collapse or hostile blow-up.

You are assertive when you stand up for your rights in such a way that the rights of others are not violated. Beyond just demanding your rights, you can express your personal likes and interests spontaneously, you can talk about yourself without being self-conscious, you can accept compliments comfortably, you can disagree with someone openly, you can ask for clarification, and you can say no. In short, when you are an assertive person, you can be more relaxed in interpersonal situations.

Some people think that assertiveness training turns nice people into irascible complainers or calculating manipulators. Not so. It's your right to protect yourself when something seems unfair. You are the one who best knows your discomfort and your needs.

Investigators such as Jakubowski-Spector (1973) and Alberti and Emmons (1970) discovered that people who show relatively little assertive behavior do not believe that they have a right to their feelings, beliefs, or opinions. In the deepest sense, they reject the idea that we are created equal and are to treat each other as equals. As a result, they can't find grounds for objecting to exploitation or mistreatment. It is likely that they learned as children traditional assumptions that implied that their perceptions, opinions, feelings, and wants were less important or correct than those of others. They grew up doubting themselves and looking to others for validation and guidance.

You did not have much choice about which traditional assumptions you were taught as a child. Now, however, you have the option of deciding whether to continue behaving according to assumptions that keep you from being an assertive adult. Each of these mistaken assumptions violates one of your legitimate rights as an adult:

| Mistaken Traditional Assumptions | Your Legitimate Rights |
| --- | --- |
| 1. It is selfish to put your needs before others' needs. | You have a right to put yourself first sometimes. |
| 2. It is shameful to make mistakes. You should have an appropriate response for every occasion. | You have a right to make mistakes. |
| 3. If you can't convince others that your feelings are reasonable, then they must be wrong, or maybe you are going crazy. | You have a right to be the final judge of your feelings and accept them as legitimate. |
| 4. You should respect the views of others, especially if they are in a position of authority. Keep your differences of opinion to yourself. Listen and learn. | You have a right to have your own opinions and convictions. |
| 5. You should always try to be logical and consistent. | You have a right to change your mind or decide on a different course of action. |
| 6. You should be flexible and adjust. Others have good reasons for their actions and it's not polite to question them. | You have a right to protest unfair treatment or criticism. |
| 7. You should never interrupt people. Asking questions reveals your stupidity to others. | You have a right to interrupt in order to ask for clarification. |
| 8. Things could get even worse, don't rock the boat. | You have a right to negotiate for change. |
| 9. You shouldn't take up others' valuable time with your problems. | You have a right to *ask* for help or emotional support. |
| 10. People don't want to hear that you feel bad, so keep it to yourself. | You have a right to feel and express pain. |

| Mistaken Traditional Assumptions | Your Legitimate Rights |
|---|---|
| 11.  When someone takes the time to give you advice, you should take it very seriously. They are often right. | You have a right to ignore the advice of others. |
| 12.  Knowing that you did something well is its own reward. People don't like show-offs. Successful people are secretly disliked and envied. Be modest when complimented. | You have a right to receive formal recognition for your work and achievements. |
| 13.  You should always try to accommodate others. If you don't, they won't be there when you need them. | You have a right to say "no." |
| 14.  Don't be anti-social. People are going to think you don't like them if you say you'd rather be alone instead of with them. | You have a right to be alone, even if others would prefer your company. |
| 15.  You should always have a good reason for what you feel and do. | You have a right not to have to justify yourself to others. |
| 16.  When someone is in trouble, you should help them. | You have a right not to take responsibility for someone else's problem. |
| 17.  You should be sensitive to the needs and wishes of others, even when they are unable to tell you what they want. | You have a right not to have to anticipate others' needs and wishes. |
| 18.  It's always a good policy to stay on people's good side. | You have a right not to always worry about the goodwill of others. |
| 19.  It's not nice to put people off. If questioned, give an answer. | You have a right to choose not to respond to a situation. |

As you continue through this chapter, keep in mind that assertive communication is based on the assumption that you are the best judge of your thoughts, feelings, wants, and behavior. Nobody is better informed than you regarding how your heredity, history, and current circumstances have shaped you into a unique human being. Therefore, you are the best advocate for expressing your positions on important issues. Because of your uniqueness, there are many times when you differ with significant people in your life. Rather than overpower the meek or give in to the aggressive, you have the right to express your position and try to negotiate your differences.

# Symptom Relief

Assertiveness training has been found to be effective in dealing with depression, anger, resentment, and interpersonal anxiety, especially when these symptoms have been brought about by unfair circumstances. As you become more assertive, you begin to lay claim to your right to relax and are able to take time for yourself.

# Time for Mastery

Some people master assertiveness skills sufficiently for symptom relief with just a few weeks of practice. For others, several months of step-by-step work are necessary to experience significant change.

# Instructions

## 1. *Three Basic Interpersonal Styles*

Assertiveness is a skill that can be learned, not a personality trait that some are born with and others are not. The first step in assertiveness training is to identify the three basic styles of interpersonal behavior.

**Aggressive style.** In this style, opinions, feelings, and wants are honestly stated, but at the expense of someone else's feelings. The underlying message is "I'm superior and right, and you're inferior and wrong." The advantage of aggressive behavior is that people often give aggressive individuals what they want in order to get rid of them. The disadvantage is that aggressive individuals make enemies, and people who can't avoid them entirely may end up behaving dishonestly toward them in order to avoid confrontations.

**Passive style.** In this style, opinions, feelings, and wants are withheld altogether or expressed indirectly and only in part. The underlying message is "I'm weak and inferior, and you're powerful and right." The advantage of passive communication is that it minimizes responsibility for making decisions and the risk of taking a personal stand on an issue. The disadvantages are a sense of impotence, lowered self-esteem, and having to live with the decisions of others.

**Assertive style.** In this style, you clearly state your opinion, how you feel, and what you want without violating the rights of others. The underlying assumption is "You and I may have our differences, but we are equally entitled to express ourselves to one another." The major advantages include active participation in making important decisions, getting what you want without alienating others, the emotional and intellectual satisfaction of respectfully exchanging feelings and ideas, and high self-esteem.

To test your ability to distinguish interpersonal styles, label person A's behavior in the following scenes as aggressive, passive, or assertive:

**Scene 1**

*A:*     Is that a new dent I see in the car?

B:   Look, I just got home, it was a wretched day, and I don't want to talk about it now.

A:   This is important to me, and we're going to talk about it now.

B:   Have a heart.

A:   Let's decide now who is going to pay to have it fixed, when, and where.

B:   I'll take care of it. Now leave me alone, for heaven's sake!

A's behavior is      ☐ Aggressive      ☐ Passive      ☐ Assertive

## Scene 2

A:   You left me so by myself at that party . . . I really felt abandoned.

B:   You were being a party pooper.

A:   I didn't know anybody—the least you could have done is introduce me to some of your friends.

B:   Listen, you're grown up. You can take care of yourself. I'm tired of your nagging to be taken care of all the time.

A:   And I'm tired of your inconsiderateness.

B:   Okay, I'll stick to you like glue next time.

A's behavior is      ☐ Aggressive      ☐ Passive      ☐ Assertive

## Scene 3

A:   Would you mind helping me for a minute with this file?

B:   I'm busy with this report. Catch me later.

A:   Well, I really hate to bother you, but it's important.

B:   Look, I have a four o'clock deadline.

A:   Okay, I understand. I know it's hard to be interrupted.

A's behavior is      ☐ Aggressive      ☐ Passive      ☐ Assertive

## Scene 4

A:   I got a letter from Mom this morning. She wants to come and spend two weeks with us. I'd really like to see her.

B:   Oh no, not your mother! And right on the heels of your sister. When do we get a little time to ourselves?

A:   Well, I do want her to come, but I know you need to spend some time without my in-laws underfoot. I'd like to invite her to come in a month, and instead of two weeks, I think one week would be enough. What do you say to that?

B:   That's a big relief to me.

A's behavior is      ☐ Aggressive      ☐ Passive      ☐ Assertive

**Scene 5**

*A:*    Boy, you're looking great today!

*B:*    Who do you think you're kidding? My hair is a fright and my clothes aren't fit for the Goodwill box.

*A:*    Have it your way.

*B:*    And I feel just as bad as I look today.

*A:*    Right. I've got to run now.

A's behavior is    ☐ Aggressive    ☐ Passive    ☐ Assertive

**Scene 6**

(While at a party, A is telling her friends how much she appreciates her boyfriend taking her out to good restaurants and to the theater. Her friends criticize her for being unliberated.)

*A:*    Not so. I don't make nearly as much as a secretary as he does as a lawyer. I couldn't afford to take us both out or pay my own way to all the nice places we go. Some traditions make sense, given the economic realities.

A's behavior is    ☐ Aggressive    ☐ Passive    ☐ Assertive

Now that you have labeled person A's responses in these scenes as aggressive, passive, or assertive, it may be useful to compare your assessment with ours:

**Scene 1.** A is aggressive. A's seemingly innocent question is actually an accusation in disguise. A's insistence on immediate action with total disregard for B's state of mind sets up a polarized conflict in which B is likely to feel wrong, withdrawn, and defensive.

**Scene 2.** A is aggressive. The tone is accusing and blaming. B is immediately placed on the defensive and no one wins.

**Scene 3.** A is passive. A's timid opening line is followed by complete collapse. The file problem must now be dealt with alone.

**Scene 4.** A is assertive. The request is specific, non-hostile, and open to negotiation.

**Scene 5.** A is passive. A allows the compliment to be rebuffed and surrenders to B's rush of negativity.

**Scene 6.** A is assertive. She stands up to the prevailing opinion of the group and achieves a clear, nonthreatening statement of her position.

## 2. *The Assertiveness Questionnaire*

(Adapted from Sharon and Gordon Bower's *Asserting Your Self*.)

Step two in assertiveness training is to identify those situations in which you want to be more effective. Having clarified the three interpersonal styles, now reexamine your responses to the six problem situations you responded to at the beginning of this chapter. Label your responses as falling primarily in the aggressive, passive, or assertive style. This is a start in objectively analyzing your own behavior and finding out where assertiveness training can most help you.

To further refine your assessment of the situations in which you need to be more assertive, complete the following questionnaire. Put a check mark in column A by the items that are applicable to you and then rate those items in column B: as:

1. Comfortable

2. Mildly uncomfortable

3. Moderately uncomfortable

4. Very uncomfortable

5. Unbearably threatening

(Note that the varying degrees of discomfort can be expressed whether your inappropriate reactions are hostile or passive.)

| | A<br>Check here<br>if the item<br>applies to you | B<br>Rate<br>from 1-5<br>for discomfort |
|---|---|---|
| **WHEN** do you behave non-assertively? | | |
| Asking for help | _____ | _____ |
| Stating a difference of opinion | _____ | _____ |
| Receiving and expressing negative feelings | _____ | _____ |
| Receiving and expressing positive feelings | _____ | _____ |
| Dealing with someone who refuses to cooperate | _____ | _____ |
| Speaking up about something that annoys you | _____ | _____ |
| Talking when all eyes are on you | _____ | _____ |
| Protesting a rip-off | _____ | _____ |
| Saying "no" | _____ | _____ |
| Responding to undeserved criticism | _____ | _____ |
| Making requests of authority figures | _____ | _____ |
| Negotiating for something you want | _____ | _____ |
| Having to take charge | _____ | _____ |
| Asking for cooperation | _____ | _____ |
| Proposing an idea | _____ | _____ |

|  | A<br>*Check here<br>if the item<br>applies to you* | B<br>*Rate<br>from 1-5<br>for discomfort* |
|---|---|---|
| Taking charge | _____ | _____ |
| Asking questions | _____ | _____ |
| Dealing with attempts to make you feel guilty | _____ | _____ |
| Asking for service | _____ | _____ |
| Asking for a date or appointment | _____ | _____ |
| Asking for favors | _____ | _____ |
| Other _____ | _____ | _____ |

**WHO** are the people with whom you are nonassertive?

| | | |
|---|---|---|
| Parents | _____ | _____ |
| Fellow workers, classmates | _____ | _____ |
| Strangers | _____ | _____ |
| Old friends | _____ | _____ |
| Spouse or mate | _____ | _____ |
| Employer | _____ | _____ |
| Relatives | _____ | _____ |
| Children | _____ | _____ |
| Acquaintances | _____ | _____ |
| Sales people, clerks, hired help | _____ | _____ |
| More than two or three people in a group | _____ | _____ |
| Other _____ | _____ | _____ |

**WHAT** do you want that you have been
unable to achieve with nonassertive styles?

| | | |
|---|---|---|
| Approval for things you have done well | _____ | _____ |
| To get help with certain tasks | _____ | _____ |
| More attention, or time with your mate | _____ | _____ |
| To be listened to and understood | _____ | _____ |

|  | A<br>*Check here<br>if the item<br>applies to you* | B<br>*Rate<br>from 1-5<br>for discomfort* |
|---|---|---|
| To make boring or frustrating situations more satisfying | _____ | _____ |
| To not have to be nice all the time | _____ | _____ |
| Confidence in speaking up when something is important to you | _____ | _____ |
| Greater comfort with strangers, store clerks, mechanics, and so on | _____ | _____ |
| Confidence in asking for contact with people you find attractive | _____ | _____ |
| To get a new job, ask for interviews, raises, and so on | _____ | _____ |
| Comfort with people who supervise you or work under you | _____ | _____ |
| To not feel angry and bitter a lot of the time | _____ | _____ |
| To overcome a feeling of helplessness and the sense that nothing ever really changes | _____ | _____ |
| To initiate satisfying sexual experiences | _____ | _____ |
| To do something totally different and novel | _____ | _____ |
| To have time by yourself | _____ | _____ |
| To do things that are fun or relaxing for you | _____ | _____ |
| Other _____ | _____ | _____ |

**Evaluating your responses.** Examine your answers, and analyze them for an overall picture of what situations and people threaten you. How does non-assertive behavior contribute to the specific items you checked on the "What" list? In constructing your own assertiveness program, it will be initially useful to focus on items you rated as falling in the 2-3 range. These are the situations that you will find easiest to change. Items that are very uncomfortable or threatening can be tackled later.

## 3. *Describing Your Problem Scenes*

Step three in assertiveness training, according to Sharon and Gordon Bower, is to describe your problem scenes. Select a mildly to moderately uncomfortable situation that suggests itself from items on the Assertiveness Questionnaire. Write out a description of the scene, being certain to include *who* the person involved is, *when* it takes place (time and setting), *what* bothers you, *how* you deal with it, your *fear* of what will take place if you are assertive, and your *goal*. Always be specific! Generalizations will make it difficult later on to write a script that will make assertive behavior possible in this situation. The following is an example of a poor scene description.

> I have a lot of trouble persuading some of my friends to listen to *me* for a change. They never stop talking, and I never get a word in edgewise. It would be nice for me if I could participate more in the conversation. I feel that I'm just letting them run over me.

Notice that the description doesn't specify *who* the particular friend is, *when* this problem is most likely to occur, *how* the non-assertive person acts, what *fears* are involved in being assertive, and a specific *goal* for increased involvement in the conversation. The scene might be rewritten as follows:

> My friend Joan (*who*), when we meet for a drink after work (*when*), often goes on nonstop about her marriage problems (*what*). I just sit there and try to be interested (*how*). If I interrupt her, I'm afraid she'll think I just don't care (*fear*). I'd like to be able to change the subject and talk sometimes about my own life (*goal*).

Here is a second poor scene description:

> A lot of times I want to strike up a conversation with people, but I worry that maybe they don't want to be disturbed. Often I notice someone who seems interesting, but I can't imagine how to get their attention.

Once again there is a lack of detail. No clear statement is made as to *who* these people are, *when* the experience takes place, *how* the non-assertive person behaves, or the specific *goal*. The described scene will become much more useful by including these elements:

> There is an attractive girl who always brings a bag lunch (*who*) and often sits at my table in the cafeteria (*when*). I would like to start a conversation by asking about her boss, who has a very hard-to-get-along-with reputation (*what*), but she looks so intent on her book I'm afraid she would be put out if I interrupted (*how, fear*). I'd like to start a conversation with her tomorrow (*goal*).

Write three or four problem scenes, and for each scene try to relive your thoughts and feelings when you were actually experiencing it. You might notice, for example, that in each problem scene you gun yourself down with negative thoughts ("I can't do it, I'm blowing it again, boy do I look stupid," and so on), or you usually feel tense in the stomach and seem to be breathing way up in your chest. Strategies in other chapters of this workbook will help you cope with habitual thoughts and physical reactions that make you uncomfortable when you act assertively. Coping skills training, deep muscle relaxation, breathing exercises, and so on should all be useful with these uncomfortable thoughts and feelings. At this point, however, we will concern ourselves with behavior—changing your habitual way of dealing with these problem situations.

## 4. *Your Script for Change*

The fourth step in assertiveness training is writing your script for change. A script is a working plan for dealing with the problem scene assertively. There are six elements in a script:

1. **Look at your rights, what you want, what you need, and your feelings about the situation.** Let go of blame, the desire to hurt, and self pity. Define your goal and keep it in mind when you negotiate for change.

2. **Arrange a time and place to discuss your problem that is convenient for you and for the other person.** This step may be excluded when dealing with spontaneous situations in which you choose to be assertive, such as when a person cuts ahead of you in line.

3. **Define the problem situation as specifically as possible.** This is essential for focusing the discussion. Here is your opportunity to state the facts as you see them and share your opinion and beliefs. For example: "It's time to make a decision about where we're going to eat tonight. I know you love Mexican food, but we've eaten at Tijuana Joe's the last three times we've gone out for dinner. We're in a rut!"

4. **Describe your feelings so that the other person has a better understanding of how important an issue is to you.** Once they are expressed, your feelings can often play a major role in helping you get what you want, especially when your opinion differs markedly from that of your listener. If nothing else, the listener may be able to relate to and understand your feelings about an issue even when he totally disagrees with your perspective. When you share your feelings, you become less of an adversary.

There are three important rules to remember when assertively expressing your feelings:

1. Do not substitute an opinion for a feeling ("I feel that Mexican food should be abolished!"). The more accurate feeling statement is "I hate Mexican food!"

2. Use "I messages" that express your feelings without evaluating or blaming others. Rather than saying "You are inconsiderate" or "You hurt me," the I message would be "I feel hurt."

3. "I messages" connect the feeling statement with specific behaviors of the other person. For example, "I feel hurt when you ignore my wishes about where we eat." Contrast the clarity of this message with the vague blame statement, "I feel hurt because you are inconsiderate."

5. **Express your request in one or two easy-to-understand sentences.** Be specific and firm! Instead of expecting others to read your mind and magically meet your needs, as in the case of the passive individual, you state clearly your wishes and needs. Rather than assuming that you are always right and entitled to getting your way, as an aggressive person might, you state your wants as preferences, not commands. Example: "I would really like to go to a French restaurant tonight."

6. **Reinforce the other person to give you want you want.** The best reinforcement is to describe positive consequences. "We'll save money . . . We'll have more time together . . . I'll give

you a backrub . . . My mother will only stay a week . . . I'll be less tired and more fun to be with . . . I'll be able to get my work in on time . . . Little Julia will do better in school," and so on.

In some cases, positive reinforcement may be ineffective. If the person you're dealing with seems resistant or you feel that you're having trouble motivating him or her to cooperate with you, consider describing some negative consequences for failure to cooperate. The most effective negative consequences are descriptions of the alternative way you will take care of yourself if your wishes aren't accommodated.

- If we can't leave on time, I'll have to leave without you. Then you'll have to drive over later on your own.

- If you can't clean the bathroom, I'll hire someone to do it once a week and add it to your rent.

- If you won't fold and put away your clothes, I'll just leave them in this box. I guess you can sort through it whenever you need something.

- If you keep talking in this loud, attacking way, I'll leave. We can talk again tomorrow.

- If you drink heavily again at these office functions, I won't go with you.

- If your check bounces again, we'll have to work on a cash basis only.

- If you keep talking during the movie, I'm going to ask the manager to come in here.

- If you can't give me an accurate idea of when you'll be home, I'm not going to cook and keep things warm for you.

Notice that these examples are different from threats. The consequence of non-cooperation is that the speaker takes care of his or her interests. The consequences are not designed to hurt, merely to protect. Threats usually don't work because they make people so angry. If you do make a threat ("You won't go to my sister's wedding? I won't go to your family reunion"), make sure you are willing and able to back it up. Even then it will often do more harm than good.

The first letters of each script element combine to spell "LADDER." You may find this a useful mnemonic device to recall the steps toward assertive behavior. The LADDER script can be used to rewrite your problem scenes so that you can assert what you want. Initially, LADDER scripts should be written out and practiced well in advance of the problem situation for which they are created. Writing the script forces you to clarify your needs and increases your confidence in success.

As an example of a LADDER script, let's say that Jean wants to assert her right to half an hour each day of uninterrupted peace and quiet while she does her relaxation exercises. Frank often interrupts with questions and attention-getting maneuvers. Jean's script goes like this:

Look at your rights, what you want, and what you need.

*It's my responsibility to make sure Frank respects my needs, and I am certainly entitled to some time to myself.*

Arrange a time and place to discuss the situation.

*I'll ask him if he's willing to discuss this problem when he gets home tonight. If he isn't, we'll set a time and place to talk about it in the next day or two.*

Define the problem specifically.

*At least once, and sometimes more often, I'm interrupted during my relaxation exercises—even though I've shut the door and asked for the time to myself. My concentration is broken and it becomes harder to achieve the relaxation.*

Describe your feelings using "I messages."

*I feel angry when my time alone is broken into and frustrated that the exercises are then made more difficult.*

Express your request simply and firmly.

*I would like not to be interrupted when my door is closed, except in a dire emergency. As long as it is closed, assume that I am still doing the exercises and want to be alone.*

Reinforce the possibility of getting what you want.

*If I'm not interrupted, I'll come in afterward and chat with you. If I am interrupted, it will increase the time I take doing the exercises.*

In another example, Harold has felt very reluctant to approach his boss to find out why he was turned down for a promotion. He's received no feedback about the reasons for the decision, and Harold is now feeling somewhat negative toward the company, and his boss in particular. Harold's script is as follows:

| | |
|---|---|
| **Look at:** | *Resentment won't solve this. I need to assert my right to reasonable feedback from my employer.* |
| **Arrange:** | *I'll send him a memo tomorrow morning asking for time to discuss this problem.* |
| **Define:** | *I haven't gotten any feedback about the promotion. The position I applied for has been filled by someone else, and that's all I know.* |
| **Describe:** | *I felt uncomfortable not knowing at all why I didn't get it and how the decision was made.* |
| **Express:** | *So I'd like to get some feedback from you about how my performance is seen, and what went into the decision.* |
| **Reinforce:** | *I think your feedback will help me do a better job.* |

These scripts, like the problem scenes earlier, are specific and detailed. The statement of the problem is clear and to the point, without blaming, accusing, or being passive. The feelings are expressed with "I messages" and are linked to specific events or behaviors, not to evaluation of Jean's husband or Harold's boss. "I messages" provide a tremendous amount of safety for the assertive individual because they usually keep the other person from getting defensive and angry. You are not accusing anyone of being a bad person, you are merely stating what you want or feel entitled to.

Successful LADDER scripts do the following:

1. When appropriate, establish a mutually agreeable time and place to assert your needs.

2. Describe behavior objectively, without judging or devaluing.

3. Describe clearly, using specific references to time, place and frequency.

4. Express feelings calmly and directly.

5. Confine your feeling response to the specific problem behavior, not the whole person.

6. Avoid delivering put-downs disguised as "honest feelings."

7. Ask for changes that are reasonably possible, and small enough not to incur a lot of resistance.

8. Ask for no more than one or two very specific changes at a time.

9. Make the reinforcements explicit, offering something that is really desirable to the other person.

10. Avoid threats or negative consequences that you're not willing or able to do.

11. Keep your mind on your rights and goals when being assertive.

Using these rules, we can now distinguish between good and bad scripts. For example, for several semesters running, Julie has wanted to take a night class in ceramics. Each time, her husband has an excuse for why he can't watch the children on the class night. Julie's script:

**L**    *I'm sick of being pushed around,*

**A**    *so I'm going to tell him tonight.*

**D**    *A year is long enough to wait.*

**D**    *He's too selfish to help*

**E**    *but he's just going to have to suffer every Wednesday night.*

**R**    *If he doesn't like it, he can just kiss this marriage goodbye.*

Julie has violated these rules for a good script:

1. By not getting agreement on the time and place for the discussion

2. By using non-specific and accusing phrases such as "pushed around"

3. By failing to specify exactly what the problem is

5. By describing her husband as selfish, rather than expressing her own feelings about specific behaviors

8. By not specifying times, or duration of the semester

9.  By threatening negative consequences that she isn't willing or able to carry out

Julie's script could be successfully rewritten as follows

**L**    *It is vital for me to have time to myself during which I can pursue interests of my own.*

**A**    *I'll ask him to discuss it after breakfast Saturday morning, or as soon afterwards as possible.*

**D**    *I've missed two previous ceramics classes because you weren't available for babysitting on the class night. I've waited a year and I would like to enroll this time.*

**D**    *I feel frustrated that I haven't been able to explore something that really excites me. I also feel hurt when you do other things rather than help me take the class.*

**E**    *I'd like you to look after the children on Wednesday nights between 6:30 and 9:00. The semester ends June 2nd.*

**R**    *If you're willing, I'll cook my special meatloaf for you on Wednesdays, but if you're not, we'll have the expense of a babysitter.*

The described problem behavior has become specific, the expressed feelings nonthreatening. Julie's reinforcements are realistic and explicit. It should be noted that negative reinforcement is often not necessary, and that positive reinforcement may require no more than the assurance that you will feel good if a certain behavior change is made. Elaborate promises can usually be avoided.

You can now write your own LADDER scripts. Using your written scripts, rehearse in front of a mirror. If possible, tape-record your rehearsals to further refine your assertive style. It is helpful to rehearse scripts with a friend, and get immediate feedback. Let yourself imagine, or better yet, act out, the worst possible response that could be made to your assertive request. Get desensitized to the "nightmare" response by facing it, and then preparing your own counter-measures.

### Short Form Assertiveness Technique

The short form assertiveness technique is designed for situations where you lack the time or energy to prepare an entire LADDER script. Assertiveness can be condensed to three basic statements:

1.  *Your thoughts* about the problematic situation. This is a non-blaming, non-pejorative description of the problem as you see it. You stick as closely as possible to objective facts, making no inferences about the motives or feelings of others.

2.  *Your feelings.* These are "I statements" about your emotional reaction to the problem. Try to avoid the implication that you're holding the other person responsible for your feelings. You're angry, sad, hurt, or disappointed. But your main message should be that you are trying to solve a problem, not blame or prove the other person wrong.

3.  *Your wants.* As in the LADDER script, make your request specific and behavioral. Don't ask your tardy spouse to be "more considerate." Request specifically that he or she call if more than 15 minutes late.

Whenever you're in a situation that requires an assertive response, quickly run through the three short form components in your mind.

I *think* . . . we've been working every night for two weeks on our bathroom remodel.

I *feel* . . . tired, grumpy, and pressured by your desire that it be done in one month's time.

I *want* . . . not to work more than three nights without one night off.

Make sure you've developed some idea of what you think, feel, and want before starting to speak. Try to express each component of your assertive statement in order. Finish one part before going on to the next.

Make the greatest effort to follow the rules about being non-blaming and making "I" statements. If you stick to these two, simple rules, you'll find the other person far less defensive and far more cooperative. Stay away from attempts to prove that your needs are more important or more legitimate than the other person's. Just keep on track with a statement of facts, feelings, and a specific request for change.

Annie invariably ate lunch with her co-worker, Marge. Once or twice a week Marge asked Annie to drop her by a bank or store on the way to eat. Annie finally reached the boiling point when Marge had her driving 40 minutes to get something notarized. Annie quickly reviewed the three statements in short form assertiveness.

I *think* . . . Once a week or more I help you with errands and we miss 15 to 30 minutes of our lunch.

I *feel* . . . tired from rushing and disappointed that I don't get to relax at lunch.

I *want* . . . to stop being a taxi service for you during my lunch hour.

The "I want" seemed a bit harsh and attacking, so Annie changed it to: "Let's eat on our own if either of us have errands."

Recall a problematic situation in your own life. As an exercise in thinking on your feet, try mentally composing an assertive message:

I *think* . . . (just the facts)

I *feel* . . . ("I" statements)

I *want* . . . (specific behavior change)

Now keep practicing. Think of at least three situations where you'd like to be more assertive. As you recall each one, pretend you are really there and have to make some response. Quickly go over the three parts of your assertive statement, then say it out loud. Listen to how it sounds. Is it blaming? Is your request specific enough? Are you saying clearly what you want? Are you criticizing the other person's motives or feelings? Correct what doesn't sound right and try saying it again.

## 5. *Assertive Body Language*

The fifth step in assertiveness training is to develop assertive body language. Practice with the mirror will help you follow these five basic rules:

1. Maintain direct eye contact.

2. Maintain an erect body posture.

3. Speak clearly, audibly, and firmly.

4. Don't whine or use an apologetic tone of voice.

5. Make use of gestures and facial expression for emphasis.

## 6. *Learning How To Listen*

The sixth step of assertiveness training involves learning how to listen. As you practice using your LADDER in real life situations, you will find that sometimes you need to deal with an issue that is important to the other person before he or she will be able to focus on what you have to say. This is especially true when what you want directly conflicts with long unspoken and unmet needs of the listener. Example: "You say you want an hour of silence when you first get home from work? Well, I haven't said this before, because you're working so hard, but I'm ready to tear out my hair after spending the day with the kids. I have needs too, you know." At this point, it might be wise to practice assertive listening.

In listening assertively, you focus your attention on the other person so that you can accurately hear the speaker's opinions, feelings, and wishes. Assertive listening involves three steps:

1. **Prepare.**  Become aware of your own feelings and needs. Are you ready to listen? Are you sure that the other person is really ready to speak?

2. **Listen and clarify.** Giving your full attention to the other person, listen to the speaker's perspective, feelings, and wants. If you are uncertain about one of these three elements, ask the speaker to clarify with more information. Examples: "I'm not quite sure how you view the situation . . . could you say more about it?" "How do you feel about this?" "I don't understand what you want . . . could you be more specific?"

3. **Acknowledge.**  Communicate to the other person that you heard the speaker's position. For example, "I hear you don't want to take on this new project because you're feeling overwhelmed with your current responsibilities and want to catch up." Another way to acknowledge the other person's feelings is to share your own about what has been said: "I'm feeling overwhelmed too, and I feel terrible about having to ask you to do more work."

Assertive listening and assertive expressing go together. Here is a sequence in which both people use assertive listening and expressing skills to solve a problem. John is unhappy about the way Carmen communicates her needs to him.

John:      Is this a good time to talk about something that's bugging me a little? (*Arrange.*)

Carmen:    Okay.

| | |
|---|---|
| *John:* | Yesterday you told me you were feeling cut off and kind of abandoned by me. (*Define.*) I felt like I was doing something horrible to you. I felt very wrong, but totally confused about exactly what I was doing. (*Describe feeling.*) Rather than making general complaints like that, could you say what I'm not doing that you need, or what I could change? (*Express request.*) I think I could be a lot more responsive that way. (*Reinforce.*) |
| *Carmen:* | What was it you needed more information about? (*Clarify.*) |
| *John:* | What you needed me to do, at that moment, to feel closer. |
| *Carmen:* | Okay, so what you're saying is that my talking about my feelings without making any specific requests for change leaves you feeling confused and responsible. (*Acknowledge.*) |
| *John* | Right. |
| *Carmen:* | Well, sometimes I'm just telling you how I feel. I don't know why I feel that way or what to do about it. Telling you is an attempt to open the discussion. (*Redefining problem.*) |
| *John:* | I see. So you really aren't sure what I could do at that point. (*Acknowledge.*) How about just saying you aren't sure and asking what *we* could do about it together? Making it we instead of me would help a lot on my end. (*New request.*) |
| *Carmen:* | That sounds right. I like it. |

Notice that Carmen clarifies and acknowledges before attempting any further explanation of the problem from her point of view. Then, in a non-blaming way, she says why she can't go along with John's request. John, in turn, acknowledges what Carmen has said. He then uses this new information to make a second proposal that works better for Carmen.

Here's the rub. You can't always expect the other person to play by the rules. There are times when you'll have to express and listen assertively in the face of defensive or hostile reactions. Consider the case of Hal and Sara.

| | |
|---|---|
| *Sara:* | I have a problem with the cash projections, can we talk? (*Arrange.*) |
| *Hal:* | Whatever. |
| *Sara:* | Currently you're only running them out to the next three months, and I can't see how sales, inventory, and costs are going to interact six-eight months down the line. (*Define.*) I'm getting pretty nervous about the big printing bills because we don't know if the money will be there. (*Describe feeling.*) Could you run out the cash projection at least six months? (*Express request.*) I think we'd all breathe easier. (*Reinforce.*) |
| *Hal:* | Forget it, Sara. There's no time. I haven't got the bodies in my department to do stuff like that. Take a Valium and cool off. |

| | |
|---|---|
| *Sara:* | How much extra work would it take? (*Clarify.*) |
| *Hal:* | (*loudly*) Forget it, Sara. Forget it, okay? |
| *Sara:* | I hear you. You're overworked and haven't the staff to take on anything extra. (*Acknowledge.*) But I'm wondering how many extra hours of work are involved? (*Clarify.*) |
| *Hal:* | At least twenty. Keep pushing, Sara. I'm up to here with everybody's demands. |
| *Sara:* | I hear how stressed you are. (*Acknowledge.*) If once a month I got a twenty hour bookkeeper from the pool for you, could you handle it? (*New request.*) |
| *Hal:* | Probably, Sara. Let me see the body first. |

In the face of sarcasm and anger, Sara continues to clarify and acknowledge until she understands Hal's problem. She doesn't get sidetracked by hostile resistance. She keeps working to understand Hal's stresses and needs so she can make a new, more acceptable proposal.

## 7. *Arriving at a Workable Compromise*

The seventh step of assertiveness training is learning to arrive at a "workable compromise."

When two people's interests are in dire conflict, a fair compromise that totally satisfies both parties is difficult, if not impossible, to achieve. Instead, look for a workable compromise you both can live with, at least for a while. Although a compromise may naturally emerge in your discussion, sometimes you might need to make a list of all the alternative solutions you can think of. Cross off the ones which are not mutually acceptable. Finally, decide on a compromise you can both live with. This brainstorming process is most effective if you let your imaginations run wild while generating ideas. It's best to agree to review a workable compromise in a specified length of time like a month. At that time, you can examine the results of your changed behavior. If you aren't both sufficiently satisfied, you can renegotiate.

Typical compromise solutions include:

- My way this time, your way next time

- Part of what I want with part of what you want

- Meeting halfway

- If you'll do _____ for me, I'll do _____ for you

- We'll do this one my way, but we'll do _____ your way.

- We'll try my way this time, and if you don't like it you can veto it next time

- My way when I'm doing it, your way when you're doing it

If you feel resistant to brainstorming and making lists of alternatives, try this simpler approach. When a person doesn't want to give you what you want, ask for a counterproposal. If the counterproposal isn't acceptable to you, make a new one of your own. But first do a little assertive listening to uncover the other person's feelings and needs in the situation. Keep going back and forth with counterproposals until something works for both of you.

A second route to compromise is to ask this question: "What would you need from me to feel okay doing this my way?" The answer may surprise you and offer solutions you never thought of.

## 8. *Avoiding Manipulation*

The eighth and final step to becoming an assertive person is learning how to avoid manipulation. Inevitably, you will encounter blocking gambits from those who seek to ignore your assertive requests. The following techniques are proven ways of overcoming the standard blocking gambits.

**Broken record.** When you find that you are dealing with someone who won't take no for an answer or refuses to grant you a reasonable request, you can carefully choose a concise sentence to use as your broken record and say it over and over again. You could say to your insistent four-year-old, "Jeff, I am not going to give you any more candy." You might say to the aggressive used-car salesman, "I am not going to buy a car today; I'm just looking." You might say to the uncooperative store clerk, "I want you to give me back my money for this defective radio." Briefly acknowledge that you have heard the other person's point, and then calmly repeat your Broken Record without getting sidetracked by irrelevant issues. "Yes, but . . . Yes, I know, but my point is . . . I agree, but . . . Yes, but I was saying . . . Right, but I'm still not interested."

**Content-to-process shift.** Shift the focus of the discussion from the topic to an analysis of what is going on between the two of you. ("We're getting off the point now." "We've been derailed into talking about old issues." "You appear to be angry with me.")

**Defusing.** Ignore the content of someone's anger, and put off further discussion until he has calmed down. ("I can see that you are very upset and angry right now. Let's discuss it later this afternoon.")

**Assertive delay.** Put off a response to a challenging statement until you are calm, have more information, or know exactly how you want to respond. ("Yes . . . very interesting point . . . I'll have to reserve judgment on that . . . I don't want to talk about it at this time.")

**Assertive agreement.** Acknowledge criticism with which you agree. You don't need to give an explanation unless you wish to. ("You're right. I did botch the Sudswell account." "Thanks for pointing out that I was smiling when I was trying to say no to that salesman. No wonder I couldn't get rid of him." "You're right, boss, I am half an hour late . . . my car broke down.")

**Clouding.** When someone is putting you down as a person, acknowledge something in the criticism with which you can agree, and ignore the rest. Agree in part: "You're right. I am late with the report." *Agree in the probability*: "You may be right that I am often late." *Agree in the principle* (agreeing with the logic without agreeing with the premise). "If I were late as often as you say, it certainly would be a problem." When clouding, rephrase the critic's words so that you can honestly concur. By giving the appearance of agreeing without promising to change, you soon deplete the critic of any reason to criticize you.

**Assertive inquiry.** Prompt criticism in order to find out what is really bothering the other person. ("I understand you don't like the way I chaired the meeting last night. What is it about it that bothered you? What is it about me that you feel is pushy? What is it about my speaking out that bothers you?")

It is helpful to prepare yourself against a number of typical blocking gambits that will be used to attack and derail your assertive requests. Some of the most troublesome blocking gambits include:

**Laughing it off.** Your assertion is responded to with a joke. ("Only three weeks late? I've got to work on being less punctual!") Use the content-to-process shift ("Humor is getting us off the point") and the Broken Record ("Yes, but . . . ").

**Accusing gambit.** You are blamed for the problem. ("You're always so late cooking dinner, I'm too tired to do the dishes afterward.") Use clouding ("That may be so, but you are still breaking your commitment") or simply disagree ("Eight o'clock is not too late for the dishes").

**The beat-up.** Your assertion is responded to with a personal attack, such as, "Who are you to worry about being interrupted, you're the biggest loudmouth around here." The best strategies to use are assertive irony ("Thank you") in conjunction with the broken record or defusing ("I can see you're angry right now, let's talk about it after the meeting").

**Delaying gambit.** Your assertion is met with, "Not now, I'm too tired" or "Another time, maybe." Use the broken record, or insist on setting a specific time when the problem can be discussed.

**Why gambit.** Every assertive statement is blocked with a series of "why" questions, such as, "Why do you feel that way . . . I still don't know why you don't want to go . . . why did you change your mind?" The best response is to use the content-to-process shift. ("Why isn't the point. The issue is that I'm not willing to go tonight") or the broken record.

**Self-pity gambit.** Your assertion is met with tears and the covert message that you are being sadistic. Try to keep going through your script using assertive agreement ("I know this is causing you pain, but I need to get this resolved").

**Quibbling.** The other person wants to debate with you about the legitimacy of what you feel, or the magnitude of the problem, and so on. Use the content-to-process shift ("We're quibbling now, and have gotten off the main concern") with the assertion of your right to feel the way you do.

**Threats.** You are threatened with statements like, "If you keep harping at me like this, you're going to need another boyfriend." Use assertive inquiry ("What is it about my requests that bothers you?") as well as content-to-process shift ("This seems to be a threat") or defusing.

**Denial.** You are told, "I didn't do that" or "You've really misinterpreted me." Assert what you have observed and experienced, and use clouding ("It may seem that way to you, but I've observed . . . ").

## Further Reading

Alberti, Robert E., and Michael Emmons. 1990. *Your Perfect Right*. rev. ed. San Luis Obispo, CA: Impact Press.

Bower, S. A., and G. H. Bower. 1991. *Asserting Yourself*. Reading, MA: Addison-Wesley.

Butler, Pamela E. 1992. *Self-Assertion for Women*. San Francisco, CA: Harper.

Fensterheim, Herbert, and Jean L. Baer. 1975. *Don't Say Yes When You Want to Say No*. New York: Dell.

Gabor, D. 1994. *Speaking Your Mind in 101 Different Situations*. New York: Simon & Schuster.

Phelps, Stanlee, and Nancy Austin. 1987. *The Assertive Woman*. San Luis Obispo, CA: Impact Press.

Smith, Manuel J. *When I Say No, I Feel Guilty*. 1985. New York: Bantam.

# 18

# Job Stress Management

The classic symptoms of job burnout include pessimism, increased dissatisfaction, absenteeism, and inefficiency at work. While you may not be on the verge of job burnout, you are probably one of the growing majority of Americans who report that their job causes them stress. A 1985 study conducted by the National Center for Health Statistics found that more than half of the workers surveyed experienced "a lot" to "moderate" stress in their jobs in the last two weeks. Job stress accounts for a tremendous amount of personal misery and billions of dollars lost annually in productivity, wages, and medical bills. Americans are waking up to the fact that job stress management makes personal and financial sense.

## What Causes Job Burnout?

Every job includes some built-in difficulties to which the worker is paid to adjust. But job difficulties alone do not cause burnout. Rather, it is the worker's lack of control over his job situation that leads to uncertainty, frustration, reduced motivation, and eventually burnout. For example, you can become demoralized because you are unable to meet the impossible expectations of your boss, because you can't get the support of your co-workers, because you are inadequately trained, or because no matter how well you do your efforts are not recognized.

Even minor factors beyond your control can have a stressful impact. Consider the many unexpected interruptions in the course of your day: special meetings, phone calls, people dropping in, and equipment breakdown. Think about having to "go through channels" and deal with bureaucratic red tape. Think about the faulty air conditioning system or the constant din of machines, elevator music, and voices. Even your daily commute can add to your accumulated stress for the day.

It is a common error to associate only excessive stress with lowered productivity. As early as 1908, Robert Yerkes and John Dodson pointed out that the symptoms of stress underload are quite similar to those of stress overload: reduced efficiency, irritability, a sense of time pressure, diminished motivation, poor judgment, and accidents. We all have a unique "performance zone" within which we experience manageable stress that stimulates our energy, motivation, decision making, and productivity.

In summary, burnout is not simply caused by too much stress in your job. If your job made no demands on you, you would be bored. Job stress management, like stress management in general, involves finding the right types and amounts of challenge to stimulate your interest and performance without overloading you. It also requires managing those distressing areas of your job that are inevitable. Finally, it includes balancing leisure and work-related activities so that they complement one another. Job stress management is a dynamic process over which you can exercise your personal control.

## Symptom Relief

Job stress management is effective in increasing your sense of control in the work setting. Increased feelings of control can improve job-related symptoms of guilt, depression, anxiety, and low self-esteem. Job stress management can also reduce job-related psychosomatic symptoms such as insomnia, ulcers, headaches, eating disorders, and lowered immunity to infection.

## Time for Mastery

The initial assessment of your job stressors and your response to them can be completed in one day. Learning how to respond more effectively to job stress will take at least a month. The habit of effective job stress management may take from two months to a year to integrate into your daily life.

## Ten Steps Toward Managing Your Job Stress

### Step 1. *Identify Your Symptoms of Job Stress*

Instructions: Rate each of the following items in terms of how often the symptom was true for you during the last three months.

0 = *Never*
1 = *Occasionally*
2 = *Somewhat often*
3 = *Frequently*
4 = *Almost always*

_____   1. I feel little enthusiasm for doing my job.

_____   2. I feel tired even with adequate sleep.

_____   3. I feel frustrated in carrying out my responsibilities at work.

_____   4. I am moody, irritable, or impatient over small inconveniences.

_____   5. I want to withdraw from the constant demands on my time and energy.

_____   6. I feel negative, futile, or depressed about my job.

_____   7. My decision-making ability seems less than usual.

_____   8. I think that I am not as efficient as I should be.

_____   9. The quality of my work is less than it should be.

_____   10. I feel physically, emotionally, or spiritually depleted.

_____   11. My resistance to illness is lowered.

_____   12. My interest in sex is lowered.

_____   13. I am eating more or less, drinking more coffee, tea, or sodas, smoking more cigarettes, or using more alcohol or drugs in order to cope with my job.

_____   14. I am feeling emotionally callous about the problems and needs of others.

_____   15. My communication with my boss, co-workers, friends, or family seems strained.

_____   16. I am forgetful.

_____   17. I am having difficulty concentrating.

_____   18. I am easily bored.

_____   19. I feel a sense of dissatisfaction, of something wrong or missing.

_____   20. When I ask myself why I get up and go to work, the only answer that occurs is "my paycheck."

If you scored 0 to 25, you are probably coping adequately with the stress of your job. If you scored 26 to 40, you are suffering from job stress and would be wise to take preventative action. If you scored 41 to 55, you need to take preventative action to avoid job burnout. If you scored 56 to 80, you are burning out and must develop a comprehensive job stress management plan.

## Step 2. Identify the Sources of Your Job Stress

Instructions: Rate your experience in your job during the past year, using the following 5-point scale:

0 = *Never*
1 = *Occasionally*

2 = *Somewhat often*
3 = *Frequently*
4 = *Almost always*

## Lack of Control

_____    1.  I lack the authority to carry out certain responsibilities.

_____    2.  I feel trapped in a situation without any real options.

_____    3.  I am unable to influence decisions that affect me.

_____    4.  There are a lot of requirements that get in the way of my doing certain tasks.

_____    5.  I can't solve the problems assigned to me.

_____    Subtotal

## Information Gap

_____    6.  I am unsure about the responsibilities of my job.

_____    7.  I don't have enough information to carry out certain tasks.

_____    8.  I am underqualified for certain tasks I'm expected to do.

_____    9.  Others I work with are not clear about what I do.

_____    10.  I don't understand the criteria used to evaluate my performance.

_____    Subtotal

## Cause and Effect

_____    11.  There is no relationship between how I perform and how I am rated.

_____    12.  I sense that popularity and politics are more important than performance.

_____    13.  I don't know what my supervisor thinks of my performance.

_____    14.  I don't know what I am doing right and what I am doing wrong.

_____    15.  There is no relationship between how I perform and how I am rated.

_____    Subtotal

## Conflict

_____    16.  I am expected to satisfy conflicting needs.

_____    17. I disagree with co-workers.

_____    18.  I disagree with my supervisor.

_____    19. I am caught in the middle.

_____    20. I can't get what I need to get the job done.

_____    Subtotal

## Blocked Career

_____    21. I feel pessimistic about opportunities for advancement or growth in my job.

_____    22. My supervisor or boss is critical.

_____    23. I feel unaccepted by the people I work with.

_____    24. My good work is not noticed or appreciated.

_____    25. My progress on the job seems less than it could be.

_____    Subtotal

## Alienation

_____    26. I experience little meaning in my work.

_____    27. I feel unsupported by my co-workers or boss.

_____    28. My values seem at odds with those of the management.

_____    29. The organization seems insensitive to my individuality.

_____    30. I find I cannot be myself at work because I feel different from my co-workers.

_____    Subtotal

## Overload

_____    31. I have too much to do and too little time in which to do it.

_____    32. I take on new responsibilities without letting go of any of the old ones.

_____    33. My job seems to interfere with my personal life.

_____    34. I must work on my own time (during breaks, lunch, at home, and so on).

_____    35. The size of my workload interferes with how well I do it.

_____    Subtotal

## Underload

_____    36. I have too little to do.

_____   37. I feel overqualified for the work I actually do.

_____   38. My work is not challenging.

_____   39. Most of my work is very routine.

_____   40. I miss contact with people in my job.

_____   Subtotal

## Environment

_____   41. I find my work environment unpleasant.

_____   42. I lack the privacy I need to concentrate on my work.

_____   43. Some aspects of my environment seem hazardous.

_____   44. I have too much or too little contact with people.

_____   45. I have to deal with many little hassles.

_____   Subtotal

## Value Conflict

_____   46. I must do things that are against my better judgement.

_____   47. I must make compromises in my values.

_____   48. My family and friends do not respect what I do.

_____   49. I observe my co-workers doing things that I don't approve of.

_____   50. The organization that I work for pressures employees to do things that are unethical or unsafe.

_____   Subtotal

_____   Grand total

If your score is over 100, you have more than an average number of job stressors. If your score is 130 or higher, the number of job stressors is unusually high. Identify the categories in which you scored 12 or more. In addition to dealing with your specific major stressors, you will want to give consideration to these general areas.

## Step 3. Identify How You Respond to Your Specific Job Stressors

What are your specific job stressors and how do you tend to respond to them? In addition to referring to your responses on the job stress inventory, reflect back over your recent experiences at work. In the far left-hand column, list your specific stressors. For each stressful item, write down your feelings when it occurs, what you say to yourself about it, and what you do in response to it.

For example, Patty, a computer programmer, wrote down the specific stressors in her job and her response to them in the following shorthand manner:

| Your Job Stressor | Your Feelings | Your Thoughts | Your Behavior |
|---|---|---|---|
| Programming | Bored, numb | "Non-stop programming makes Patty a dull girl." | Plodding, inefficient; eat sweets, drink coffee |
| Deadlines | Anxious | "I'll never make it!" | Work faster and longer; mistakes |
| Meetings | Annoyed, impatient | "What a waste, I've got work to do." | Critical, resistant to suggestions |
| Vague supervisor | Insecure, confused, annoyed | "What does it take to please this jerk?" | Guess what he wants; complain |
| Chatty co-worker | Angry | "Why does he keep interrupting me? He's so inconsiderate!" | Respond politely and return to my own work |
| Uncooperative secretary | Angry, frustrated, dissatisfied | "She's lazy, slow, and utterly useless." | Refuse to talk to her |
| No privacy | Annoyed | "Hard to focus." | Tense my muscles; neck and backache |
| Terminal | Strained, tired | "I wish I didn't have to do this." | Eye strain, headache |
| Down time | Frustrated, refreshed | "Damn, I lost it!" | Eat, drink coffee, socialize |
| No raise | Angry, frustrated | "I deserve better than this!" | Complain bitterly |

**Exercise:**  List your specific stressors and how you respond to them. Use as little or much detail as you need.

| *Your Job Stressor* | *Your Feelings* | *Your Thoughts* | *Your Behavior* |
|---|---|---|---|
| _____ | _____ | _____ | _____ |
| _____ | _____ | _____ | _____ |
| _____ | _____ | _____ | _____ |
| _____ | _____ | _____ | _____ |
| _____ | _____ | _____ | _____ |
| _____ | _____ | _____ | _____ |
| _____ | _____ | _____ | _____ |
| _____ | _____ | _____ | _____ |
| _____ | _____ | _____ | _____ |
| _____ | _____ | _____ | _____ |
| _____ | _____ | _____ | _____ |
| _____ | _____ | _____ | _____ |
| _____ | _____ | _____ | _____ |
| _____ | _____ | _____ | _____ |
| _____ | _____ | _____ | _____ |

Now that you have written out your specific job stressors and how you typically respond to them, review your list and see if any patterns emerge. When Patty did this, she noticed the following patterns:

1.  I respond to boredom and frustration by eating and drinking coffee.

2.  Working at a computer terminal for long periods of time and having to concentrate in spite of a lack of privacy causes me to have a variety of physical and emotional symptoms of stress.

3.  I waste time because I'm not assertive enough to ask questions of my supervisor, say no to my office mate, or firmly request secretarial support.

4.  I tend to be highly critical of myself, others, and my environment, but rarely do anything constructive to improve my situation. I can see why I feel chronically irritated and tense at work.

In looking over your list of specific job stressors and your responses to them, what patterns did you pick out?

1. _____
   _____
   _____

2. _____
   _____
   _____

3. _____
   _____
   _____

4. _____
   _____
   _____

## Step 4. Set Goals To Respond More Effectively to Your Job Stressors

Now that you have identified your patterns of stress, you can begin to formulate a more effective plan for responding to the stressors that you can anticipate. Maybe you can avoid some of them altogether. Perhaps you can be better prepared for them when they happen. The name of the game is taking more control. And this is where you begin to do it.

You will probably want to make changes in one or more of these general areas:

1. Change the external stressor (quit the job, assertively tell the boss not to overload you, take regular breaks, reorganize your time).

2. Change your thoughts (turn off the job when you go home, alter your perfectionist attitude, stop assuming that you are responsible for others' problems).

3. Change physically (relax, exercise, eat properly, get sufficient sleep).

When you are designing goals for yourself, remember the following guidelines. Useful goals are generally:

- Specific
- Observable
- Achievable within a certain time frame
- Broken down into small intermediate steps
- Compatible with long-term goals

- Written down in simple self-contract form
- Reevaluated at specified intervals
- Rewarded when achieved

**Example:** Patty decided to set a new, more effective response to each of her four stress patterns as a goal for herself. She wrote out the following self-contract:

---

I, Patty Bowers, agree to change the following four old patterns of responding to stress as follows:

*Patterns 1 and 2.* Rather than eating or drinking coffee when I am bored or frustrated, I will take regular breaks once an hour in which I either do a brief relaxation exercise or get up and walk around and talk to people. I'll take advantage of flex time and go to an aerobics class three days a week and run personal errands two days a week in the middle of the day. I will eat three nutritious meals, rather than snack on junk.

*Pattern 3.* I will take a one-day workshop on Assertiveness Training and ask my supervisor more questions until I am sure I know what he wants. I also will tell my co-worker not to interrupt me with small talk, other than when I get up and walk around. I will assertively ask the secretary for help.

*Pattern 4.* I will take each one of my critical thoughts and turn it into a constructive action thought. For instance, rather than saying about meetings, "What a waste, I have work to do," I could say, "Whew, a break from programming! What constructive contribution can I make here?"

I will revaluate my progress for each goal on a weekly basis. I plan to spend a weekend at a local hot springs as a reward for changing these four patterns for one month.

*Patty Bowers*

---

If it would increase your motivation, make this contract with a friend or co-worker. Then report back weekly on your progress toward each goal.

**Exercise:** Using the form on the next page, write out goals to modify a few of your responses to specific stressors in your life in the form of a self-contract.

## Step 5. Motivate Yourself

Create specific rewards for every goal you establish:

- Give yourself one point for each relaxation break you take. 25 points means a new dress or car radio.
- You'll buy that book you've wanted to read after clarifying with your boss some of his expectations.

I, _____ , agree to:

1. _____
   _____
   _____

2. _____
   _____
   _____

3. _____
   _____
   _____

I will monitor my progress every _____ (*length of time*).

I will reward myself with _____ .

- You'll rent that spicy new murder mystery after you tell John not to interrupt you when you're writing.

- You'll call Rebekah for a little chat after you write that memo requesting flex time.

- After you've requested a limit on the number of cases you're expected to take, you'll call Art and invite him to dinner at Walker's.

- You'll assign one dollar toward a shopping spree for each stress-producing thought you catch and change (see step 6).

Here's a way of motivating stress reducing activities that you normally feel too rushed to do. Sometimes a work-related task that you enjoy has no immediate pay-off, so you postpone it and focus your attention on tasks that have immediate deadlines. Such was the case with Marty who kept putting off writing a professional article he had outlined two years earlier. Administrative responsibilities swallowed up his time. He decided to deal with the problem by setting aside half an hour each morning to work on his article before letting himself tackle the demands of the day. He used the motivating power of immediate deadlines to prompt him to accomplish something fun and rewarding.

## Step 6. Change Your Thinking

Job stress occurs because your thoughts trigger a painful emotional reaction. There are three generic thoughts that do you in:

1. I've got to do _____ (*a certain task*) _____ (*perfectly*) (*on time*) (*so my boss will be pleased*) or (*something painful*) will happen.

2. They're doing this to me and it's not fair.

3. I'm trapped here.

Thought 1 makes you anxious, thought 2 triggers anger, and thought 3 generates depression. You can do something about these thoughts and the job stress they create. Right now, list the things you tell yourself about your job that fit into each of the above three categories.

**Category 1**

_____

_____

_____

**Category 2**

_____

_____

_____

**Category 3**

_____

_____

_____

Here's how you cope with these stress-producing thoughts.

1.  Make a *realistic appraisal* of what exactly will happen if the task isn't on time, flawless, or totally pleasing to your boss. A realistic appraisal means looking at what has happened to yourself and others in the past when tasks such as this were late, had errors, and so on. Realistic also means being specific. It's time to get rid of that vague sense of doom. Exactly what is your boss likely to say to you? What, if anything, is likely to happen to you?

Now complete this sentence: "If _____ isn't (*perfect, on time, totally acceptable*), the boss's response will likely be _____ . I can handle it."

Mentally repeat this coping statement each time you catch yourself catastrophizing about vague and dire consequences. Note: If you have no idea how your boss would respond, ask him. "If I'm a day late with the Crocker report, will that be a problem?"

2.  There's absolutely no good that can come from blaming anybody for your job stress. Blaming maintains your sense of being stuck and helpless. You see yourself as a victim who has no alternatives and has lost the power of choice. Blaming triggers anger and stress hormones such as noradrenalin that deplete your energy and over the long run damage your health.

Reread the chapter on Refuting Irrational Ideas: "The conditions for things or people to be otherwise than they are don't exist . . . Things are what they are because of a long series of causal events." Saying to yourself that your boss or the company president *should* act differently is like saying Nixon should never have authorized Watergate. The conditions necessary for Nixon to be fearful and obsessed with secrecy existed, the means and opportunity existed. His values, needs, ambitions, advisors, and personal history all pushed him toward the break-in.

No one is *supposed* to take care of or protect you on this job. They are all busy taking care of and protecting themselves. This is natural. This is the inescapable fact of working life. So what can you say to yourself to avoid chronic blaming and anger?

The first thing you can do is ask yourself this question: "What steps can I take to change the conditions I don't like?" If you can't think of any way to change the job, you have two rational choices. You must either adapt to and accept the conditions or look for another job.

If you decide to accept the current situation, the second coping statement you can make is: " _____ is acting exactly as he should. The conditions necessary for him to act this way (*his needs and coping strategies to meet those needs, past successes and failures, fears, attitudes toward our relationship*) all exist, and this is why he did _____ (*to*) (*with*) me."

3. You are not trapped. You may have difficult choices, but you aren't trapped. Right now the pain of this job seems less than the pain associated with other available choices. Is this really true? Here's a chance to list your options for change. What specific steps could you take to change a major stress producer on your job?

_____

_____

What would you risk in attempting that change?

_____

_____

What steps could you take to change jobs altogether?

_____

_____

What would you risk in attempting that change? (See step 10, "Know When to Quit," for help in exploring these fears.)

_____

_____

Rather than "I'm trapped," the more accurate thing to say to yourself is: "I *choose* to stay with the current conditions on this job because right now it seems less painful than _____ _____ (*the steps to change*). I may choose differently in the future."

## Step 7: Deal With Your Boss

Since one of the primary sources of job stress is ambiguity about what is expected of you, the time has come for a conference with your boss. Here are some suggested questions to use during the interview. The main thing you want to do is to get enough information so you no longer have to mind-read his or her reactions.

1. What is expected of me in my position?

2. Where is this organization going and how do I fit into the plan in the near and long-term future?

3. How am I doing? What are my strengths? What areas do I need to improve?

4. What additional skills or education do I need to progress?

5. What happens if something goes wrong? What can I expect from you if a problem develops?

6. If I continue my current level of performance, what can I expect?

If your boss is a clear, straightforward communicator, the above discussion may significantly reduce your job stress. But if your boss is indirect, irascible, or highly demanding, you have more work to do. You'll have to learn what motivates him or her and how to use that to your benefit.

Look beneath the surface of your boss's actions to understand what motivates him. Does your boss have a difficult boss or a miserable home life or does your boss also find you impossible? Is he just marking time until he retires, and thus views any new ideas as unnecessary or threatening? Is he a guy who needs to be liked, and therefore always says nice things about you but fails to give constructive criticism? Is he the silent type who never lets you know what he expects? Does he lack management skills? Is he buried under his own heavy workload? Or is it something else? Is he a slave driver who was raised to expect perfection of himself and others? If your boss insists on always being right and criticizes any idea that is not his own, he may be suffering from low self-esteem and secretly crave recognition and approval.

You can often use your knowledge of what motivates your boss to get what you want. For example, with a critical boss you can satisfy some of his need for recognition by praising his successes. You can have a candid talk with him about how his put-downs make you feel and how you need positive feedback as well as constructive criticism. If your boss is a perfectionistic slave driver, it would take some of the pressure off of him if certain decision-making responsibilities were shifted to a committee or delegated down. One powerful, yet relatively low-risk way to give a slave driver feedback is in the form of a questionnaire filled out by all his employees. If your boss is the silent type, you may need to confront him regarding his expectations of you in the job.

**Exercise:** Describe what is difficult about your boss's behavior:

_____

_____

_____

Describe what you think motivates his behavior:

_____

_____

_____

Describe how you might use your understanding of what motivates him to anticipate his next move and deal with him more effectively:

_____

_____

_____

Changing your boss is unlikely; changing yourself is the easiest way to improve your relationship with him. Through trial and error, you can develop strategies for effectively influencing your boss. Perhaps you will look for common ground upon which to build your relationship. Maybe you will decide to support your boss on points that are important to him and confront him only on the points that are vital to you, and only when he is in a good mood.

## Step 8. When in Conflict, Negotiate

Whether you disagree with your boss regarding your salary or with your co-workers about who is going to get the coffee, you need to present your position and negotiate a compromise you can all live with.

Read chapter 17 on "Assertiveness Training" for a more in-depth understanding of how to express your opinions, feelings, and wants as you negotiate for change. The following is a brief four-step model for you to follow when you want to discuss specific problems with your supervisor or co-workers with the aim of arriving at a mutually acceptable outcome.

1. State the problem (what you perceive to be the cause of your stress).

2. State how you feel about the problem.

3. State how it affects your productivity and motivation.

4. State win-win solutions (both sides of the conflict get something positive from your solution).

For example, Randy, a creative high school teacher, was refused compensation for the time he spent developing new courses.

Randy told his boss, "Ever since I realized I wouldn't receive money for my course development work, my enthusiasm for teaching has deteriorated. I think my students have gained tremendously from my special classes. They're now suffering as a result of my lost motivation. It's important to me and the school to continue creating new classes and to be compensated in some way. Since the money isn't available, I would be satisfied if I could take one class period each day for a semester to develop my new class."

The principal's response was, "I can't spare you a period every day, but I would agree to three hours a week." Randy accepted this workable compromise.

**Exercise:** Write out a script to negotiate a win-win solution to a job related conflict or problem, using the following four-part model.

1. State a work related problem:

   _____

   _____

2. State how you feel about the problem:

   _____

   _____

3. State how it affects your motivation and productivity:

   _____

   _____

4. State a win-win solution:

   _____

   _____

## Step 9. Pace and Balance Yourself

Do you pace yourself at work? If you are a sprinter, you can afford to throw everything you've got into the race. This is because at the end of a fast short run you know you have plenty of time to recover from your intense effort. Most jobs, however, require you to be more like a marathon runner who must pace himself in order to get across the finish line in a timely manner without collapsing. Like the marathon runner, you need to maintain a certain detachment from the immediate demands of your job so that you will remember to reserve enough energy to deal with what you anticipate down the road as well as any surprises.

Here are eight tips for pacing and balancing yourself.

1. Pay attention to your natural rhythm to determine when you tend to perform optimally and schedule your most difficult tasks for then.

2. Try to set up your day so you shift back and forth between pleasant and more difficult tasks. After something tough, make an effort to schedule something you enjoy.

3. Schedule inviolate periods of time into your day for work-related tasks that are pleasurable, even though not terribly productive. Try to do this even when you feel rushed.

4. Take advantage of your coffee breaks and lunches to do things that will reverse the stress response. For example, go to a quiet place and do a relaxation exercise. A ten-minute brisk walk will give you as much energy as a cup of coffee. A light conversation with your co-workers will release tension and may be just what you need to get a fresh perspective on a problem that was weighing you down.

5. If you are fortunate enough to have a flexible schedule, consider taking a long break in the middle of the day to do aerobic exercise, a relaxation exercise, or personal errands.

6. Take mini-breaks throughout your day to reduce or prevent symptoms of tension and stress. These breaks never take more than a few minutes and pay for themselves in terms of increased mental alertness and productivity. See the Brief Combination Techniques chapter for exercises appropriate to short breaks.

7. Choose leisure activities that balance the unique stresses of your job.

| If your job requires: | Consider a complementary leisure activity such as: |
| --- | --- |
| Much sitting or mental concentration | Aerobic exercise |
| Mindless repetition | Intellectually challenging hobbies and interests |
| A controlled environment | Hiking in nature; adventure |
| Boring tasks or no recognition | Competitive or achievement-oriented activities |
| Responding to people demands | Solitary activities |
| Dealing with conflicts | Peaceful activities |
| Working alone | Social activities |

8. Carefully plan the timing and type of vacations that you take to maximize their recuperative effects.

## Step 10. Know When To Quit

After making a genuine effort to modify your own thinking, behavior, and work conditions, you may find that your job is still dissatisfying. It may be that you are just not suited to your job. Ask yourself whether the price you are paying emotionally is worth the material benefits. Visualize yourself continuing in the same manner for another five years. Will your job make you a stronger, happier person in five years or a weaker, more miserable person? Your time is precious. Is this how you want to spend it?

**Exercise:** Describe your ideal job. Include your job title, your job responsibilities, your boss, your co-workers, your environment, and the management.

_____

_____

_____

_____

_____

_____

_____

Although you may have yearned to quit for years, you probably have several fears that stand in the way of making your move. Perhaps you think that you are too old or too young, too inexperienced or over-qualified, the wrong sex, or that you interview poorly, or there aren't any jobs that you want out there, or the economy is going to hell and you're lucky just to be employed.

**Exercise:** List your fears about leaving your job:

_____

_____

_____

_____

_____

Each one of your fears is a barrier that stands between you and finding your ideal job. Turn each one of your fears into a goal designed to get around the barrier. For example, if the fear is that you are too old, your goal statement might be: "I will talk to someone my age who has a job like my ideal one and find out if age really makes a difference." If your fear is that you will do poorly in an interview, your goal statement could be, "I will take an interview class and improve my skills."

Now your turn:

My fear: _____

My goal statement: _____

_____

_____

My fear: _____

My goal statement: _____

_____

_____

My fear: _____

My goal statement: _____

_____

_____

Carefully explore your alternatives. Looking at your options can either make you realize how good you have it or motivate you to plan for change.

## Further Reading

Davis, Martha. 1984. "Job Stress Management." In *Relax: The Stress Reduction System.* Richmond, CA: Synapse Software Corporation. (Parts of this chapter were duplicated with the permission of the author.)

Kemper, Donald, Jim Giuffre, and Gene Drabinski. *Pathways: A Success Guide for a Healthy Life.* Boise, ID: Healthwise, Inc., 1983.

Potter, Beverly A. 1987. *Preventing Job Burnout: Transforming Work Pressures Into Productivity.* Los Altos, CA: Crisp Publications.

Veninga, Robert L., and James P. Spradley. 1981. *The Work/Stress Connection: How To Cope With Job Burnout.* Boston, MA.: Little, Brown.

# 19

# Nutrition

Eating is one of the natural joys in life, but it is not without its stresses. Preparing and anticipating a meal and enjoying its colors, aromas, and tastes are delightful ways of giving yourself pleasure as well as taking good care of yourself. Since meals are often a time to relax and socialize, they can help to reduce stress. Most cultures celebrate holidays and the passages of life with feasting; these times bring people together and give life meaning. Unfortunately, the foods that people eat for pleasure are not always nutritionally sound. Eating right is a learned skill and not something that just comes naturally.

America's love affair with snack foods has led some to joke that the four food groups are candy, cookies, coke, and chips. The average American diet, with its emphasis on convenience foods, often does contain too much fat, sugar, and sodium. Obesity is only one of the risks run by physically inactive people who eat a high-fat, high-calorie diet. These habits also increase the danger of degenerative joint diseases and high blood pressure, and research indicates that diets high in fat may contribute to cardiovascular disease and some cancers.

This chapter will help you assess your present eating habits and provide you with guidelines for a healthy diet. You can compare your current diet with these recommendations and set goals for retraining your eating habits. By taking charge of your nutritional health, you can enjoy healthy eating. You will find that it is not hard to eat a balanced diet, even if you are not a chef at heart.

## Symptom Relief

A healthy body responds better to the inevitable stresses of life, and good nutrition is a building block of good health. Eating well can help prevent or control high blood pressure, heart disease, indigestion, constipation, hypoglycemia, diabetes, and obesity. Good eating habits may also reduce irritability, PMS, headaches, and fatigue.

## Time for Mastery

Plan to keep track of your food intake for three days. After reading the guidelines for a healthy diet, you will go on to compare them with your own eating habits and decide what changes you want to make in your diet. You can begin to apply the recommendations in this chapter in a matter of hours. To make lasting changes in your diet, plan on *gradually* introducing a few changes at a time that you can stick with for a minimum of one month.

## Ten Steps to Positive Eating

The first five of these ten steps to positive eating follow the format of the food guide pyramid illustrated below, starting at the top of the pyramid and working toward the base. The top represents the fat, sugar, and salt that we tend to overindulge in because of the flavor and fun that they add to our diets. The middle level of the pyramid represents milk, meat, eggs, legumes, and nuts, which provide protein. The bottom level contains fruit and vegetables, and the base represents grains like bread, rice, cereal, and pasta. The last five of the ten steps cover weight control, caffeine, alcohol, vitamins, and tips for making food preparation and eating less stressful.

### 1. *Cut Back on Fats*

Despite all the bad press that fat receives, the average American still ingests 37 to 42 percent of their calories from fat, instead of the recommended 20 to 30 percent. We talk about cutting fat, but when we get hungry we reach for our old high-fat favorites, despite the presence

## Recommended food guide pyramid versus common food pyramid.

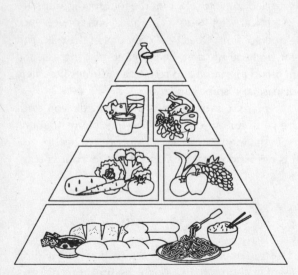

Recommended Pyramid                    Common Pyramid

Source: U.S. Department of Agriculture.

of so many alternatives. The food industry has come up with dozens of new lower fat snack and cookie products to help you make the change (and fruit is still one of the best low-fat snacks). Any bookstore has shelves full of low-fat cookbooks that offer a menu of tasty and creative dishes. Fat-free salad dressings or flavored vinegars provide still another attractive way to reduce the fat in your diet. Even those with no time to cook can fall back on "lean" frozen entree products (but be sure to check the label and select items with three grams or less of fat per serving).

There are three kinds of fat. Saturated fat is solid at room temperature and usually of animal origin. Examples are meat fat, butter, and Crisco. Unsaturated or monosaturated fat is liquid at room temperature but solidifies when chilled, as do olive oil and margarine. Polyunsaturated fats like corn oil and safflower oil remain liquid even when refrigerated. Although the exact relation of fats to hypertension and heart disease is still controversial, the most widely accepted theory is that saturated fats contribute to heart disease and strokes by elevating the body's cholesterol level.

**How do you score on fat intake?** Answer the following questions by circling the number in the column that best describes how often you select or limit the foods listed on the scorecard. Add up the numbers you circled for your total score.

## Your Fat Scorecard

| Your fat score: Do you . . . ? | Rarely | Often | Almost always |
| --- | --- | --- | --- |
| Choose lean meat, chicken, or fish? | 1 | 5 | 10 |
| Eat high-fat meats like bacon, lunch meats, or sausage? | 10 | 5 | 1 |
| Limit eggs to four yolks per week? | 1 | 5 | 10 |
| Read labels and select foods with less than three grams of fat per serving? | 1 | 5 | 10 |
| Choose low-fat or nonfat dairy products? | 1 | 5 | 10 |
| Limit fried foods? | 1 | 5 | 10 |
| Choose doughnuts, croissants, or sweet rolls for breakfast? | 10 | 5 | 1 |
| Choose reduced-fat or fat-free products when they are available? | 1 | 5 | 10 |
| Limit margarine, butter, salad dressings, and sauces on foods? | 1 | 5 | 10 |
| Balance a high-fat dinner with a low-fat breakfast and lunch? | 1 | 5 | 10 |

**Scoring.** If you scored 10 to 59 points, you can do better. At 60 to 79 points, you're on your way. If you scored over 80 points, keep up the good work!

## 2. *Avoid Too Much Sugar*

Americans have a sweet tooth. If you've been abroad, you've probably noticed that American desserts tend to be much sweeter than Mexican or European desserts. Including table sugar, sugar in soft drinks, canned foods, baked goods, and other sweets, the average American eats 130 pounds of sugar and sweeteners annually. And many of these items provide few nutrients.

As children, we were given sweets to comfort us. So now, when we are stressed, we still reach for cookies, candy, or sweets. Studies indicate that women are more likely to seek solace in sweets than men. Other evidence suggests that sweets trigger the release of endorphins, natural opiates that create euphoric feelings. Though sugar may provide a temporary "high," it also stimulates the pancreas to secrete insulin to process the sugar. In some people, the pancreas overreacts and secretes excess insulin. The result is hypoglycemia, a condition characterized by dizziness, irritability, nausea, and hunger pangs that may in turn prompt another sweet treat.

Cravings for sweets are better satisfied with a piece of fruit. Fruit provides the complex sugars, fiber, and vitamins that sugar will not.

**Clues for cutting sugar:**

- Use less sugar, raw sugar, honey, and syrup.
- Eat fewer foods that contain sugar such as candy, cookies, and soft drinks.
- Select fresh fruit or fruits canned in juice or light syrup.
- Read labels and avoid foods listing sucrose, glucose, maltose, dextrose, lactose, or fructose as one of their first four ingredients.

## 3. *Limit Sodium Intake*

Sodium is an essential mineral, but adults in the United States ingest about ten to twenty times more sodium than the body needs. Sodium is used to regulate body fluids, maintain pH balance, and control nerve and muscle activities. Although our major sodium sources are table salt (composed of 40 percent sodium and 60 percent chloride) and processed foods, sodium is also a natural component of milk, cheese, meats, and bread. A single slice of bread actually provides the minimum daily requirement for salt (230 milligrams). Recommended sodium intake is 3,000 milligrams daily. A low-sodium diet of 2,000 milligrams is often prescribed for people with high blood pressure.

Though research is inconclusive, a high intake of sodium correlates with high blood pressure and increased risk of stroke. Since stress also aggravates these conditions, you will be wise to reduce your salt intake. Salt also increases edema, an excess accumulation of fluid that adds to the stress of PMS.

**Tips for shaking the salt habit:**

- Avoid salty snacks like chips, pretzels, and nuts.

- Limit your intake of salty condiments like soy sauce, pickles, and cheese.

- Restrict use of cured meats, sausages, and bacon.

- Learn to savor less salt and to substitute spices and herbs.

- Do not cook with salt and add little or no salt at the table.

- Read labels carefully and avoid foods with salt or sodium listed in the first three or four ingredients.

## 4. *Eat a Variety of Foods*

You need over forty nutrients for optimum health. These are classified as macronutrients (proteins, carbohydrates, and fats) and micronutrients (vitamins and minerals). As the names suggest, you need the former in larger quantities and the latter in smaller amounts. While an excess of macronutrients will lead to weight gain, an excess of micronutrients may actually be toxic for you, or at least a waste of the money you spend on unnecessary vitamin or mineral supplements.

There is no perfect food. Even milk, which provides the backbone of a baby's diet, does not supply vitamin C or iron (which is why we include juice and cereal among baby's first foods). Although natural foods are favored by many health-conscious individuals, these can sometimes have toxic components. Again, varying your diet helps to maximize your nutrients and minimize your exposure to any one toxic substance or contaminant.

A wide variety of foods supply a wide variety of nutrients. Level two of the pyramid adds protein to the diet, but may provide too much fat. The best precaution is to select low-fat or nonfat meat and dairy products whenever possible. Read labels and choose items that have less than three grams of fat per serving. Using beans and legumes liberally in your diet will help keep protein up and fat down. But don't limit your choices based on erroneous information. Despite the widespread perception that fish is a better source of protein than red meat, some fish actually has more fat than lean red meat, and red meat also contains the iron that most women need. Informed food preparation can also help. Take the skin off chicken, since the skin alone on a chicken breast has five grams of fat. Bake, broil, or barbecue to reduce fat.

Level three of the pyramid reminds us to eat at least five fruits and vegetables daily for the valuable fiber and vitamins they provide. An appropriate serving is usually half a cup. Add up juice at breakfast, an apple for lunch, and a potato, a salad, and a vegetable for dinner, and your five servings are taken care of for the day. Spaghetti sauce for dinner is the equal of one to two servings of tomato all by itself. Make "five a day" your rule and remember to follow it.

The pyramid base is composed of bread, rice, and cereal and pasta products, all variants of the proverbial "staff of life." Six to eleven servings are suggested daily. That may seem like a lot, but it really isn't. Many people eat two servings of cereal at breakfast. A sandwich provides two more servings of bread, and a plate of spaghetti easily provides three to four more "servings" of pasta of a half a cup each. A few pretzels for a snack is another serving. Total: nine servings.

## 5. *Eat More Complex Carbohydrates*

Eating foods with adequate starch and fiber will add to your sense of well-being. You'll notice that complex carbohydrates and fiber make meals filling and satisfying. Eating lots of fresh fruits and vegetables is also good for your peace of mind, since these "power foods" contain the fiber, vitamins, minerals, and nutrients that can protect you against chronic illnesses, including diabetes, cancer, and heart disease.

Choose whole grain breads or pastas more often. Enriched grain products restore the known nutrients that may be removed by milling. Yet although some enriched foods actually provide more nutrients than natural foods, unrefined foods may well contain nutrients that we have not yet discovered. When you do buy refined foods, be sure they are enriched to restore the B vitamins and iron lost in milling.

Evidence continues to build that dietary fiber (including cellulose, gums, pectin, and lignin) is an essential component of a healthy diet. Fiber helps to reduce constipation by increasing stool bulk and water absorption, to control blood sugar and blood lipids by binding nutrients, and to decrease stool transit time, thus reducing the risk of colon cancer and diverticulitis. Unfortunately, although the recommended intake of dietary fiber is 25 to 40 grams daily, the average American consumes only 5 to 10 grams. For most of us, fresh vegetables and fruits and whole grains and legumes are the chief sources of fiber in our diets. You can supplement your fiber intake by increasing your use of legumes and bran products or by adding bran to homemade foods. Plan to increase fiber gradually, as rapid increases may lead to bloating and flatulence.

## Dietary Fiber in Common Foods

| Food group | Dietary fiber content |
|---|---|
| Legumes and bran cereals | 5 to 8 grams per serving |
| Fruits and vegetables | 2.5 grams per serving |
| Grains and starches | 2.5 grams per serving |
| Nuts | 2.5 grams per ounce |

Source: *Journal of the American Dietetic Association.*

Carbohydrates also seem to function as edible tranquilizers. They contain tryptophan, an amino acid that stimulates the production of serotonin in the brain. Serotonin has a calming effect that eases tension and may cause drowsiness. Is this the explanation for that happy full feeling that a big spaghetti dinner usually seems to create?

## 6. *Attain or Maintain Your Ideal Weight*

What happens when the infant or toddler cries and receives a cookie in response? The child learns that eating is a comfort, that it soothes troubles away. Another way of stating this lesson is to say that he or she learns to eat not as a response to the internal stimulus of hunger, but as the result of external stimuli or cues. And now, as adults, we eat because it's lunch time, or because we smell pizza cooking, or because we pass an ice cream shop in the mall. We eat because we're tired or bored or angry. None of these responses to the world around us have a direct connection to what our bodies need.

Positive eating means paying attention to internal hunger cues. This is so because people who eat in response to external cues are more likely to become overweight. Remember that overeating stresses your body and that carrying extra weight around is a continuing physiological strain. The psychological stress of an overweight body image can be even more pervasively damaging. Healthy Weights for Men and Women

## Healthy Weights for Men and Women

| Height | Men | Women |
|--------|-----|-------|
| 4'10" | | 91-199 lbs. |
| 4'11" | | 94-122 lbs. |
| 5'0" | | 96- 125 lbs. |
| 5'1" | | 99-128 lbs. |
| 5'2" | 112-141 lbs. | 102-131 lbs. |
| 5'3" | 115-144 lbs. | 105-134 lbs. |
| 5'4" | 118-148 lbs. | 108-138 lbs. |
| 5'5" | 121-152 lbs. | 111-142 lbs. |
| 5'6" | 124-156 lbs. | 114-146 lbs. |
| 5'7" | 128-161 lbs. | 118-150 lbs. |
| 5'8" | 132-166 lbs. | 122-154 lbs. |
| 5'9" | 136-170 lbs. | 126-158 lbs. |
| 5'10" | 140-174 lbs. | 130-163 lbs. |
| 5'11" | 144-179 lbs. | 134-168 lbs. |
| 6'0" | 148-184 lbs. | 138-173 lbs. |
| 6'1" | 152-189 lbs | |
| 6'2" | 156-194 lbs. | |
| 6'3" | 160-199 lbs. | |
| 6'4" | 164-204 lbs. | |

Source: U.S. Department of Health, Education, and Welfare.

Your ideal weight is probably the weight you had between the ages of 20 and 25, if you were lean at that time. Check your weight against the chart of healthy weights for men and women.

Although there are thousands of weight-reduction diets, the best weight-control strategy is a lifelong sensible eating plan. Diets just don't work. In fact, research now indicates that "yo-yo" dieting damages health and makes each successive weight-loss effort even harder.

First of all, diets don't work because most dieters don't reach their diet objectives. After all, diets represent food deprivation, which is emotionally difficult for most of us. In addition, your body interprets the diet as a famine, which means that it goes into a reduced metabolic state to decrease the severity of the impact on your overall well-being. The harder you diet, the more your body resists losing weight.

Even worse results await most of those who do manage to lose weight. Since over 95 percent of these dieters do not keep the weight they lost off for even a year, most end up deciding to go on a diet again. This sets the yo-yo spinning, as with each new diet the body lowers the energy required for maintenance a little bit more, making weight control even harder.

What these findings suggest is that it is better for you to maintain a moderate weight gain than to continually diet to lose the same ten pounds over and over again. The simple math is that you must expend more calories than you eat in order to avoid gaining weight. The ideal combination is to eat a little less and exercise a little more. (It's also possible to eat the same quantity of food, or even more, if you cut the fat content of your food.) The best approach to weight control is to reduce your daily intake by 100 calories and to increase your exercise by 100 calories. This means that you cut out one slice of bread and butter and walk one mile a day more than you walk now. If you continued this same regimen for a year, you would be twenty pounds lighter than you are now!

The underlying problem is that diets are just a temporary quick fix, when weight control is really a lifestyle issue that we face throughout our lives. Dealing with that issue means making a commitment to learning to cook using low-fat methods, to consistently choosing low-calorie, low-fat foods, and to deciding that small portions are just as satisfying as large ones.

A program that provides good nutrition education and realistic exercise goals may be a help in making that commitment. Weight Watchers, one of the most reputable programs, advocates eating lots of vegetables and cutting down on fat, while increasing exercise. It also offers behavior modification and support. There are chapters in most cities and an 800 number (listed at the end of this chapter) for help in identifying a convenient location. Other organizations that provide educational and support programs include Overeaters Anonymous, the YMCA and YWCA, and many health insurance programs, local colleges, and community centers.

Good weight-control programs emphasize behavioral changes that enhance weight control:

- **Eat slowly.** Take small bites and truly enjoy the color, taste, and texture of the food. Remember that it takes twenty minutes for the hypothalamus (your "appestat") to provide feedback on satiety.

- **Concentrate on eating.** Don't read or watch TV while eating. Enjoy eating as a primary activity so you can be aware of flavors, colors, and portion size.

- **Eat regularly.** Studies show that people who eat three to five meals daily control their weight successfully. This may be because they do not get excessively hungry and overeat. Studies also indicate that people who eat breakfast consume fewer total calories daily.

- **Control portion size.** Portions are generally a half a cup. You can eat anything you want as long the portion fits in a four-ounce Pyrex custard cup!

- **When you're bored:** Substitute a pleasurable activity such as a walk, a phone call, or engaging in a hobby.

- **When you're angry:** Write a letter to the person you're angry with (but don't send it) or go jogging or do some gardening. If you must bite down on something, make that something a carrot or some sugarless gum.

- **When you're tired:** Go to bed or take a hot bath. You may be surprised to find that a walk or a bike ride may reenergize you.

- **When you're anxious:** Engage in physical activity, go to a movie, or find a way to deal with the issues causing the anxiety.

## 7. *Avoid or Limit Caffeine*

Coffee, tea, chocolate, colas, and some medications are all high in this stimulant, which can make some people feel irratable or nervous, interfere with sleep, and contribute to gastrointestinal distress. If you drink regular coffee, a daily limit of 200 milligrams of caffeine is recommended by the American Medical Association.

## Caffeine Counter

| *Beverage* | *Serving* | *Caffeine* |
|---|---|---|
| Regular brewed coffee | 10 oz | 170-200 mg |
| Decaffeinated brewed coffee | 10 oz | 10 mg |
| Instant coffee | 10 oz | 90-140 mg |
| Brewed tea | 10 oz | 60-100 mg |
| Canned ice tea | 12 oz | 25-35 mg |
| Cola drinks | 2 oz | 40-60 mg |
| Dark chocolate | 1 oz | 20 mg |
| Milk chocolate | 1 oz | 6 mg |

Source: *Journal of the American Dietetic Association*, August 1987.

# Recommended Dietary Allowances

|  | Men | | Women | |
|---|---|---|---|---|
| Age | 25-50 | 51+ | 25-50 | 51+ |
| Weight (lbs) | 174 | 170 | 138 | 143 |
| Height (inches) | 70 | 68 | 64 | 63 |
| Protein (grams) | 63 | 63 | 50 | 50 |
| *Fat-soluble vitamins* | | | | |
| Vitamin A ($\mu$g RE) | 1,000 | 1,000 | 800 | 800 |
| Vitamin D ($\mu$g) | 5 | 5 | 5 | 5 |
| Vitamin E ($\mu$g TE) | 10 | 10 | 8 | 8 |
| Vitamin K ($\mu$g) | 80 | 80 | 65 | 65 |
| *Water-soluble vitamins* | | | | |
| Vitamin C (mg) | 60 | 60 | 60 | 60 |
| Thiamine (mg) | 1.5 | 1.2 | 1.1 | 1.0 |
| Riboflavin (mg) | 1.7 | 1.4 | 1.3 | 1.2 |
| Niacin (mg) | 19 | 15 | 15 | 13 |
| Pyridoxine (mg) | 2.0 | 2.0 | 1.6 | 1.6 |
| Folate ($\mu$g) | 200 | 200 | 180 | 180 |
| Vitamin B12 ($\mu$g) | 2.0 | 2.0 | 2.0 | 2.0 |
| *Minerals* | | | | |
| Calcium (mg) | 800 | 800 | 800 | 800 |
| Phosphorous (mg) | 800 | 800 | 800 | 800 |
| Magnesium (mg) | 350 | 350 | 280 | 280 |
| Iron (mg) | 10 | 10 | 15 | 10 |
| Zinc (mg) | 15 | 15 | 12 | 12 |
| Iodine ($\mu$g) | 150 | 150 | 150 | 150 |
| Selenium ($\mu$g) | 70 | 55 | 55 | 55 |

Source: National Research Council, Food and Nutrition Board, National Academy of Sciences. Revised 1989.

## 8.  *If You Drink, Drink in Moderation*

As a tool for reducing stress, alcohol has the bothersome side effect of reducing reality as well. Although some research indicates that a drink a day will increase longevity, reliance on alcohol to deal with daily life is a dangerous practice. Alcoholic beverages are high in calories and low in nutrients. In excess, alcohol depletes B vitamins, alters blood sugar, elevates blood pressure, and disrupts relationships. When you drink, limit yourself to one to two drinks.

## 9.  *Take a Multivitamin Tablet Daily*

Vitamins and minerals are the micronutrients we mentioned earlier. They are necessary in small amounts, and without them metabolism is impaired. The recommended dietary allowances listed here reflect considerable research by the academic community and are approved by the National Research Council. The quantities given include allowances for individual variation.

Since we do not all eat according to the food guide pyramid every day, a multivitamin tablet is recommended as an "insurance policy." However, taking vitamins is not a substitute for not eating well. There are undoubtedly compounds in foods that we have not yet identified that are nutritionally important adjuncts to the functioning of vitamins and minerals in metabolism.

A multivitamin can provide you with extra amounts of the B vitamins linked to stress and vitamins A, E, and C, which seem to have anti-cancer properties. In addition, it can supplement any minerals that have been bound by fiber in the diet. Keep in mind that vitamins marketed as "stress tabs" or as stress formulations are meant for physical stress, rather than psychological stress. More is not better when supplementing vitamins and minerals. Fat-soluble vitamins are known to become toxic because they accumulate in the liver. New evidence indicates that water-soluble vitamins may also be toxic. We do know that consistent doses of over three grams of vitamin C a day increase the risk of kidney stones. Vitamin and mineral function is interrelated: vitamin C enhances iron absorption; vitamin D, calcium, and phosphorus work together in bone metabolism; and B vitamins are necessary for burning glucose as a fuel for the body. Trace minerals are interrelated, so increasing intake of one mineral often causes an imbalance in another. Supplements should supply no more than 1 RDA of each metal, because the metals can become toxic.

## 10.  *Eat Frequent, Calm Meals*

Positive eating includes taking the time to prepare and eat frequent meals or snacks and relaxing as we eat them. Our fast-paced society, along with our many available fast-food options, encourages eating on the run and denies us the time to relax as we eat. Our bodies run better if we refuel them frequently. Blood sugar is like gasoline to a car, and we all know a car does not run if the fuel lines are empty. Eating three to five small meals a day will help to maintain an even blood-sugar level.

To reduce the daily stress of meal preparation, plan and shop weekly. When you cook, cook with the idea of leftovers or snacks in mind. It's cheaper, quicker, easier, and healthier to reheat something in the microwave than to run out to buy fast food. Reheated leftovers can make tasty lunches at the office.

At work, take time away from your workstation to sit and relax with your meal or snack. Likewise, take some time alone to relax and reflect during your breaks. Learn to savor the flavors, textures, and colors of your food.

## Self-Assessment

### Daily Food Diary

If you are interested in making significant changes in your eating habits, it will be worth your while to keep a record of everything you eat and drink for the next three days. You will discover exactly how much you neglect certain food groups and overindulge in others. You will be amazed to see how sugars and fats sneak into your diet. You will see important connections between the circumstances in which you eat and drink, your feelings, and your diet. With this factual account of your eating habits, you will also be motivated to use the guidelines in this chapter to create a more nutritionally balanced diet. You may want to repeat this exercise periodically to measure your progress.

Before you start, look at the first day of the diary that Sharon kept as an example of how to do this. In addition to writing down everything that she ate, she also noted the setting in which she ate and how she felt while she was eating.

Refer to Sharon's diary and to the food guide pyramid to fill in the "Food Guide Points" column of your diary. Sharon's example shows you how to use the pyramid to count servings. Here are some specific guidelines to keep in mind:

- Note that low-fat milk counts as one milk serving and one fat serving, since nonfat milk is a basic milk serving.

- Similarly, count all cookies, donuts, or danish as one serving each of bread, fat, and sugar. (These treats actually may have more fat and sugar, but counting them this way will help you begin to realize how these items sneak into your total diet.)

- Four ounces of ice cream counts as one-half serving of milk and one serving each of fat and sugar.

- If you put butter or margarine on vegetables or potato, don't forget to count it. One teaspoon of either equals one fat serving.

- Note that french fries contain at least three teaspoons of oil (equal to three servings of fat).

- Salad dressing is one serving of fat serving for every two tablespoons of dressing.

Make some extra copies of the blank daily food diary and use them to record your intake for at least the next three days. Be sure to write down where and when you eat, the setting and the people with you at the time, and your feelings. What a person eats is often tied to internal and external cues, and keeping track of this information may give you clues why you eat as you do.

# Sharon's Food Diary

| Meal | Food | Amount | Food guide points | Setting | Feelings |
|------|------|--------|-------------------|---------|----------|
| Breakfast | Cereal<br><br>Low-fat milk | 1/2 cup<br><br>1 cup | 1 bread<br><br>1 milk<br>1 fat | Kitchen, alone | Hungry, hurried |
| Snack | Crumb donut<br><br>Coffee | One<br><br>2 cups | 1 bread<br>1 fat<br>2 sugar<br>2 caffeine | Coffee room | Happy, social |
| Lunch | Tuna sandwich with mayo<br><br>Diet Coke<br><br>Apple | 3 oz<br>2 tsp<br><br>One<br><br>One (lg) | 1 fish<br>2 fat<br>2 bread<br>1 caffeine<br><br>1 fruit | Alone at my desk, working | Busy, pressured |
| Snack | Cookie | One (lg) | 1 bread<br>1 fat<br>1 sugar | Coffee room | Tense, headache |
| Dinner | Hamburger with lettuce, tomato, mayo, catsup, bun<br><br>French fries | 6 oz<br><br>2 tsp<br><br>4 oz | 2 meat<br>1 veg<br>2 fat<br>2 bread<br><br>1 veg<br>3 fat | Home, with family | Tired, grumpy |
| Snack | Rocky Road ice cream | 8 oz | 1 milk<br>1 fat<br>1 sugar | TV, alone | Tired, bored |

# Daily Food Diary

| Meal | Food | Amount | Food guide points | Setting | Feelings |
|------|------|--------|-------------------|---------|----------|
|      |      |        |                   |         |          |

# Sharon's Food Diary Summary

| | Day 1 | Day 2 | Day 3 | Daily average | Ideal servings |
|---|---|---|---|---|---|
| Breads and grains<br>A serving equals<br>1 slice of bread;<br>½ cup rice, cereal,<br>or pasta | 7 | 4 | 7 | 6 | 6-11 |
| Vegetables and fruits<br>A serving equals<br>½ cup or 1 small<br>apple, orange,<br>or potato | 2 | 3 | 1 | 2 | 5-9 |
| Milk, cheese, yogurt<br>A serving equals<br>1 cup low-fat milk;<br>1 oz cheese | 2 | 2 | 2 | 2 | 2-3 |
| Meat, poultry, fish<br>A serving equals<br>2½-3 oz meat or<br>fish; 1½ cup legumes;<br>1 cup nuts | 3 | 2 | 4 | 3 | 2-3 |
| Fats and sweets<br>A serving equals<br>2 tbs salad dressing;<br>1 tsp butter or<br>margarine; 1 oz candy | 11 | 9 | 6 | 8+ | 2-5 |
| Alcohol<br>A serving equals<br>12 oz beer, 3 oz<br>wine, 1 bar drink | 0 | 1 | 0 | ⅓ | 0-1 |
| Caffeine<br>A serving equals<br>1 cup regular coffee<br>or tea | 4 | 5 | 3 | 4 | 0-1 |

# Food Diary Summary

|  | Day 1 | Day 2 | Day 3 | Daily average | Ideal servings |
|---|---|---|---|---|---|
| **Breads and grains**<br>A serving equals<br>1 slice of bread;<br>½ cup rice, cereal,<br>or pasta |  |  |  |  | 6-11 |
| **Vegetables and fruits**<br>A serving equals<br>½ cup or 1 small<br>apple, orange,<br>or potato |  |  |  |  | 5-9 |
| **Milk, cheese, yogurt**<br>A serving equals<br>1 cup low-fat milk;<br>1 oz cheese |  |  |  |  | 2-3 |
| **Meat, poultry, fish**<br>A serving equals<br>2½-3 oz meat or<br>fish; 1½ cup legumes;<br>1 cup nuts |  |  |  |  | 2-3 |
| **Fats and sweets**<br>A serving equals<br>2 tbs salad dressing;<br>1 tsp butter or<br>margarine; 1 oz candy |  |  |  |  | 2-5 |
| **Alcohol**<br>A serving equals<br>12 oz beer, 3 oz<br>wine, 1 bar drink |  |  |  |  | 0-1 |
| **Caffeine**<br>A serving equals<br>1 cup regular coffee<br>or tea |  |  |  |  | 0-1 |

*Summarizing Your Food Diary*

For each of the three days that you kept your daily food diary, add up the total number of points in each food group and write it in the appropriate box on your food diary summary. At three. Write this number in the "daily average" column for each food group. You will then be able to compare your daily averages for each food group with the ideal servings listed in the sixth column of the summary form. Refer to Sharon's food diary summary as an example and then go on to fill out the blank food diary summary from the data in your daily food diary.

## Taking Charge of Your Nutritional Well-Being

The food guide pyramid provides a goal for daily food choices. Review your food diary summary and compare your average servings per food group against the ideal servings. Put a check in the margin of the groups in which you were below the recommendation. Put a star in the margin by the groups in which you were over the recommendation.

Having digested the facts presented in this chapter, you shouldn't be too surprised to find that your usual food intake looks a lot more like the typical American diet than like the recommended pyramid. Chances are good that it is top heavy with fats and sugars and skimpy on fruits, vegetables, grains, bread, and cereals.

When Sharon had reviewed her own summary, she sat down and filled out her goal-setting chart. The solutions she developed may suggest some positive steps that you can take.

## Sharon's Goal-Setting Chart

| *Food group* | *Problem* | *Solution* |
|---|---|---|
| Sugar | Too much sugar | Replace sweets with fresh fruit |
| Fat | Too much fat:<br>Salad dressing<br>Mayonnaise<br>Fried foods<br>Ice cream | Fat-free dressing<br>Omit<br>Bake, broil<br>Use low-fat frozen<br>yogurt instead |
| Vegetables | I hate vegetables | Add one new vegetable<br>per month |
| Portions | My portions are huge | Use the custard cup<br>to measure |
| Caffeine | I'm using four times<br>too much | Switch to herbal teas,<br>take walks |

Now fill in your own positive eating goals on the form on the next page.

Now go back to your daily food diary again and review the settings in which you ate. Note anything about the setting that might contribute to unhealthy eating behavior. For example, it's clear from Sharon's sample diary that eating alone at her desk provided no break from work and may have actually made her less efficient as her tension level grew in the afternoon. Lunch with friends or at least in a different locale could have provided a change of scene. She takes her breaks in the coffee room, where high-fat, high-sugar snacks are a constant temptation. If she plans to take a piece of fruit to the coffee room, she can still have the benefits of socializing, but markedly improve the nutritional value of her break.

What changes or improvements would you make regarding the setting in which you eat?

_____

_____

_____

Now review the feelings that you recorded in your daily food diary. Note any feelings that contributed to unhealthy eating behavior. For instance, looking at Sharon's food diary, you can see that she uses comfort food to try to feel better when she has negative feelings and sensations (tension, a headache, boredom, fatigue). Aerobic exercise, socializing, or a relaxation exercise might have been more effective in alleviating these symptoms without adding unneeded fat and sugar. She can also plan ahead to have a favorite low-calorie substitute available for those times when she knows she is likely to feel down. Going to bed earlier might also help prevent snacking when she feels bored or tired at night. If an earlier bedtime led to getting up earlier in the morning, she would also have time for a less hurried breakfast.

How do your feelings contribute to your dietary intake? What changes can you make?

_____

_____

_____

Changing your eating habits will take some time. Concentrate on no more than a few goals at a time for a minimum of one month. When you have integrated these new eating habits into your daily life, move on to a few more goals. Depending on how many habits you wish to change, you should be enjoying a healthier diet in one to six months. Making too many changes at a time can be stressful, so insure your success by going slowly. The changes you make also need to be tasty ones, otherwise you will feel deprived and have difficulty sticking with your plan.

## Final Thoughts

You have the power to take charge of your eating habits, and taking charge will make a positive difference. Just keep the ten steps of positive eating in mind and gradually make changes in your food selections. Put a copy of the food pyramid on the refrigerator as a reminder and keep it in

# Your Personal Positive Eating Goals

| Food group | Problem | Solution |
| --- | --- | --- |
| | | |

mind when you shop. Go to your local bookstore and check the cookbook section for a new low-fat cookbook or magazine to inspire you. If you need a personalized nutrition plan, consult a registered dietitian at your medical clinic or check the yellow pages of the phone book. If you have a nutrition question, call the Center of Nutrition and Dietetics Hotline listed below. Food is a necessity and a pleasure in life, so make positive, healthy choices!

## Further Reading

Brody, Jane. 1982. *Jane Brody's Nutrition Book*. New York: Bantam Books.

————. 1985. *Jane Brody's Good Food Book, Living the High Carbohydrate Way*. New York: W. W. Norton.

Clark, Nancy. 1983. *The Athlete's Kitchen*. New York: Bantam Books.

Lappe, F. M. 1991. *Diet for a Small Planet*. New York: Ballantine Books.

National Academy of Sciences. 1989. *Recommended Dietary Allowances*. Washington, DC: National Academy of Sciences.

Ornstein, R., and D. Sobel. 1989. *Healthy Pleasures*. New York: Addison-Wesley.

Oxmoor House. 1993. *Cooking Light Cookbook*. Menlo Park, CA: Oxmoor House.

"The Vitamin Pushers." 1986. *Consumer Reports*, March, 170-175.

U.S. Congress. Senate. Select Committee on Nutrition and Human Needs. 1977. *Dietary Goals for the United States*. 2nd ed. Washington, DC: U.S. Government Printing Office.

## Other Resources

Center for Nutrition and Dietetics Nutrition Hotline:
1-800-366-1655.

Weight Watchers Program locations: 1-800-726-6108.

# 20

# Exercise

Exercise is one of the simplest and most effective means of stress reduction. Vigorous physical exertion is the natural outlet for the body when it is in the "fight or flight" state of arousal. Exercise returns your body to its normal equilibrium by releasing natural chemicals that build up during the stress response.

## Types of Exercise

There are three broad categories of exercise: aerobic exercises, stretching exercises, and toning exercises. All three types should play a role in any balanced exercise program.

### Aerobic Exercises

Aerobic exercises are repetitive, rhythmic, and varied. They involve sustained use of the large muscles in your body, especially the legs and arms. The goal of aerobic exercise is to strengthen your cardiovascular system and increase your stamina. To produce this effect, you need to exercise at least three days a week. Each time you do aerobic exercise, your heart rate should reach the target heart rate appropriate for your age and remain at that rate for twenty minutes. (Instructions for determining your target heart rate are given later in this chapter.) Exercising below your target heart rate will not strengthen your cardiovascular system, and exercising consistently above that rate could put too much strain on your heart.

---

### Prescription for Aerobic Exercise

*Frequency:* Three to five days per week.

*Duration:* A minimum of twenty minutes uninterrupted, continous exercise.

*Intensity:* 60 to 75 percent of your maximum heart rate.

---

Popular aerobic exercises include running, jogging, brisk walking, swimming, bicycling, dancing, and a number of other activities. Fortunately, this wide variety of choices offers alternatives to suit every lifestyle and a range of physical conditions.

You probably get a certain amount of exercise each day in activities such as slow walking, housecleaning, shopping, some office duties, and light gardening. To find out how much activity you get in a day, you can use a pedometer. When adjusted to your walking stride, this device clips to your clothing and measures the number of miles that you walk or run. Wear it for one week, removing it when you do aerobic exercises, and record how far you have walked at the end of each day. If you walk less than 2½ miles per day, you should consider yourself an inactive person and begin your exercise program slowly.

In addition to these everyday activities, both stretching and toning exercises should be incorporated into your exercise program.

## Stretching and Toning Exercises

Stretching and toning exercises are not vigorous or prolonged enough to produce the cardiovascular strengthening that results from aerobic exercise. They can be used to increase muscle strength and flexibility and joint mobility. If you are very sedentary or in poor physical condition, stretching and toning exercises will help prepare you for aerobic exercise with minimum risk of cardiovascular strain.

**Stretching exercises** are slow, sustained, and relaxing. Specific stretches are available to decrease muscle tension, improve the flexibility of specific muscle groups, and help maintain joint mobility. Stretching also improves circulation and helps to prevent injury when used during the warm-up and cool-down periods before and after aerobic exercise. They also help you feel good, by soothing your mind and body and helping to focus and center your thoughts. You can also stretch before going to bed in preparation for a good night's sleep.

Many yoga positions are good stretching exercises. The greatest attraction to stretching exercises is their convenience. You need no special clothing or equipment. Weather is irrelevant, because you can do them indoors at any time.

---

### Prescription for Stretching Exercises

*Frequency:* Stretch both before and after aerobic exercise, during your warm-up and cool-down periods. You can also stretch whenever you're feeling stressed, tense, stiff, or tired.

*Duration:* Begin by holding the stretch position for thirty seconds. Gradually increase to two minutes over a period of a few weeks. Breathe rhythmically and notice how your body feels.

---

**Toning exercises** focus on specific muscles that need to be firmed or tightened. Some good examples are crunches for stomach muscles, partial squats for thigh muscles, toe raises for calf muscles, and push-ups for arm and chest muscles.

Most toning exercises can be placed in one of these two categories:

1. *Isotonics* involve the contraction of muscles against resistance through a range of movement. Weight lifting is the most popular form of isotonic exercise. Istonics can be used to increase the size of the muscle or simply for toning. Bigger muscles can mean more power, endurance, and speed. Toned muscles yield a firmer looking body and are important in protecting joints.

2. *Isometrics* require the contraction of muscles against resistance, without movement. For example, you can push your two hands together at chest level. Isometrics do not make muscles larger, but they do increase muscle strength.

---

### Prescription for Toning Exercises

*To tone muscles*, rather than increase muscle size, use less resistance and do more repetitions.

*To increase muscle size*, use more resistance and do fewer repetitions.

---

## Symptom Relief

Regular and adequate exercise is the best choice for increasing muscular strength, endurance, and flexibility. It is also an excellent way to relieve chronic muscle tension. The greater flexibility and better posture gained through exercise can relieve lower back pain. Improved metabolism can relieve indigestion and chronic constipation. Exercise will fight both chronic fatigue and insomnia. It also decreases emotions such as depression and anxiety.

## Time for Mastery

You need to set up a schedule of at least three exercise sessions per week over a six-to-eight-week period. Make the commitment to stick with it in order to make exercise a regular part of your life. Keeping a diary similar to the diary described later in this chapter will help give you a picture of the progress you are making during this initial period.

## Precautions

Abruptly starting a strenuous program of aerobic exercise could overstrain your heart if you are not used to the exertion. If you lead a sedentary lifestyle, are somewhat overweight, eat a great deal of fatty or salty foods, or smoke, begin slowly with low intensity exercises such as walking and easy stretches. Likewise, if you are resuming an exercise program after a serious illness or an operation, start gradually and follow any special precautions suggested by your doctor or health care provider.

Do not start any regular exercise program without seeing a doctor for a complete physical examination if you are obese (more than 20 percent over your ideal weight), or have any medical problems that require regular medications and regular checkups with your doctor.

Once you have begun your exercise program, contact your doctor if you develop any of the following symptoms:

- Your heart rate becomes irregular and begins to skip beats.

- Your heart rate takes longer than fifteen minutes to slow down.

- You feel a tightness, pressure, or pain in your chest, shoulders, arms, or neck.

- You feel dizzy or nauseous.

- You feel extreme breathlessness after only mild exertion.

- You feel exhausted long after you have stopped.

# Developing Your Own Exercise Program

## *Overcoming the Barriers*

The benefits of exercise are easy to understand and commonly appreciated. Unfortunately, the many barriers to beginning an exercise program are also widely shared. Do any of these excuses sound familiar?

- I'm too tired.

- I don't have enough time.

- I'm feeling rushed

- I get enough exercise in my job.

- I don't want to look like a body builder.

- It will increase my appetite and I'll just gain more weight.

- I'm too old.

- I'm too fat or too out of shape.

- The weather is bad.

- Exercise is boring.

- I have more important things to do.

- My other obligations don't leave me enough time.

- I don't want to look silly.

- I'd be embarrassed in front of others.

- I'm afraid I'll hurt myself.

The reasons you give yourself for not exercising are powerful–they have succeeded in depriving you of one of your basic needs. Facing up to these excuses is an essential step in overcoming an inactive lifestyle.

You can begin by keeping a daily exercise diary to discover times in your schedule when you can increase your exercise. Make a note in your diary each time you have at least ten minutes free to take a walk or do some other kind of exercise. Also write down the things you say to yourself that hold you back or give you an excuse for not exercising.

Angela, a 32-year-old administrative assistant, kept the following diary on a typical day.

## Daily Exercise Diary

| Time | Opportunity to exercise | Reasons for and against exercising |
|------|------------------------|-----------------------------------|
| 7:45 | Let dog out to run in the yard. | I'm running late, so I can't walk the dog this morning. |
| 8:15 | Drive to work. | It's too far to walk, and my bike has a flat. |
| 10:00 | Drive with co-worker to a special conference three blocks away. | I would have walked, but I couldn't very well say no to a friend offering a ride. |
| 12:00 | Drive to lunch. | I want to save time. Besides, it looks like rain. |
| 1:00 | Make calls to people who work on different floors of my building. | It's more efficient to phone. |
| 3:00 | Walk to Post Office. | I need to stretch my legs. |
| 5:00 | Collapse on sofa at home. | I could go jogging, but I'm exhausted and too out of shape since gaining those five pounds at Christmas. |
| 7:30 | Back on the sofa. | I could walk the dog, but it's dark and this isn't a safe neighborhood. Also, I have a headache. Maybe tomorrow . . . |

Look over your diary and examine the statements that you made to yourself. Are they really valid reasons for not doing something that is essential to your health and well-being? Consider the implications of the following common excuses.

*"I don't have enough time."*

*"I'm feeling rushed."*

*"I have more important things to do."*

*"My other obligations don't leave me enough time."*

If these excuses sound familiar, it may mean that exercise is at the bottom of your list of priorities. Instead of saying "I *can't* exercise," try saying "I *choose* not to exercise." What does that statement say about you?

If exercise really is important to you, you will create a space for it in your life. Remember that for a busy person, exercise is an especially important outlet for your daily pressures. Without exercise, you will become increasingly tense, out of shape, and low on physical energy. Your ability to cope with the stresses of your busy life will be jeopardized.

For help in sorting out your priorities and finding ways to schedule in the activities that really do matter to you, see chapter 16 on "Goal Setting and Time Management."

*"I'm too old to exercise."*

*"I'm too fat to exercise."*

*"I'm too out of shape to exercise."*

Even though you recognize the advantages of exercise, you may persist in a sedentary lifestyle because you see yourself as too out of shape to engage in an activity that would make you sweat or allow others to see how uncoordinated you are. Such beliefs can make it hard for you to initiate an exercise program on your own. You should take a class, join a group, or get together with a friend who already exercises regularly. Others will soon show you that exercise is for all ages and shapes.

*"I'm afraid I'll hurt myself."*

*"I'm afraid that I'll look silly."*

*"I'm afraid of embarrassing myself."*

Of the many fears associated with exercise, fear of a heart attack is one of the most common. You need have no fear if you get a physical exam first and start slowly under a doctor's supervision. You may be afraid of injuring yourself. In this case, books, classes, and experienced people can provide you with information about how to exercise safely, what to expect as you progress, and how to cope with any difficulties you encounter.

When Angela reviewed her exercise diary, she took a close look at the things she was saying to herself. Since she knew they were a barrier to doing something that she needed and wanted to do, she took the time to write out ways of overcoming these obstacles.

If your own excuses for not exercising seem particularly hard to dispute, try reading chapter 14 on "Refuting Irrational Ideas."

## Choosing the Best Type of Exercise for You

If you aren't sure which forms of exercise you'd like to try, then there are a few key questions that can help you decide. Think carefully about your answers and write them down in the space provided. Be honest with yourself, since the answers to these questions may determine how successful your exercise program is.

# Responses to Reasons for Not Exercising

| Reason for not exercising | Response or solution |
| --- | --- |
| Running late . . . can't walk the dog. | I rarely have time to walk the dog in the morning because I don't get up early enough to do it. I'll set the alarm fifteen minutes earlier and get up as soon as it goes off. |
| Can't bike to work . . . flat tire. | It's not a matter of "can't": I just don't want to bike to work. But I can fix the flat so that I can bike on weekends, when I do enjoy biking in the country. |
| Can't decline a ride from a friend. | I'm full of "can'ts." Obviously I can say no, but sometimes I choose not to. I'll ask my friend to walk to meetings in the future. |
| Save time by driving to lunch. | An hour is plenty of time to walk to lunch, eat, and walk back. |
| Drive to lunch because it looks like rain. | This is the dumbest excuse yet! So what if it's cloudy? If I'm so concerned about the weather, I'll carry an umbrella or eat in the cafeteria downstairs. |
| It's more efficient to phone. | True, but face-to-face contact is valuable. And I do have the time to make the rounds in person. |
| I'm too exhausted, out of shape, and overweight to jog. | These are all signs of exercise deprivation and the very reasons why I should jog. |
| The neighborhood is unsafe after dark. | I could ask my husband to walk with me, or do some indoor exercises, or join a health club, or plan my exercises for earlier in the day. |
| I have a headache. | Another possible sign of exercise deprivation and stress accumulation. |
| Maybe tomorrow . . . | My favorite strategy for avoiding exercise! I'll go walk the dog right now! |

1. How physically fit are you already?

_____

_____

_____

2. What do you want out of your exercise program?

_____

_____

_____

3. Would you prefer to exercise alone or with others?

_____

_____

_____

4. Would you prefer to exercise indoors or outdoors?

_____

_____

_____

5. How much time are you willing to spend?

_____

_____

_____

6. When can you best fit your chosen exercise into your schedule?

_____

_____

_____

7. How far are you willing to travel to exercise?

_____

_____

_____

8. How much money are you willing to spend on exercise equipment?

_____

_____

_____

Your answers to these questions should give you a sense of which kinds of activities are appropriate for you. Walking may be the best way to start if you are middle-aged or somewhat overweight or have been inactive. Swimming is good for people who are substantially overweight or have bone or joint problems. The list of common aerobic exercises on the following page highlights some of their typical advantages and disadvantages.

## Establishing Goals

Your daily exercise diary should have given you a sense of the time already available to you for exercise. (If you feel that you need more time than you have now, read chapter 16 on "Goal Setting and Time Management.") You're now ready to use this information to set goals and develop a plan for increasing the amount of exercise that you get during the day. Make sure that the goals you set are realistic and achievable, taking into account your current exercise level, the resources available to you, your time limitations, and your personal interests.

In establishing your goals, you'll want to pick the times that are most convenient for you. Bear in mind these considerations:

- Morning offers the advantage of cooler weather and fewer people. On cold days, be sure to wear several layers of clothing and a hat that will prevent heat loss.

- Midday offers warmer weather and more people. On hot and humid days drink lots of water and beware of signs of heat stroke: feelings of dizziness, weakness, light-headedness, or excessive tiredness. If sweating stops, your body temperature can become dangerously high.

- Evening again offers cooler weather, but probably more people.

- If your schedule requires you to exercise at night on city streets, be sure wear reflective clothing, travel on well-lighted streets, and carry identification, a loud whistle, and enough change for a phone call. (This is a good time to exercise with a friend.)

- Plan to exercise before meals or at least two hours after your last meal.

- Exercise any day during the week, but not more than five out of seven days.

Once you have determined the optimal times for you, use them consistently. Set a short-term goal for each week. Discuss your goals with a good friend or family member who will be supportive and help you to attain your goals.

Here are a few more suggestions to help you stay on track.

- Make a promise to yourself to stick with your program at least three times a week for three months.

# Types of Aerobic Exercise

| Exercise | Advantages | Disadvantages |
| --- | --- | --- |
| Basketball | Challenging as a game | Cannot be done alone<br>Requires a court to play on |
| Bicycling (outdoors) | Changing scenery keeps your interest up<br>Good for the environment<br>Not stressful on bones or joints<br>Good exercise for the legs and heart | Requires a bicycle and a helmet<br>You need to know how to fix a flat<br>Traffic can be dangerous<br>You need an alternative when the weather is bad<br>Your arms don't get exercised |
| Bicycling (stationary) | Weather or traffic make no difference<br>No flat tires | Requires access to a stationary bicycle<br>Can be monotonous |
| Dancing | It's fun, especially if you enjoy music<br>Can be an excellent whole-body exercise | If done on a non-wooden floor, can cause harm to bones and joints |
| Hiking | Takes you outdoors into the fresh air and lets you experience nature | Requires hiking boots<br>May require other equipment or precautions if hiking in remote or unfamiliar territory |
| Racquetball | An excellent whole-body exercise | Requires access to a court<br>Requires some skill<br>Requires a partner<br>May be too strenuous for beginners |
| Rope jumping | Cheap and convenient<br>Equipment is small and portable<br>Can be done alone<br>Can be done almost anywhere | Requires some skill |
| Rowing a boat | Can be very relaxing<br>A scull with a sliding seat provides an excellent full-body workout | Requires a boat and access to water |

| | | |
|---|---|---|
| Rowing (stationary) | Can be done indoors | Requires access to equipment<br>Can be monotonous |
| Running or jogging | You can enjoy changing scenery<br>You only need a pair of running shoes<br>You can do this alone or with others<br>An excellent full-body workout | Can increase wear and tear on joints<br>Can lead to injuries if not properly done<br>May be too difficult for beginners or overweight individuals<br>Takes a longer time to learn to enjoy than other forms of exercise (but once you're hooked, you won't easily give it up) |
| Skating (roller skates or on ice) | Can be done alone or with others | Can give you skinned knees and elbows<br>Requires some skill<br>Requires equipment and access to facilities |
| Skiing (cross-country, outdoors) | An excellent way to enjoy nature | Requires some skill<br>Requires equipment and access to snow |
| Skiing (cross-country, indoors) | Can be done indoors | Requires access to equipment |
| Stair climbing | Requires no skill | Can be very monotonous |
| Swimming | A good way to stay cool<br>Good for joint pain or muscle weakness<br>Good for large muscles in arms, legs, and chest | Requires an ability to swim and access to a pool<br>Not a good choice if you are sensitive to chlorine |
| Tennis (singles) | A good whole-body workout<br>Can be done with others | Requires some skill<br>Requires equipment and access to a court<br>Cannot be done alone |
| Walking briskly | Can be done anytime, anywhere<br>Requires only a pair of shoes<br>Can provide an excellent whole-body exercise | It takes longer to reach your target heart rate than other forms of exercise |

- Tell your friends, family, and co-workers who you know will offer support and encouragement about your plans.

- Choose a time in the day that is convenient for you.

- Write down your goals and post them where you'll see them each day.

- Continue to write down your excuses for not exercising and how you'll deal with them when they arise in your diary.

## Sample Exercise Program

This program will take you from thirty to eighty minutes to complete and will stretch and tone the major muscle groups in your body. For best results, do a full set of exercises three to five days each week. If you don't have time for such an ambtitious program, try exercising every other day. Whenever you exercise, always do the warm-up stretches first to avoid putting too much sudden stress on your body.

### Begin by Warming Up

*Length:* Ten minutes before aerobic exercise.

Warm-up exercises increase your metabolism and your body temperature and prepare your muscles and your heart and lungs for vigorous exercise. They also decrease your chance of injury. The stretching and the toning exercises described later in this chapter are all excellent as warm ups.

### Follow With Aerobics

*Easy length:* Ten to twenty minutes.
*Intermediate length:* Twenty to forty minutes.
*Advanced length:* Forty to sixty minutes.

The simplest, most readily available form of aerobic exercise is brisk walking or jogging. Accordingly, a walking and jogging program is used in this section to illustrate the principles of aerobic exercise. You can use a similar graduated approach for running, bicycling, swimming, cross-country skiing, jumping rope, or any other aerobic exercise that you choose to do.

As you exercise, your large skeletal muscles rhythmically tense and relax, stimulating the blood flow through your vascular system, heart, and lungs. Your heart rate is particularly important. Much like the speedometer in your car that tells you how fast you are going, your heart rate tells you how hard you are working. If you are travelling too fast in your car, you slow down; likewise, if you are going too slow, you speed up.

Just as the speed of your car is measured in miles per hour, the work of your heart is measured in beats per minute. You can find out how fast your heart is going by taking your pulse. Practice taking your pulse while sitting quietly. Wear a watch with a sweep second hand on your left arm. Turn the palm of your right hand toward you. Firmly place the fingertips of your left hand on your right wrist near the bone that joins your thumb to your wrist. You will feel your pulse. To determine your heart rate for one minute, simply take your pulse for ten seconds and then multiply this number by six. (You can also find this number by referring to the chart.)

## Heart Rate in Beats Per Ten Seconds and Per Minute

| If you got this number in ten seconds | 10 | 11 | 12 | 13 | 14 | 15 | 16 | 17 | 18 | 19 | 20 | 21 | 22 | 23 | 24 | 25 |
|---|---|---|---|---|---|---|---|---|---|---|---|---|---|---|---|---|
| This is your heart rate in beats per minute | 60 | 66 | 72 | 78 | 84 | 90 | 96 | 102 | 108 | 114 | 120 | 126 | 132 | 138 | 144 | 150 |

A normal resting pulse may range from 40 to 100 beats per minute.

In order to benefit from aerobic exercise, your heart must reach and stay within a range known as your *target heart rate* for at least twenty minutes. You reach this range when your heart is beating at a rate of between 60 to 75 percent of its maximum rate. It is the safest exercise range for you, and exercising at this pace stimulates the relaxation response. The following table shows the estimated heart rates for different age groups.

Exercise at your target level level places a moderate stress on your heart that will gradually improve its efficiency. By monitoring your heart rate during exercise and comparing it to your target rate, you have immediate feedback about whether you are doing too much

## Estimated Heart Rates for Selected Ages

| Age (years) | Average maximum heart rate (beats per minute) | Target heart rate (60 to 75 percent of maximum rate) |
|---|---|---|
| 20-24 | 200 | 120-150 |
| 25-29 | 195 | 117-146 |
| 30-34 | 190 | 114-142 |
| 35-39 | 185 | 111-138 |
| 40-44 | 180 | 108-135 |
| 45-49 | 175 | 105-131 |
| 50-54 | 170 | 102-127 |
| 55-59 | 165 | 99-123 |
| 60-64 | 160 | 96-120 |
| 65-69 | 155 | 93-116 |
| 70+ | 150 | 90-113 |

# Stretching Exercises

**A. Side body stretch.** (1) Stand erect, arms at sides, feet shoulder width apart, and legs relaxed with knees slightly bent. (2) Raise one arm over your head to the side. Keeping stomach tucked in and chest high, continue to bend your arm and trunk to the side until you feel a stretch in your waist. Hold this position for five seconds. (3) Return to starting position. (4) Repeat on the other side. *Begin with five repetitions on each side.*

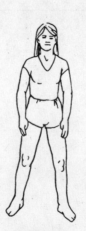

figure A-1    figure A-2

figure A-3    figure A-4

**B. Leg and back stretch.** (1) Stand with feet together, arms at sides, and eyes looking straight ahead. (2) Squat down, keeping heels on floor and reaching your arms straight ahead. Hold ten seconds. (3) Reach hands forward between knees and slide body forward onto knees. (4) Continue sliding forward until front of body touches floor. (5) With hands on floor in front of shoulders, press chest away from floor by straightening elbows. Keep front of hips in contact with floor. Keep head and neck relaxed, eyes looking at the floor. Hold ten seconds. (6) Push back into the squatting position. Hold for another ten seconds. (7) Return to starting position. *Begin with five repetitions.*

**C. Full body stretch.** (1) Lie on the floor with legs straight and arms overhead. (2) Stretch right arm and leg in opposite directions. Hold five seconds. (3) Stretch left arm and left leg in opposite directions. Hold five seconds. (4) Stretch left arm and right leg in opposite directions. Hold five seconds. (5) Stretch right arm and left leg in opposite directions. Hold five seconds. (6) Stretch both arms and legs in opposite directions. Hold five seconds. *Begin with five repetitions.*

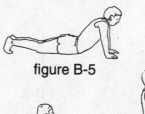

figure B-1

figure B-2     figure B-3

figure C-1     figure C-2     figure C-3

figure B-4

figure B-5

figure B-6          figure B-7

figure C-4     figure C-5     figure C-6

## Toning Exercises

**D.  Arm and upper back toner.** (1) Place hand about shoulder width apart on the wall. Move your feet back until your legs and back are in a straight line, your body supported by your feet and hands. Always keep head up. (2) Bend arms at elbow, lowering your body until your chest touches the wall. (3) Push up, straightening arms, and return to starting position. *Begin with ten repetitions.*

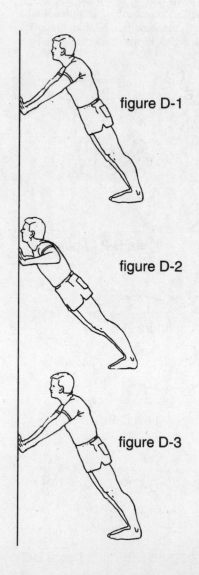

figure D-1

figure D-2

figure D-3

**E.  Leg toner.** (1) Stand with feet comfortably apart, hands on hips. (2) Bend knees to half-squat position as you bring arms forward with palms down. Be sure to keep your heels on the floor. (3) Return to starting position. *Begin with ten repetitions.*

**F.  Tummy toner.** (1) Lie on back with knees bent and feet flat on the floor. Interlace fingers behind head. (2) Tucking chin into chest, curl forward, lifting only head, neck, and shoulders. Hold for five seconds. (3) Return to starting position. *Begin with ten repetitions. Start slowly and gradually increase pace. Do not pull on your neck!*

figure E-1

figure E-2

figure E-3

figure F-1

figure F-2

figure F-3

exercise or not enough. If your heart rate is greater than your target rate, you slow down; if your heart rate is less than your target rate, you speed up.

If you are out of shape, brisk walking may push your pulse over 60 percent of the maximum heart rate for your age group. As your cardiorespiratory system becomes conditioned, you will have to exert more effort (by walking faster or jogging) to attain your target rate. Here are three simple tests that you can do to determine how fast you should walk or jog in order to reach your target rate.

1. Walk five minutes at a comfortable pace. Take your pulse immediately, because the rate falls off rapidly. If it is less than the target rate for your age group, go on to the second test. If you have already reached your target rate, continue to walk at this pace every other day until your heart rate falls below 60 percent of your maximum rate and then go on to the second test.

2. Walk five minutes at a vigorous pace. Again, take your pulse immediately. If you have not reached 60 percent of your maximum heart rate, go on to the third test. If your pulse is within your target range, continue at this pace with aerobic walks every other day until your pulse falls below your target rate and then go on to the third step.

3. Alternate one minute of slow jogging with one minute of brisk walking for five minutes and then take your pulse. If you still haven't reached your target rate, you are ready to continue with slow jogging every other day. If you have reached 60 percent of your maximum heart rate, continue to alternate one minute of jogging with one minute of brisk walking every other day until your pulse falls below the target level. Then increase the amount of time you spend jogging as you decrease your time walking.

You will need to check your pulse frequently until you find a a pace that will keep your heart rate within your target range for at least twenty minutes. After that, monitor your pulse once per week to make sure that you are maintaining your target rate.

You will find that you need to gradually spend more time jogging or even running in order to stay within your target heart rate. A good rule of thumb is to continue to jog until you feel winded and then slow to a brisk walk for about a minute. If you can sing while exercising, you're not exercising hard enough. Note, though, that you should be able to carry on a conversation while you're jogging without becoming excessively short of breath. If you can't, you're going too fast.

## End by Cooling Down

*Length:* Ten minutes after your aerobic exercise.

A period of cooling down helps decrease your metabolism and body temperature and prevents your muscles from becoming sore. When jogging or running, always end your session with five minutes of slow walking. Take long exaggerated steps, stretching your legs. Let your arms dangle loosely and shake your hands. The stretching and toning exercises that you used to warm up are also excellent for cooling down.

# Special Considerations

## *Daily Opportunities for Additional Exercise*

In addition to your regular program, don't neglect these additional opportunities:

- Walk instead of driving to your destination. Or drive to within two or three blocks and walk the rest of the way.

- Take the stairs instead of the elevator.

- Use the bathroom farthest from your workstation.

- Park at the farthest end of the parking lot.

- Get off the bus or train one stop early and walk the rest of the distance.

- Stretch or tone while watching the morning or evening news.

- Walk a pet. If you don't have a pet, arrange to walk a friend or neighbor's pet.

- Take a walk on your lunch break with a co-worker or friend.

## *Avoiding Injury*

Here are a few things to consider in order to avoid injury:

- Have a physical checkup to make sure that you are healthy. Get cleared by a medical professional (doctor, nurse practitioner, or physician's assistant) before beginning a regular exercise program.

- Start slowly and build up gradually. Progress at a steady pace.

- Always warm up and cool down.

- Wear comfortable shoes that offer good support to your feet and ankles.

- Do not exercise if you are feeling sick. Your body needs rest at this time.

- After a serious illness or an operation, get cleared by your medical professional before resuming your exercise program. Start slowly and build up gradually.

- Wear comfortable, lightweight, loose-fitting layers of clothing. Be prepared to remove clothing as your body temperature increases during the warm-up and aerobic phases and to add clothing as your body temperature decreases when you are cooling down.

- Exercise within your target heart rate zone. Remember, you should be able to talk comfortably while you are exercising. If you are too breathless, you need to slow down.

- Drink plenty of fluids to replace those lost during vigorous exercise.

- Pace yourself. Set goals that are realistic for you.

- Spread your exercise over the week, rather than exercising only on weekends.

- Use any equipment that is recommended for your protection.

- Don't use ankle or arm weights that can place added stress on your back and joints.

- Don't exercise after a large meal, because blood flow to the large muscles is limited.

## Keeping at It

There are two major obstacles to overcome in undertaking an exercise program. The first is just to get started. The second is to keep at it. If you have followed the instructions in the preceding sections, you have jumped the first hurdle. The second may be more difficult. The following suggestions will help you keep at your exercise program until it becomes as automatic as eating or sleeping.

- Choose exercise activities that you enjoy. If you enjoy what you're doing, you'll be more likely to do it.

- Start slowly and never overdo. Your body will not tolerate too much exercise without adequate preparation.

- Keep your exercise diary up to date.

- Give yourself small rewards. Put a gold star on your calendar or in your diary, take a bubble bath instead of a shower, go out to a movie, or buy a new pair of walking shoes.

- Focus on the benefits of exercise. Notice that you feel relaxed, energized, and refreshed, and how your concentration and sleep have improved.

- Post your goals where you can see them each day at home or at the office. Put up some pictures of yourself or others doing your favorite exercise. Put up affirmations.

- Visualize success. See yourself as already having attained the benefits of exercise. See yourself dancing gracefully or walking down a country road, looking radiant, healthy, and slender.

- Get support from your family and friends by telling them about your goals or enlisting them to join you in your exercise program.

- Join an exercise class, running club, or fitness center. Participate in group activities like footraces or other exercise-related events.

## Some Final Thoughts

- Exercise with a good friend to renew and maintain your support system.

- Exercise alone to get in touch with your thoughts and feelings.

- Don't burden yourself with "shoulds." Choose exercises that you find fun, playful, pleasurable, and refreshing.

- Keep track of your program either by jotting down each time you exercise on your calendar or keeping a diary where you can record your thoughts and feelings.

- If you believe that variety is the spice of life, then select several exercises that you enjoy and alternate them during the week.

# Exercise Diary

Week of _____

Target heart rate: _____

Remember to WARM UP and COOL DOWN.

| Day | Activity | Location | Distance or Duration | Comments, Thoughts, Feelings |
|---|---|---|---|---|
| Monday | | | | |
| Tuesday | | | | |
| Wednesday | | | | |
| Thursday | | | | |
| Friday | | | | |
| Saturday | | | | |
| Sunday | | | | |

**Further Reading**

Anderson, B. 1980. *Stretching*. Bolinas, CA: Shelter Publishers.

Bailey, C. 1991. *Fit or Fat*. Boston: Houghton Mifflin.

Cooper, K. 1982. *The Aerobics Program for Total Well Being*. New York: Bantam Books.

Dworkis, S. 1994. *Extension: The 20-Minute-a-Day Yoga-Based Program To Relax, Release, and Rejuvenate the Average Stressed-Out Over-35-Year-Old Body*. New York: Poseidon Press.

Fixx, J. F. 1980. *Jim Fixx's Second Book of Running*. New York: Random House.

Katz, J. 1992. *Swimming for Total Fitness*. New York: Doubleday.

Lyons, P., and D. Burgard. 1990. *Great Shape: The First Fitness Guide for Large Women*. Palo Alto, CA: Bull Publishing.

Meyers, C. 1992. *Walking*. New York: Random House.

Sprague, K. 1993. *The Gold's Gym Book of Weight Training*. New York: Perigie Books.

**Fitness and Aerobic Exercise Brochures**

For a catalog, write or call:

Krames Communications
312 90th Street
Daly City, CA 94015-8800
1-800-333-3032

# 21

# When It Doesn't Come Easy—
# Getting Unstuck

This book has covered many techniques to reduce stress and tension. Essentially they provide alternatives to our old stressful habits. You may have found that just practicing the new skills and observing the positive effects has caused you to give up the old habits. For instance, you may have found that practicing slow, deep breaths rather than short, constricted breaths results in a relaxed sense of well being. This positive feedback from your body may have provided ample motivation for you to give up your old anxiety provoking shallow breathing habit. However, if you are like most people, at some point you probably encountered some difficulty in exchanging old familiar habits for new ones. This chapter takes a look at why old habits are hard to part with, even when they are obviously contributing to your stress. It also offers some suggestions for how to deal with your own resistance to change.

If you find yourself skipping an exercise session you have contracted with yourself to do, or are aware that you are just going through the motions of the exercises, ask yourself some of the following questions:

- Why am I doing these exercises?

- Are these reasons really important to me?

- What am I doing or would I like to be doing instead of these exercises?

- Is this alternative activity more important to me than my doing the exercises?

- Can I schedule my life so that I can do the exercises *and* this alternative activity?

- If I do not want to do the exercises now, exactly when and where will I do them next?

- What would I have to give up if I succeeded with my exercises?

- What would I have to confront if I succeeded with my exercises?

## Taking Responsibility for Your Decisions

It is difficult to learn new habits on your own, especially when, at least at first, the rewards for your efforts may be minimal. When distractions occur, decide whether you want to be detoured or you want to continue on your chosen route. If you decide to take the detour, do so with full awareness, after weighing the pros and cons. Before going off on the detour, make an appointment with yourself for when and where you are next going to do your exercises. In this way you are taking responsibility for your decision. In addition, you are less likely to feel bad about yourself for not following through on your original plan, if that is your conscious choice.

## Questioning Your Excuses May Prove Enlightening

When you slack off on your exercises, it is often illuminating to examine the reasons you tell yourself this is happening. Typical reasons are: "I'm too busy today," "I'm too tired," "Missing once won't hurt," "David needs my help," "This isn't working," "This is boring," "I feel relaxed and unstressed today, so I don't need to exercise," or "I feel too bad today to do exercises." These excuses are seductive because they are partially true. That is, you may really feel very busy or tired, somebody may want your help, and missing one session probably won't hurt. The part that isn't true is the implication that because you are busy or tired or someone needs your help, you cannot do the exercise sessions. A more truthful statement would be, "I am tired. I could do the exercises, but I choose not to," or "I could do my exercises, but I choose to help David rather than do them." The important point here is that you take responsibility for your decision to choose one activity over another, rather than pretend that you are the passive victim of circumstances such as your fatigue, David's demands or other priorities that keep you busy.

You may find yourself repeatedly using the same reason or similar reasons for not doing your exercises. A common theme with many variations is: "I'm indispensable. Things won't get done without me and may even fall apart." For example, one very bright, middle-aged housewife and mother could rarely find time to do her exercises because her housework was never done. She believed that she could not take time out for herself or the pile of chores would grow rapidly into an unassailable mountain. After years of doing continuous housework with no time set aside to relax, she was run down, depressed, anxious, having migraines and lower back pain, and getting work done at a fraction of her previous rate. Her perfectionistic belief that she had to do all of her work before she had a right to relax had caused a gradual depletion of her energy. The result was inevitable physical and emotional signs of stress.

The excuses you give yourself for not doing your exercises are likely to be the same ones that you have used for years to keep yourself locked into a stressful situation. These excuses are based on faulty premises. For example, the middle-aged woman mentioned above believed erroneously that she had no right to relax until all her work was done. But the work of a housewife and mother is never done; therefore she could never relax. Furthermore, she had overlooked her innate right (and some would call it an obligation) to relax and replenish her vital store of energy. This woman had defined her priorities as being "housewife first" and "me second," without taking into account the importance of relaxation and getting away from stressful activities for maintaining good mental health and physical health.

If you are an energetic person who likes to succeed, who likes to get things done yesterday, slow down your pace when learning these exercises. Enthusiasm may push you to take on many exercises at once and do the sessions for too long. You run a high risk of burning out and losing interest if you do too much too fast. Furthermore, you are likely to feel guilty for not keeping up the rigorous program you have set for yourself. Soon you will find yourself coming up with excuses to avoid exercising at all ("I'm over-extended already in many areas of my life. Why add to the burden?").

You may feel confused when you begin to experience *more* energy as a result of doing the relaxation and stress reduction exercises. Resist the temptation to pour this extra energy back into your work. Rather, use it for further rest and enjoyment.

## Common Roadblocks in the Road to Relaxation

If you read this workbook without doing any of the exercises, you have reason to expect that you are only dabbling. Intellectually, you see the value of the exercises, but you somehow never get much past the stage of thinking about them; or you may actually do some of the exercises, but never apply them to everyday situations. For the dabbler, this is just another book with some interesting ideas, rather than a workbook promoting experiential learning of new ways to deal with stress.

There are some individuals who are frightened by novel experiences, and this fear becomes a roadblock to success. You might become overwhelmed by some side effect of a relaxation technique such as tingling in your arms and legs. Unfortunately, you may then stop the exercise instead of going on to find that the tingling is not harmful and goes away with time. You can get turned off by a single element of an exercise and, rather than changing the exercise to fit your needs, drop the exercise. Perhaps you don't understand a step in the instructions and rather than ad lib, you chuck the whole thing. It can be a valuable growth experience to work through these difficulties on your own.

## When Symptoms Persist

Sometimes symptoms of stress persist in spite of regular relaxation and stress reduction. If you are a conscientious person, and have been practicing regularly, this is disheartening. The following are just a few of the most common reasons why this might be happening to you.

Some people are highly suggestible and begin to experience every symptom that they hear about. For example, one very tense policeman joined a relaxation group to overcome his tendency to hyperventilate when under stress. He found himself experiencing all of the physical symptoms described by the other group members: migraines, lower back pain, rapid heartbeat, and so forth. These tendencies may be combatted by combining thought stopping or coping statements with progressive relaxation.

A surprising number of people are attached to their symptoms, which serve a very definite purpose. For example, your headaches may get you out of interpersonal situations you want to avoid, without having to take responsibility for disappointing others. You can soon find out whether your symptoms rescue you from more unpleasant experiences by keeping a log of when you get your symptoms and the activities (or would-be activities) that surround them. If you suspect that your symptoms provide you "secondary gain" in this manner, refer to the chapter on assertiveness training. It should provide you with the incentive and the tools to be more direct in saying "no."

Your symptoms of tension may be a signal that you are not dealing effectively with something in your life and that you are covering up your feelings. For example, you may be angry with your family but not sharing this fact with them. You might be putting off talking about a particular conflict because you don't see any way of improving matters. A nurse was visited every other weekend by a very spoiled stepdaughter. She had agreed to the arrangement when she married and now felt trapped by it. Within three years the visits invariably produced a migraine headache. To counteract this symptom, she finally negotiated a new contract with her husband to spend Sundays on her own while he babysat.

The people around you are apt to be aware that you are withholding stressful feelings and that something is wrong. Nevertheless they cannot read your mind, and are unlikely to come to your rescue. You know best what you need. Letting others know your feelings and what you want opens the way to engaging them in helping you make a change.

Your symptom may be a way of getting taken care of when you feel that you cannot directly ask for help or consideration. If you feel tired and have a backache, someone else may have to do the cooking and cleaning and keeping the house quiet. Ask yourself when your symptoms first began. What was going on in your life that might have contributed to them? One elderly woman who had suffered from periodic colitis since childhood recalled that her abdominal cramps began when her younger twin brothers were born. She remembered that the only time her busy mother ever held her and rocked her was when she had the symptoms. She noted that she tended to get colitis only when her husband left her alone in the evenings.

It is possible that you have developed a symptom of an important person in your life as part of your identification with them. For example, you may not only have learned to be hard working and successful from your father, but also to deal with stress in a similar manner. Carrying your tension in your stomach, you may come to the point of getting an ulcer just like your father. Since characteristic ways of responding to stress are generally learned, ask yourself who in your family shares your same symptoms. It's often easier to learn how they are not dealing effectively with the stress in their lives than to see it in yourself. The next step is to observe and see if the same is true for you.

If you continue to have difficulty reducing the stress in your life, consider consulting a professional. You may be interested in one-on-one sessions, or in joining one of the relaxation and stress reduction groups that are becoming more and more common. Your medical doctor, company health plan, community health organization, adult education program, or community college are good places to start looking for professional help.

## Persistence Pays

Finally, don't give up. Your ability to relax, learn to handle stress, and heal yourself is a tremendous power. Change might not always come easy—you may feel stuck in your old stressful habits—but you can do it. All it takes is patience, persistence . . . and time.

# Other New Harbinger Self-Help Titles

*Natural Women's Health: A Guide to Healthy Living for Women of Any Age*, $13.95

*I'd Rather Be Married: Finding Your Future Spouse*, $13.95

*The Relaxation & Stress Reduction Workbook, Fourth Edition*, $14.95

*Living Without Depression & Manic Depression: A Workbook for Maintaining Mood Stability*, $14.95

*Belonging: A Guide to Overcoming Loneliness*, $13.95

*Coping With Schizophrenia: A Guide For Families*, $13.95

*Visualization for Change, Second Edition*, $13.95

*Postpartum Survival Guide*, $13.95

*Angry All The Time: An Emergency Guide to Anger Control*, $12.95

*Couple Skills: Making Your Relationship Work*, $13.95

*Handbook of Clinical Psychopharmacology for Therapists*, $39.95

*The Warrior's Journey Home: Healing Men, Healing the Planet*, $13.95

*Weight Loss Through Persistence*, $13.95

*Post-Traumatic Stress Disorder: A Complete Treatment Guide*, $39.95

*Stepfamily Realities: How to Overcome Difficulties and Have a Happy Family*, $11.95

*Leaving the Fold: A Guide for Former Fundamentalists and Others Leaving Their Religion*, $13.95

*Father-Son Healing: An Adult Son's Guide*, $12.95

*The Chemotherapy Survival Guide*, $11.95

*Your Family/Your Self: How to Analyze Your Family System*, $12.95

*Being a Man: A Guide to the New Masculinity*, $12.95

*The Deadly Diet, Second Edition: Recovering from Anorexia & Bulimia*, $11.95

*Last Touch: Preparing for a Parent's Death*, $11.95

*Consuming Passions: Help for Compulsive Shoppers*, $11.95

*Self-Esteem, Second Edition*, $13.95

*Depression & Anxiety Mangement: An audio tape for managing emotional problems*, $11.95

*I Can't Get Over It, A Handbook for Trauma Survivors*, $13.95

*Concerned Intervention, When Your Loved One Won't Quit Alcohol or Drugs*, $11.95

*Redefining Mr. Right*, $11.95

*Dying of Embarrassment: Help for Social Anxiety and Social Phobia*, $12.95

*The Depression Workbook: Living With Depression and Manic Depression*, $14.95

*Risk-Taking for Personal Growth: A Step-by-Step Workbook*, $14.95

*The Marriage Bed: Renewing Love, Friendship, Trust, and Romance*, $11.95

*Focal Group Psychotherapy: For Mental Health Professionals*, $44.95

*Hot Water Therapy: Save Your Back, Neck & Shoulders in 10 Minutes a Day* $11.95

*Older & Wiser: A Workbook for Coping With Aging*, $12.95

*Prisoners of Belief: Exposing & Changing Beliefs that Control Your Life*, $10.95

*Be Sick Well: A Healthy Approach to Chronic Illness*, $11.95

*Men & Grief: A Guide for Men Surviving the Death of a Loved One.*, $12.95

*When the Bough Breaks: A Helping Guide for Parents of Sexually Abused Childern*, $11.95

*Love Addiction: A Guide to Emotional Independence*, $12.95

*When Once Is Not Enough: Help for Obsessive Compulsives*, $13.95

*The New Three Minute Meditator*, $12.95

*Getting to Sleep*, $12.95

*Leader's Guide to the Relaxation & Stress Reduction Workbook*, $19.95

*Beyond Grief: A Guide for Recovering from the Death of a Loved One*, $13.95

*Thoughts & Feelings: The Art of Cognitive Stress Intervention*, $13.95

*The Divorce Book*, $11.95

*Hypnosis for Change: A Manual of Proven Techniques, 2nd Edition*, $13.95

*The Chronic Pain Control Workbook*, $14.95

*My Parent's Keeper: Adult Children of the Emotionally Disturbed*, $11.95

*When Anger Hurts*, $13.95

*Free of the Shadows: Recovering from Sexual Violence*, $12.95

*Lifetime Weight Control*, $11.95

*The Anxiety & Phobia Workbook*, $14.95

*Love and Renewal: A Couple's Guide to Commitment*, $12.95

*The Habit Control Workbook*, $12.95

Call **toll free, 1-800-748-6273**, to order. Have your Visa or Mastercard number ready. Or send a check for the titles you want to New Harbinger Publications, Inc., 5674 Shattuck Avenue, Oakland, CA 94609. Include $3.80 for the first book and 75¢ for each additional book, to cover shipping and handling. (California residents please include appropriate sales tax.) Allow four to six weeks for delivery.

*Prices subject to change without notice.*